"Relevant for multiple disciplines, *Popular Culture as Everyday Life* offers readers a unique (and even experimental) perspective on popular culture that at times reads like a diary, at other times like a history lesson, and at still other times promises to be a time capsule or snapshot representing popular culture as it currently exists in the early twenty-first century. Whether they are embracing the culture, resisting the culture, or merely co-existing with the culture, the authors in this volume collectively document and examine the place, function, meaning, and value that the culture in question has in their everyday lives."

—Carol Rambo, University of Memphis

"Peter Berger argued that the most important thing you can know about someone is what they take for granted, and these days, it is largely about popular culture. The gripping essays show the richness of "the mundane doings of people and their ways of life" in constructing social and moral orders, even as they celebrate the profoundly trivial. The chapters will motivate students to do their own investigations of everyday life."

—David Altheide, Arizona State University

"*Popular Culture as Everyday Life* celebrates how daily commonplaces can become rich subjects for deep sociological insights. The diverse chapters reveal the mundane doings of people to be anything but. A must read for anyone who has ever slept, gotten dressed, drank coffee, put on makeup, gone to the bathroom, has never smoked or kicked ass, has watched television, or has had sex."

—Eugene Halton, University of Notre Dame

Popular Culture as Everyday Life

In *Popular Culture as Everyday Life* Dennis D. Waskul and Phillip Vannini have brought together a variety of short essays that illustrate the many ways that popular culture intersects with mundane experiences of everyday life. Most essays are written in a reflexive ethnographic style, providing both observation and personal narrative, and convey insights at an intimate level that will resonate with readers. Some of the topics are so mundane that they can legitimately be called universal (sleeping, getting dressed, going to the bathroom, etc.), while others are common enough that most readers will directly identify in some way (watching television, using mobile phones, playing video games, etc.). Some topics will appeal more or less, depending on the reader's gender, interests, and recreational pastimes (putting on makeup, watching the Super Bowl, homemaking, etc.). The book reminds readers of their own similar experiences, provides opportunities to reflect upon them in new ways, as well as to compare and contrast how experiences described in these pages relate to lived experiences. The essays will easily translate into rich and lively classroom discussions that shed new light on familiar, taken-for-granted aspects of everyday life—both individually and collectively.

A grid is provided at the beginning of the book that shows the topics and themes of each article. This work is intended for popular classes; it will also be an asset in courses on the sociology of everyday life, ethnography, and social psychology.

Dennis D. Waskul is a Professor of Sociology and Distinguished Faculty Scholar at Minnesota State University, Mankato. He has authored or edited six books and is editor of the book series *Interactionist Currents* (Ashgate). He has published many empirical studies, including various investigations of the use of new media technologies for sexual purposes, sensual sociology, and the intersections of fantasy and lived experience. Dennis serves on the editorial board for multiple journals, including *Sexualities* and *Qualitative Sociology*.

Phillip Vannini is Canada Research Chair in Public Ethnography and Professor of Communication and Culture at Royal Roads University. He is the author of five books and editor of seven, as well as the editor of two book series, including *Interactionist Currents* (Ashgate). All of his scholarship deals with cultural and everyday life issues. Several of his journal articles and chapters for edited books have also dealt with popular culture and everyday life issues, such as research studies on camping, eating, drinking, traveling, building, consuming, body modification, experiencing the weather, and more.

Popular Culture as Everyday Life

**Edited by Dennis D. Waskul
and Phillip Vannini**

NEW YORK AND LONDON

First published 2016
by Routledge
711 Third Avenue, New York, NY 10017

and by Routledge
2 Park Square, Milton Park, Abingdon, Oxon, OX14 4RN

Routledge is an imprint of the Taylor & Francis Group, an infor business

Library of Congress Cataloging in Publication Data

A catalog record for this book has been requested.

ISBN: 978-1-138-83338-8 (hbk)
ISBN: 978-1-138-83339-5 (pbk)
ISBN: 978-1-315-73548-1 (ebk)

Typeset in Adobe Caslon and Copperplate
by codeMantra

Contents

FOREWORD

This book is intended as a supplement for popular culture courses, although its contents may have a broad range of pedagogical applications, especially for those interested in the sociology of everyday life, ethnography, and social psychology. Our primary objective is to provide a wide variety of highly accessible short essays that illustrate the many nuanced ways that popular culture intersects with mundane experiences of everyday life. The essays that comprise the bulk of this book are intentionally written in a reflexive ethnographic style, primarily through observation and personal narrative, to convey insights at an intimate level that will resonate with most readers.

As a textbook, our primary objective is to help facilitate *talking points* in class. Some of the topics addressed are so mundane they are legitimately universal (sleeping, getting dressed, going to the bathroom, etc.), others are common enough that most readers will directly identify in some way (watching television, using mobile phones, playing video games, etc.), while some topics will appeal more-or-less depending on a reader's gender, interests, and recreational pastimes (putting on makeup, watching the Super Bowl, home-making, etc.). Regardless, the primary content of this book ought to frequently remind readers of extremely similar experiences of their own, provide opportunities to reflect upon them in new ways, as well as compare and contrast how experiences relayed in these pages relate to experiences that are lived. Pedagogically, those talking points should easily translate into rich and lively classroom discussions that can gainfully shed new light on a familiar, taken-for-granted everyday life—both individually and collectively.

While our objective is to help facilitate discussion and reflection, we also aim not to determine the content of the conversation. Most of the essays in this book make *practical* use of an interactionist approach to popular culture and everyday life—just enough to hint at interesting nuances and illustrate ways of understanding. Course instructors may wish to more fully develop those interactionist foundations, aiming for as much depth as their specific course focus warrants, or take the discussion in a different direction altogether by launching a more critical critique, perhaps illustrating functional aspects, or some combination thereof. Alternatively, through those talking points users may also explore other related substantive topics. To give just a few examples: in what ways can Michael Ian Borer's insights (Essay 29) on Big Beer and micro brews inform our understandings of wine or even soda? Rebecca F. Plante (Essay 16) writes intimately on the feminine experience of putting on makeup. Is there a male equivalent? If so, what? If not, why? In these ways, *Popular Culture as Everyday Life* facilitates talking points that are intentionally designed to be highly adaptable so as to open opportunities for many possible ways of learning, knowing, and stimulating the sociological imagination.

The essays that comprise the bulk of this book are extremely short in order to allow instructors to assign them impromptu during class, if they so choose, without consuming too much class time. Students can write personal reflections on what they read, have pointed questions for small group discussions, or engage a classwide, free-for-all conversation. Most authors make incisive use of humor and irony, so however they are used the majority of readers ought to find the essays engaging if not downright entertaining.

One brief warning: the titles of the essays are deceptively simple, and each is about significantly more than one might expect—something that readers will have to discover for themselves. For example, Simon Gottschalk writes about playing music, but equally about a video game (*Guitar Hero*). That kind of blending and blurring should to be expected, considering that the main goal of the book is to illustrate the *intersections* of popular culture and everyday life; authors move deftly between and among commercials, consumer activity, media, and ultimately what people do with all that "stuff" in daily life. Consequently, the organization of the essays is somewhat arbitrary—or at least more so than the simple titles might imply. To assist we have provided a general guide that identifies some of the major themes in each essay.

	Advertising	Phones	Coming of age	Consumerism	Gender	Games	Health	Holidays	Identity	Internet	Media	Music	Ritual	Social media	Sports	Technology	TV	Transport	Video
1			x										x			x	x		x
2			x														x		
3	x			x	x		x		x								x		
4		x							x	x				x		x			
5		x							x	x			x	x		x			
6			x						x										
7																			
8		x							x	x	x			x		x			x
9						x						x							
10				x					x			x	x			x			
11						x						x	x			x			
12				x									x			x			
13			x	x	x				x	x	x						x		
14					x								x						
15				x	x				x				x						
16			x	x	x				x				x						
17													x					x	
18							x		x		x		x		x				
19					x		x		x		x		x		x				
20				x	x			x					x		x		x	x	
21				x						x					x				
22									x	x	x								
23			x																
24							x				x		x						
25				x				x					x						
26				x			x	x			x		x						
27				x							x							x	
28	x						x		x		x		x						
29	x			x					x										

INTRODUCTION
POPULAR CULTURE AS EVERYDAY LIFE
Dennis D. Waskul and Phillip Vannini

Sociologists of everyday life make a living out of people watching. And for us that's a damn good thing because, to be quite honest, we are too shamelessly curious to help ourselves. Maybe it's a little creepy to confess that we enjoy observing people in public without their knowledge but, at some base level, you must confess that it is something we all do: watching patterns of interaction, body language, how people assemble their clothing, overhearing other people's conversations (especially that annoying person speaking loudly on a cell phone in a public space), catching a whiff of someone's perfume, reading the words written on t-shirts, carefully averting our eyes lest someone think we are gawking, perceiving the soft rhythmic beats of the music people are listening to in the solitary acoustic world of the earbuds, watching people so artfully exchange reciprocating smiles, nods, and glances. For those who do not make it a part of their occupation, people watching can be a hobby—or at least an enjoyable pastime— and in recent decades social media have brought people watching to a whole new level; we suspect that at this moment there are millions of people who are unknowingly being observed on Facebook alone (at least when we observe people in public spaces we adhere to the rules of decorum and tact!).

But what is it that we primarily observe when we are people watching? Let us share a few brief observations of one sunny, warm afternoon as Dennis D. Waskul strolls outside and takes a seat on a bench at his university campus.

1

A young, buff shirtless guy jogs by me—he is wearing loose blue running shorts, the telltale three angular bars on the side of his shoes strongly suggest he is wearing black Adidas, and his only other accessories are white earbuds that are attached to a small iPod affixed to his muscular arm on an elastic band. The jogger moves to his left to pass a brunette woman walking toward me. The brunette is wearing tight jeans with calf-high boots; her turquoise shirt ironically reads "Love Pink." In one hand she carries a disposable cup of some iced beverage that bears the distinctive green logo of Starbucks and, as she gets closer, I notice in her other hand a blue textbook with an interesting cover: The World of Psychology[1], *featuring an image of a white Chinese restaurant take-out box, only filled with colorful marbles. As she passes by, we exchange a brief friendly smile at about the same time a couple walks past in the opposite direction. The couple is holding hands and only engaged in casual conversation, since I do not see a diamond ring on her left hand; all I hear is, "Jimmy invited us to his place after the game tonight." As she turns to say something to her boyfriend, her blonde highlighted hair gently blows across her face as the slaps of her flip flops smack against the back of her heel with each step. Her boyfriend reaches into a front pocket of his saggy jeans—I notice the name "Calvin Klein" written across the waist band of his boxers—and pulls out a smart phone to check the time. Lots of people walk by with their eyes and attention focused on small but powerful communication devices, but only a few are listening or speaking into them. A dingy-looking fellow with ratty hair slowly walks past wearing loose, faded jeans and a plaid shirt—the heels of his sandals dragging against the concrete with every slow step—and it appears to me that he needs to change his bong water more frequently; I know it's a stereotype, and I don't know if he smokes pot, but he sure looks the part (and it doesn't help that he's devouring a bag of Cool Ranch Doritos either!). As two men firmly shake each other's hand and loudly and greet one another as "bro!" (I doubt they are related), I stand up and walk back to my office—eight minutes is enough time to gather sufficient observational illustrations for what will surely be a long paragraph.*

Clearly, popular culture is saturated in the *mundane doings of people*—music, commercial logos, clothing trends, fashion labels, vending machine goodies, name brands, sporting events, communication and new media technologies, and whatever the significance of a Chinese take-out box has for "the world of psychology." Popular culture is also rooted in commonplace rituals—from the friendly exchange of a smile to a firm handshake between "bros"—that are informed by habits, routines, loosely scripted customs, and informal social and cultural performances. The meanings that we assign to what we observe are also, no doubt, interpreted in the context of popular culture. Most importantly for this book, popular culture is emergent within the quotidian experiences, practices, and expressions of people. Or more simply, as we emphasize, the "stuff" of popular culture is less important than what people do with and amongst it.

Of course, the presence of popular culture can be observed not only in public spaces, the people within them, and what they are doing—it is equally apparent in our private lives and even within our most intimate relationships. Popular culture streams into our private spaces on cables, satellites, and through wireless networks. Popular culture is printed in the newspapers, magazines, and books that we read. We bring home popular culture in grocery bags while likely listening to it in the car on the drive. Our bedroom closets and dresser drawers are filled with a multitude of artefacts of popular culture that adorn our body for the vast majority of our life; indeed, we only come *in* to this world naked. Clearly, popular culture is intimately woven into our private life and there is, perhaps, no better example of this than our cell phones. According to a 2013 study by Pew Research Center's Internet & American Life Project, 91% of Americans own a cell phone. 81% of Americans use their cell for text messaging (97% of 18 to 29-year-olds), 60% use their cell to access the Internet (84% of 18 to 29-year-olds), 52% use it for mobile email (75% of 18 to 29-year-olds), and 50% to download apps (77% of 18 to 29-year-olds). Given how many uses there are for cell phones today, we venture a strong hunch that on any given day you interact more with your cell than with your loved ones. In fact, we strongly suspect that virtually every night you sleep with your cell phone within arm's reach—and for those of you in a sexual relationship, you sleep with your phone as much, if not more, than with your lover. Indeed, we even take popular culture to bed with us.

Of course, all of this begs for a definition. What is popular culture? It turns out that this is a surprisingly difficult question with a multitude of possible answers (see Bennett 1980; Parker 2011; Storey 2006). For our purposes, without belaboring the point too much, it is sufficient to identify three main approaches to defining and understanding popular culture. Popular culture is most often defined as, more or less, the sum product of the media and entertainment industries. Thus, the first two approaches we wish to mention are closely related to one another. First is a critical approach that focuses on the *production* of media and entertainment commodities—the industry that makes music, television, movies, sports, fashion, and so on. Second is an equally critical but institutional approach that focuses on the *organization* and *consumption* of media and entertainment commodities, as well as related industries— ranging from the creation of cultural standards at a macro-level to the micro-commercial choices we make in our efforts to both identify and differentiate ourselves from others.

From either point of view, popular culture is necessarily a modern innovation with origins in the Industrial Revolution, and that betrays what is implied by the word "popular:" commonplace, general, widespread. Surely, throughout history people have listened to common songs and played common games, even when they didn't pay for those commodities that were mass-produced by for-profit industries. Hence a third approach emphasizes popular culture as that which *originates from the people* and, especially, the things they commonly do—and that makes for the broadest definition of all; one that closely resembles what we often call "folk culture."

Any one of these approaches has its merits and critics. Yet ultimately, popular culture necessarily concerns all three: things are *produced* by some process of production and are, in turn, *consumed* by people who *do something* with them. Sometimes that process is distinct: a new video game is created, hyped by advertising, and released; consumers purchase the game at a store or online; people then play the game to their delight or disappointment. Sometimes that process is experienced more instantaneously: we turn on the radio and music that was produced and already consumed by others comes streaming to us for the paltry price of having to endure some commercials. Most importantly, all three—the production of commodities, their consumption, and what people do with them—profoundly influence one another, and that is precisely what we illustrate in the pages of this book.

Yet culture, which we simply define as people's way of life, is more than the sum of the material products people consume and what they do with them. Just as important are the immaterial elements: words, rituals, patterns of expectations, and so on. A decade ago, "sexting" would have been flagged as misspelled on a word processing program; a decade prior you might have thought a "wardrobe malfunction" was a punch line for one of Jay Leno's monologues on the *Tonight Show*. And a decade prior to that the word "groovy" had already disappeared from common everyday speech. As will be illustrated throughout this book, ritual is among the most prevalent elements of culture. For some rituals, such as formal rites of passage (symbolic markers showing that a person has become someone different), it is fairly clear to see the influences of popular culture. Recall the couple that Dennis observed earlier: he assumed they were not engaged because she was not wearing a diamond ring that her fiancé would have purchased and she would have accepted. Yet, that convention was not popularized until the post-Depression and post–World War II era when De Beer Consolidated Mines managed to gain control over the most of the world's diamond supply and, needing to boost demand, launched their highly successful "A Diamond is Forever" campaign. Certainly, the diamond engagement ring has a long history. But, as a standard convention to symbolize a commitment to marriage, it is something we literally bought into from popular culture, and rather recently at that. Seldom do we think of the much more subtle and mundane rituals that structure our everyday life—and those, too, are influenced by popular culture. Recall the two men greeting with a handshake: a common, long-standing ritual greeting in our culture, but only recently punctuated with the word "Bro!"

In sum, popular culture is meaningful in light of the fact that it matters to us—not just on special occasions but on any given day, and perhaps at any given moment as well. And in many cases it matters so deeply that to ignore it, contest it, or re-invent it would be utterly impossible. In those cases where popular culture can somehow be ignored, contested, or re-invented, interestingly enough we observe something else that is very powerful and important: the birth of a new culture, a subculture, counterculture, or perhaps an alternative lifestyle. No matter what, it seems, popular culture is inescapable; it percolates through our mundane existence so deeply that our entire way of life could not be imagined, lived, and practiced without it. In the increasingly secular societies of the Western hemisphere popular culture is like a religion: its meaningfulness is so pervasive and its presence so widespread that our very individual and collective being has become inseparable from its many expressions—much like the Qur'an is inseparable from Islamic society, or the Bible from Christian culture, or the Torah from Jewish tradition.

What This Book is About

As you may have gleaned already, this is a book about popular culture *in* everyday life. Or, if you like, it is a book about everyday life *in* and *through* popular culture. We do not really care which comes first; the distinctions between popular culture and everyday life—given our perspective rooted in the mundane *doings* of people and their ways of life—are in fact more or less arbitrary and irrelevant, and it would be nonsensical to view one as the cause or effect of the other. Therefore, more broadly, the purpose of this book is to examine the domain of everyday life and popular culture *simultaneously* in order to reflect on what is common about our shared collective existence in the twenty-first century. Ours is not a dominant approach in sociology, communication studies, or cultural studies. Popular culture and everyday life are often treated as separate fields of inquiry by scholars with different interests and different methods. We, on the other hand, propose that popular culture and everyday life are inseparable and impossible to understand unless analyzed in relation to one another.

In addition to our relatively original approach, our book is characterized by an important theoretical constant that distinguishes it from many others. All of the essays included in this book originate from a broadly-defined *interactionist* perspective. Interactionism is a simple idea rooted in the belief that social realities emerge as the outcomes of social actors interacting with one another—that is, establishing relations and doing things together. These social realities are infinite: from the most fundamental beliefs, ideals, and values that specify what is right, true, good, and beautiful, to the most commonly lived and practiced habits, routines, feelings, sensations, and actions. Social actors are a similarly broad category. Social actors are individuals, groups, larger collectives, and institutions, but also nonhumans such as animals, materials, and consumer objects. From the most fleeting and ephemeral situations to the more durable relations amid all these actors, in all kinds of contexts and settings, and with all kinds of intents and purposes, thus do social life and popular culture as we know them take shape.

Stated in the familiar manner articulated by its many practitioners over the years, interactionism resides in the threefold idea that: (1) humans act toward things in relation to the significance those things hold for them, (2) that significance arises in social interaction, and (3) that significance is subject to ongoing processes of interpretation (Blumer 1969). Obviously, this perspective is ideal for our approach, because it is so deeply rooted in what "ordinary" people do on any given day of their lives. From an interactionist approach, in fact, both popular culture and everyday life are the emergent outcome of what we all do, think, feel, and sense together.

To put our idea in slightly more sophisticated terms, we might say that from an interactionist perspective *we may understand popular culture as an assemblage of ideas, practices, experiences, representations, material objects and other "things" and phenomena that comprise the mainstream, ordinary ways of life of large groups of people.* We believe that this assemblage permeates everyday life, that is, the day-to-day existence of people. Therefore, rather than conflate popular culture with media culture, and rather than deconstruct mediated popular culture's images, discourses, codes, regimes of signification, and production as many scholars do, in this book *we examine popular culture as it becomes embedded within the quotidian experiences, practices, and expressions of people.* We, in other words, treat popular culture simply as what people do routinely, as something they share with one another, and as a domain constituting the basis of all social relations.

Drawing upon the interactionist tradition, we approach popular culture as everyday life from an *ethnographic* perspective—that is, from the perspective of insiders rather than of detached outsiders. But rather than present full-blown ethnographic studies in the typical presentation format (comprised of introduction, literature reviews, research design, data analysis, and conclusions) our book features what we might call *narrative reflections*. By narrative reflections we refer to short, evocative, insightful essays that are inspired by informal observation of, and participation in, everyday life practices, experiences, and representations. Anchored in a relevant domain of existing knowledge, and properly contextualized historically, politically, culturally, and socially, these short and lively narrative reflections describe and interpret in pithy and captivating ways the significance of their topics utilizing a first person voice and a dynamic, off-the-cuff style. The key strength of these narrative reflections, we argue, is their readability and immediate resonance with many audiences of readers. Much more than typical theoretical essays in popular culture studies, these narrative reflections resemble, in a way, the popular culture expressions they discuss. We find it in fact unfortunate that the fun and pleasures of popular culture are so often deflated by typically overly abstract, dry, and highly theoretical accounts. In contrast the essays in this book, we hope, resemble in tone and style popular communication media and genres.

Essay topics focus on the features of everyday life in the Western world. From play and hobbies to texting and exercising, from enjoying drink and food to dressing oneself in the morning, from going to the bathroom to interacting with one's pets, from watching a TV show to updating one's Facebook profile; the subjects treated in this book constitute a time capsule of everyday life and popular culture in our hemisphere and historical time. Not every medium and not every possible topic is discussed, of course, and for that we have no one to blame but ourselves as editors and our inevitably limited space. Yet, we hope that the range of essays presented here will provide our readers with a variety of topics and an arsenal of concepts from social and cultural theory that will allow them to reflect and learn a great deal about the subject.

In treating popular culture as everyday life, and everyday life as popular culture, the essays advance the idea that culture and life are what people do together anytime, anywhere, any day. Such a focus on collective doing, feeling, and the expressiveness and performativity of shared cultural processes is intended to downplay (but not deny) the importance of abstracted economic or discursive dimensions of popular culture. Such a focus also simultaneously highlights how actions, values, sensations, beliefs, codes, feelings, emotions, and ideas implicit in all of popular culture are revealed, enacted, and shared in the multiple-lived engagements, habits, and scripts of ordinary interaction by ordinary people. For these reasons the authors have chosen to write not so much from an elevated and distant "know-it-all" position but rather about things that personally matters to them, things they are familiar with, things they have a strong passion or curiosity about, and things of biographical significance to them. Each essay oscillates between the mundane and the historical, the personal and the social, the quirky and the ordinary, the realm of media communication and the domain of face-to-face interaction.

The study of everyday life, both within sociology and cultural studies, is a strong, dynamic, and captivating research field with long and rich theoretical traditions. From its outset symbolic interaction has played a central role in the development of this field by allowing researchers to examine ordinary and mundane topics, and by allowing them to take a unique methodological and theoretical approach to the pragmatics of day-to-day life. Yet, broadly ranging symbolic interactionist volumes on everyday life have been very rare, if existent at all. Similarly, popular culture studies attract very large numbers of students, as well as professional scholars across a vast number of disciplines such as sociology, anthropology, ethnology and folklore, communication, cultural studies, and the humanities. Amongst students of popular culture are many interactionists who study topics that range from music and identity development to fandom, and from the use of new consumer technologies to the mediated presentation of self. Yet, no broadly ranging books that treat symbolic interaction and popular culture have ever been published. By combining the study of everyday life and the study of popular culture our book is the first to offer a broad panoramic scope of this vibrant field.

What the Essays Teach Us

Approaching popular culture and everyday life as an assemblage requires occupying ourselves with *disentangling* the various pieces comprising the whole in order to understand better the units and the whole, as well as the relations amongst them. Disentangling means untying, taking apart, disconnecting, and extricating. We disentangle something in order to get a better view—much like an imploded diagram can help us comprehend and then piece together the parts of something (like pre-made IKEA furniture). The activity of disentangling is similar in principle to other activities common in the social and natural sciences, like deconstructing or decoding. But while the interpretive practices of deconstructing and decoding are useful for theoretical models based respectively on social constructionism or semiotics, the process of disentangling is especially useful for models likes ours founded on ideas of relationality.

Relationality is a simple principle grounded on the idea that through interaction social agents establish and maintain meaningful rapports with one another. Rather than discussing in abstract terms what these kinds of rapports might be and how they might work, let us highlight in what follows six possible types based on the key themes of the essays contained in this book: embodiment, ritualization, performance, creativity, biography, and bonding. These six kinds of relations are not the only ways in which popular culture and everyday life can become entangled, of course, but they are very common ones that we will find taking shape in variety of contexts and across a multitude of subjects.

The first (in no particular order) of the six key instances of entanglement between popular culture and everyday life is *embodiment*. Embodiment is a process whereby something becomes part of our bodily experiences, practices, emotions, sensations, feelings, moods, and affects. Take the act of putting on makeup, for example. As Plante discusses in her essay, the ordinary routine of applying makeup is a powerful process through which we imagine how other people will perceive our bodily presence and therefore how they will impute significance to our social identity. Consequently, by applying certain types of makeup in certain ways we will fashion a physical self. Embodiment is therefore the process whereby our physical being acquires social and cultural significance. Take for example the ways in which the women studied by Montemurro in her essay incorporate popular media discourses on sexual expression. Montemurro writes:

> Watching television, seeing movies, paging through *Cosmopolitan* magazine, perusing the Victoria's Secret catalogue provide Robin

and women like her a specific image of "sexy." And so Robin feels inhibited while having sex. She does not know how to "talk dirty" to her husband, but confided she wishes she did. Robin grapples with the image of the sexy woman in popular culture versus who she sees in the mirror. These dueling visions come into play when she has sex.

(Montemurro, this volume)

In this sense the sexual scripts portrayed in popular media ooze into everyday life and become entangled with what we do in bed or the way we look at ourselves in the mirror. Now, this doesn't have to be the case, of course. Popular media are not omnipotent; it is sometimes possible to disregard them and choose for ourselves how we, for example, want to live our sexual lives. But when these discourses and images become entangled with our day-to-day existence it is quite common for them to become deeply embodied as well.

Instances of embodiment abound in this book. Adams for example tells us how relating to a reality TV show can take place at a profound emotional and carnal level. Borer explains how the act of drinking a certain beer brand rather than another can serve as a way of embodying a certain set of ideas about taste and flavor while rejecting others. Edgley and Ellis in their respective essays show us how advertising and the consumption of specific products—medicines and mattresses respectively—become embedded in our bodily perception of a normal state of being, that is, a healthy and rested body and mind. Equally useful in helping us understand the nature of consumption, Martin's essay allows us to understand vaporizing—as opposed to smoking cigarettes—as the natural evolution of the intersection between discourses on health and seduction. Spencer—providing in a way the proverbial exception that confirms the rule—tells us how choosing *not* to kick somebody's ass (despite the abundance and seeming acceptability of violent acts on television and in the movies) is way of *not* choosing to embody dominant images of aggressive comportment (while choosing to embody alternative discourses on civility and propriety). And finally, Dennis shows us in his essay how consumer items and everyday bodily activities are entangled even in the most private domains, such as the bathroom.

A second common form of entanglement is that of ritualization (see Bell 1992). Ritualization is the process whereby something becomes ritual, habitual, and part of our recurrent actions. Just like the kinds of things that people do on Halloween, for instance, things—or better yet, ritual behaviors—that seem normal only because we have grown to accept them for what they are, no matter how strange (see Force, this volume). Think about it this way: By ritualizing something, you find yourself becoming familiar with it, you learn to depend on it and live with it, you become accustomed to it. Ritualization may be so deep that to live without that ritual may feel strange to you, and depending on how meaningful that rite is, you may even find living your life without it unthinkable. Take for example cell phone technology. Twenty or maybe even only 10 years ago you might have thought that walking around carrying your own telephone would have been a strange thing to do. I (Phillip) have never owned a cell phone and to a great degree I still find the act of carrying around a telephone for texting or calling people, or posting on Facebook (I'm not on Facebook either), very bizarre indeed. After all, who or what—I think—could be *that* important? The reason why I feel this way is because the phone or social media have never become *ritualized* into my own life. Newmahr's essay gives us an insight into the opposite (and much more common) ritualization scenario by articulating how the most common moments of her life and her friends' lives have "become so intertwined with a desire to share them on Facebook." And Klein, in her essay on selfies, outlines how taking photographic self-portraits is a way of sharing common daily experiences and therefore a way of creating a sense of sociality.

Ritualization is first and foremost a form of common habituation. The word "ritual" or "rite" may bring to mind foreign and mysterious—dare we say "exotic?"—coded behaviours whose scripts and significance have been passed down from generation to generation. But in contemporary Western societies like North America, rituals may be so ordinary that they escape our attention. Thus we have TV-watching rituals centered around the end of a sports season (see Glowinski and Kotarba, this volume), generation-defining shows (see Berry, this volume), concerts drawing cult-like audiences (see Boyd, this volume), daily domestic routines (see Ellis, this volume), rites of decorum (see Pruit and Plante, both this volume), rituals that mark the arrival and departure of the seasons (see Redmon, this volume), and rituals (like drinking coffee) that become so deeply-embodied that living a typical day without them might feel downright unthinkable (see Strobaek, this volume). In sum, for our purpose in this book, ritualization is a commonly practiced mundane behavior that typically occurs in the context of media or cultural production and/or consumption. Or, if you like to switch the idea around, ritualization is a type of media or cultural production and/or consumption that typically occurs in the context of daily habits, routines, and customs (also see Couldry 2003).

The third typical relation between everyday life and popular culture takes the shape of *performance*. Performance is a common idea in the social and cultural sciences. This elegant and powerful concept refers to at least two different phenomena. The first, generally associated with the dramaturgical theory of Erving Goffman, highlights how impressions are constantly managed by people in the various "stages" (metaphorical, but also very real) of day-to-day life. Extended to the realm of popular culture, the dramaturgical metaphor captures how production teams create impressions for their audiences through strategically-planned roles and scripts—and how audiences in turn utilize popular culture productions to stage meaningful identities in day-to-day interaction.

The second version of performance can be traced to the work of performance theorists such as Richard Schechner (2013) and Victor Turner (1975), for whom performativity is a characteristic quintessential to all kinds of rituals, activities, and stories. In Schechner's terms performance is action unfolding after people have gathered somewhere to take part in a common activity, and before they have dispersed to return to their homes or places of origin (think of the act of going to a concert, taking in the show, and then driving home together). What happens in between gathering and dispersal, for both Schechner and Turner, is extremely powerful and transformative, often generative of strong communities (no matter how small) and unique identities, scripts, and roles for their participants (such as concert-goers—see Boyd, this volume). Performance—whether one goes by Goffman's ideas, or Turner and Schechner's—is therefore a deeply spatial practice. Performance happens here, not over there, and as a result the here and the there become very different places with different norms, expectations, and roles.

In Löfgren's essay, for example, we learn how hotels work as stages for the performance of a unique self: the "holiday me." Similarly concerned with crafting key impressions for others are individuals who produce and upload high-quality adventure videos on the Internet, as described in Phillip's essay. The power that performance has in setting spaces apart is also clear when we think of what goes on in the bathroom and in dressing rooms as a form of backstage domestic ritual—as described respectively in Dennis's essay and in John Pruit's essay—as well as when we think of homes as "fronts" for the style and taste that homeowners wish to display to neighbors and passers-by (see McCormack, this volume).

Performance-related ideas are also important for Boyd, Martin, Redmon, and Schneider. Boyd, for example, tells us how transformative the experience of taking part in a music concert or festival can be, and how cohesive the subcultural communities that gather there can become over time. A similar same type of relationality between strangers can take place in much more profane spaces, such as the curb sides surrounding building entrances where exiled smokers congregate for a quick puff, a friendly chat, and incidentally for an increasingly stigmatized performance of deviant identities (see Martin, this volume). For a different take on performance we may then turn to Redmon's essay on snow. In his essay the snow becomes—far from being an inert "prop"—an actor whose entrance on the urban stage marks the arrival of a treasured season with all its beloved time-sanctioning rituals and unique atmosphere, informed in large part by the consumption of leisure and popular entertainment as well. The timing in which we perform certain acts—such as speaking on a cell phone or sending a text with it—is also important (see Schneider, this volume). Because most of us seem to use our cell phones all the time, private and public stages become easily confused, re-shaping roles and scripts in ordinary interactions.

If there is one key theme that distinguishes our work from many of the available books on either popular culture or everyday life, it is that of *creativity*—our fourth key relation. While new media and Web 2.0 have resuscitated the notion of creativity in cultural studies (see Gauntlett 2013) and shown how people are active content producers, as interactionists we find that creativity is a fundamental component of our life, regardless of technology or medium. In fact, the very idea of interpretive agency—one of the key cornerstones of interactionism—highlights the active roles that individuals and groups play in cultural production and social transformation. A sustained attention to creativity, which may manifest itself in acts ranging from making something new to combining things together in original assemblages, can show us how encounters between users of popular culture and products of popular culture are always potentially alive, inventive, and ingenious.

For instance, in Phillip's essay on video production we learn about the complexities of creating HD video and how those technical challenges serve as media and lessons for the sharing and teaching of skills with others. With a similar interest in doing-it-yourself rather than consuming what others can make for you, McCormack focuses on home improvement as a productive act shaping both a material object (a home) and its users (or dwellers, in this case). In an entirely different context Berry shows us how mundane grocery shopping can be a way of crafting a unique subjectivity, not to mention a consumer's sense of health and body image. In his essay Gottschalk reflects on the ironies of the creative agency and improvisation skills displayed by Guitar Hero players. And in what is possibly the clearest display of creativity as a resistant or at least counter-hegemonic act, Borer teaches us how the making and drinking of craft beers is done to challenge the boorishness of the dominant, mass-manufactured beer industry. Thus creativity, in all of these cases, becomes a key lens for the performance and observation of taste and distinction.

The next theme is *biography*. Certain popular culture products and activities become meaningful in the everyday life of certain individuals, whereas they may remain entirely meaningless in the lives of others. This difference is due in large part to how different people personally relate to something, that is, how they establish associations, how they make connections, how they sympathize with something. When we relate to a film, a TV program, a rock band, or any popular culture object, we typically do so from a biographical perspective. A particular show may remind us of growing up as a child and spending carefree evenings in the living room in the company of our parents and siblings. A song may remind us of a first kiss or a wedding dance. A place of consumption may reconnect us with who we used to be, or whom we once aspired to become, evoking feelings of nostalgia and melancholia.

It is precisely in light of nostalgia that Conroy examines the changing landscape of home entertainment, with the current fragmentation of the TV-watching experience brought about by on-demand content, niche program offering, and the consequent disappearance of video stores. It is with similar nostalgia that Schwalbe recalls reading a special book as a child and catching glimpses, through its pages, of the adult world. Nostalgia is not always an entirely positive feeling. While we may look to the past and its rituals as good times, recalling the past through the lens of popular culture can bring about difficult memories, contested roles and identities, challenging circumstances, and hard choices. Kleinman, who recalls growing up as a nondriver, uses her memories to reflect on how our life in the past can inform the choices we make today as consumers of popular culture. Along the same lines, the essay by Adams challenges us to explain to ourselves why we become attracted to certain reality shows.

Biography, of course, is constantly being written, performed, and revised as we live our day-to-day life. Interactionists believe in a constantly developing self that is continuously emerging and reshaped as a result of different encounters, situations, and environments. Who we were as children and what we experienced during our primary socialization does not determine who we are today, how we live our daily life, or the popular culture we produce or consume now. Rather, our mundane existence over the years is something that is regularly woven into a complex story whose twists and turns make sense only when we look at our biography holistically: with a past or beginning, a middle or present, and a future end.

We cannot talk about biography without talking about how we *bond* with others—our sixth and final relation between popular culture and everyday life. As Daniel Miller (1998) has articulated in his insightful theory of shopping, the activity of consuming is not as self-indulgent, narcissistic, and egotistical as early critics of consumerism made it out to be. Shopping, Miller teaches us, is a way of establishing and maintaining relations with others, often based on bonds built in love and care. The same can be said about popular culture in everyday life. Popular culture becomes meaningful within our mundane existence because of the way it allows us to be with significant others—both those physically close to us, as well as farther away. Popular culture allows us to develop collective identities, group affiliations, and statuses we could not otherwise establish without it.

It is therefore in light of such affordance for bonding—or in other words in light of how certain popular culture objects have the potential to become tools for tackling specific interpersonal tasks—that we become fans of something, frequent consumers, regular watchers or users, and so on. In Schwalbe's essay, for example, we learn about how cult literature can be used to make friends and maintain friendships. In Strobaek's essay we discover how coffee drinking—far from being a mindless routine—works as a social occasion for relationship-maintenance. Through Schneider's attention to the minutia of texting or Klein's attention to selfies we learn how the cell phone has become such a popular consumer item because of the way it allows us to keep in touch with friends at a moment in history when personal relationships are made so difficult by busyness and distance. Newmahr tells us that the same goes for Facebook, of course, which has built its popularity on the same principle by which public squares have worked as meeting spaces throughout human history. And Williams explains how games can be played to establish and maintain relationships.

The idea of bonding is a powerful one for a different reason as well. Not only can we understand the relation between popular culture and everyday life by examining whom we bond with, how, and why, but also whom we do *not* bond with, how, and why (and also why sometimes popular culture is *not* all the fun it seems to be—see Williams's essay, this volume). In spite of an obsessive popular fascination with cars, and indeed an outright fetishization of automobiles—especially in relation to how they express our social and personal identity and how they allegedly enable individual freedom—Kleinman explains how she never came to bond with a car of her own. And it is in light of the absence of that bond that in her case, as well as in the case of many other people who reject dominant trends (like Phillip and his antipathy toward Facebook and cell phones!), we can get a glimpse of that agency, that (relative) freedom to choose, that characterizes interactionist understandings of subjectivity. But there are constraints in place as well, of course. For example, in Irvine's essay we get a sense of the stereotypes (e.g., "crazy cat ladies") that are directed at some pet lovers—largely because they are believed to be individuals who fail to bond with other human beings. And through Mike Atkinson's essay we learn how daily life's temporal and spatial constraints profoundly limit the commitment one can make to popular practices such as sports in light of the interpersonal relationships simultaneously demanding our presence.

Together, these six relations give us a small glimpse into the complex assemblages of popular culture and everyday life. We could have chosen different themes and different essays, of course, but we would have come up with the same conclusion: popular culture dynamics and the way our daily life is lived are simply inextricable. This book itself—not only in content but also in form and identity—is the result of this entanglement.

Note

1. Samuel E. Wood, Ellen Green Wood, and Dennis Boyd. 2010. *The World of Psychology* (7th Ed.). New York, NY: Pearson.

References

Bell, Catherine. 1992. *Ritual Theory, Ritual Practice*. New York, NY: Oxford University Press.

Bennett, Tony. 1980. "Popular Culture: A Teaching Object." *Screen Education 34*: 18.

Blumer, Herbert. 1969. *Symbolic Interactionism: Perspective and Method*. Englewood Cliffs, NJ: Prentice-Hall.

Couldry, Nick. 2003. *Media Rituals: A Critical Approach*. London, UK: Routledge.

Gauntlett, David. 2011. *Making is Connecting. The Social Meaning of Creativity, from DIY and Knitting, to YouTube and Web 2.0*. Cambridge, UK: Polity Press.

Miller, Daniel. 1998. *A Theory of Shopping*. Ithaca, NY: Cornell University Press.

Parker, Holt N. 2011. "Toward a Definition of Popular Culture." *History and Theory 50*(2): 147–170.

Pew Research Project. 2013. "Cell Phone Activities 2013." Washington, DC: Pew Research Center's Internet & American Life Project.

Schechner, Richard. 2013. *Performance Studies: An Introduction (3d. ed.)*. Abington, UK and New York, NY: Routledge.

Storey, John. 2006. *Cultural Theory and Popular Culture: An Introduction*. Athens, GA: University of Georgia Press.

Turner, Victor. 1975. *Dramas, Fields, and Metaphors: Symbolic Action in Human Society*. Ithaca, NY: Cornell University Press.

ESSAYS ON THE DAILY LIFE OF POPULAR CULTURE

1

WATCHING TELEVISION

Thomas Conroy

This essay focuses on the one-time popular pastime of video consumption from video/DVD rental stores, which included the always enjoyable experience of browsing shelves and discovering obscure video content. During its heyday, one specific characteristic of the local video store experience, for me, was the expansion of my tastes and preferences, including the cultivation of the kitschy and the obscure as well as the classical and the iconic. Video stores also fed my nostalgia, providing me with old television programs and old movies, the watching of which evoked earlier eras of my childhood and adolescence. Video stores also allowed me the opportunity to seek out critically acclaimed films from around the world, including those recommended by a number of best-selling video guides.

As a child of the 1960s growing up in blue collar New Jersey, television was very much a part of the fabric of my everyday life. With an aunt and uncle who lived upstairs from us and who enjoyed employee discounts from working for an RCA plant in Edison, New Jersey, our house was not lacking for well-functioning TV sets. I am old enough to remember the shift to color programming ("The following program is brought to you in living color on NBC"), as well as the mix of network and local stations and their range of programming. I can remember—reading everything from science, nature, and history books for kids to *Classic Comics*, *Mad* magazine, and *Famous Monsters of Filmland*—I watched television on my own, particularly shows geared toward kids and popular 1960s sitcoms, as well as shows in the company of my family. On my own, I tended to like informative science shows, but also the pop-kitsch of shows like *The Munsters*, *F-Troop*, *Bewitched*, *Batman*, *The Flintstones*, and *Rowan and Martin's Laugh-In*.

My childhood sense of the possible meaning of the protest-filled Vietnam War era of the late 1960s was undoubtedly shaped by such pop culture representations, even their catch phrases and quirky and sometimes random juxtapositions of square and hip. I also tend to associate particular programs with particular family members: my father and uncle watched sporting and outdoor shows like *The American Sportsmen*, *The Wide World of Sports*, *The Undersea World of Jacques Cousteau*, Yankees baseball and Giants football games and shows depicting war or the Wild West. One aunt watched soap operas, movie melodramas from Hollywood's golden age, and *The Lawrence Welk Show*; another aunt watched the talk shows of David Susskind, Mike Douglas, and Joe Franklin. My older siblings watched music or variety shows like *Shindig*, *American Bandstand*, *The Ed Sullivan Show* (particularly when rock bands were featured), and later *Don Kirshner's Rock Concert* and *The Midnight Special*. To these lists, I will also add game shows, specials, movie programs (e.g., *The Million Dollar Movie*, *The 4:30 Movie*, *Chiller Theater*, etc.), and even the various commercials and station identification moments that I can recall seeing and hearing as evocative signifiers of a TV-watching past. I also retain vivid memories of the adults in our house liking to watch TV news broadcasts, particularly local news broadcasts, and tending to watch the same particular news broadcasts night after night. To this day, I can still rattle off the names of the WABC *Eyewitness News* crew (Roger Grimsby, Bill Beutel, Tex Antoine, etc.) and I have continued my family's habit of watching TV news, including local news, and of connecting, as an audience member, with particular local news personalities.

The television set in our house was a large (for its day) RCA console color TV, built into a wooden cabinet. It was of its time, looking a bit more like a piece of furniture than an electronics gagdet, and it fit right in with the space-age decor of our 1950s and 1960s living room. It sat against a side wall and was thus visibly accessible to anyone who sat in that room (we also had a cabinet-style stereo record player in the same room). On the top floor of my house, where my two aunts and one uncle lived, there were multiple TVs in different rooms, often each tuned to different programs. In fact, my uncle's lair was the upstairs kitchen where I remember him, on a nightly basis, sitting in his kitchen chair, wearing his white t-shirt and slippers and watching a movie or a ball game. He usually sat there watching television while sipping from a can of Horlacher pilsner or from a glass of Seagram's whiskey, which he kept within an easy reach of his seat. When I was upstairs visiting my relatives, as I did nearly every day, I could "sample" the shows that they might each be watching, getting small impression-istic glimpses of their televisual worlds. I also associated the sound of a TV with both floors of our house and occupied by my family members, a happy and comforting association.

With the above notions in mind, I seek here to reflect on some of my own particular experiences of TV and video viewing and, in particular, to reflect on them within the shifting contexts of TV watching as this practice has evolved from the era of large living room TVs receiving signals from broadcast towers to the era of Google TV and of Netflix and Amazon streaming services. In considering such changes, largely through a discussion of some of my own experiences as a TV-viewing child of the 1960s who grew up to become a cultural sociologist who continues to be interested in watching TV, I narratively reflect on the possibilities and potentialities of viewing TV as it now is experienced in the still-evolving digital age. In various ways, watching TV today is not unlike the past practice of video store shopping and browsing—namely, a potentially consciousness-expanding activity grounded in multiple aesthetics, multiple and diverse mass audiences, and the principle of expanded consumer choice.

As I reached adulthood, I watched a bit less TV than I did as a younger person, but this is probably very typical. I found sociology and philosophy while an undergraduate and also came to political awareness at the time of Ronald Reagan's first term—thus in an era of growing conservatism, from which I felt a particular alienation. I also found myself immersed in the art, music, and literary worlds of nearby New York City, and I took advantage of my proximity to the city to explore alternative culture. This included listening to punk, new wave, and experimental music and seeing my share of art and indie films. The 1980s were also proving to be a decade of rapidly changing technological shifts, particularly in the area of personal computing. But with television, it also meant shifts to better quality television sets, the rapid expansion of cable broadcasting, audience size, and to the growing use of home recording and playback systems, such as Betamax and, in particular, Video Home Systems (VHS).

One truly transformative effect of videotaping is that it allowed for recording a show and watching it at some later time after it was broadcast, thus freeing one from having to be home at a particular time for a particular show. I had a 13-inch Sony Trinitron TV in the early 1980s and it was a prized possession, with its rich colors and improved sound system. This made it perfect for watching such stylized content as *Miami Vice* or music video shows. Of course, a mention of the latter suggests MTV, and while I would not become a regular cable TV subscriber until the tail end of the 1980s, I was very much aware of cable from the beginning of the decade and enjoyed the novelty whenever I was visiting someone who had it. My own experiences reflect the general pattern in the United States, in which only around 6% of households were wired for cable by the end of the 1970s, with that number then climbing to 23% in the early 1980s, and 60% by the late 1980s (Thompson, 2014).

The growth in the use of VCRs was rapid over the span of the 1980s, going from merely 1% of all households to nearly 70% (Thompson, 2014). Over this period of time, and into the 1990s, the cost of owning both a VCR and of a prerecorded video tape dropped rapidly. In fact, when I scour used markets and notice that videotapes tend to sell for perhaps one dollar or 50 cents, I am reminded of how expensive they once were. So, the 1980s era of hypercapitalism and the explosion of information and entertainment technologies was very much in keeping with many of the claims which had been made by Jean-François Lyotard (1984) in his massively influential book, *The Postmodern Condition*, in which Lyotard reflects upon such themes as the disintegration of metanarratives, that is, the rapid decline of a shared public consensus about meaning brought on, in part, by technology and novel systems of mass communication. His thinking thus parallels the reality that the once-standard system of mass communications, largely shaped by media companies and directed toward relatively passive receivers, had started to give way to a newer understanding of a media consumer who, aided by technology, constructed his or her own meanings for what was being consumed. In fact, I can recall as a grad student reading and discussing Lyotard with fellow students by day and going home with a videotape for some evening entertainment, thus experiencing my own form of postmodernism as I went about juxtaposing various and disparate forms of media content on one another.

Videos, video rental stores, and regular access to cable TV, along with later immersion in the world of the Internet in the mid-1990s, transformed my viewing habits in a profound and long-lasting way. They allowed, for example, for the possibility of watching videotaped programs in small, fragmentary bites or all the way through. They allowed for freeze framing, so as to more carefully examine the details of a scene. And eventually, after purchasing a second-hand VCR, that allowed for source material examine for building up a private collection of dubbed videos.

As I experienced the 1990s and began researching an eventual doctoral dissertation, I was also introduced by both peers and by circumstances to Usenet and to the World Wide Web. This, for me, along with the continued consumption of both cable and of video, ignited a desire to go deeper into particular genres or auteurs (such as obscure 1970s and 1980s Euro horror films or films by particular, acclaimed directors like Luis Buñuel or Wim Wenders), as well as to connect with a (mostly cyber-) community of like-minded aesthetes (or, perhaps as some analysts might put it, with various "taste cultures"). The 1990s—a decade with both a Baby Boomer in the White House and the revival of a variety of 1960s signifiers, from tie-dye to Woodstock to hippy jam bands—for me also was an irony-oriented decade. For example, network shows like *Seinfeld*, *The Simpsons*, and *Married with Children*, MTV's *Beavis and Butthead*, Comedy Central's *South Park*, and the retro-filled rebroadcasts of Nickelodeon's *Nick at Night* programming, all played off irony, with their witty, sarcastic, and largely youth-oriented observational humor reigning supreme. For me, personally, the best expression of 1990s TV-watching irony was probably the series of "bad movie" gatherings that I would host for my grad student friends in my Boston apartment. Our definition of fun was watching movies like *Dr. Butcher, MD*, or *Glen or Glenda?* and riffing on the scenes as the movie played. It helped to have a good trash aesthetic, and there were certainly lots of available resources for developing one. And this example of video-watching parties also reminds me of the one-time phenomenon of going to the video rental store as a social activity, done in groups or by couples, where the ultimate goal was nearly always trying to negotiate what everyone would like to watch.

Today, as I reflect on the even more hypercapitalist and more advanced tech-driven world of the twenty-first century and on what it means to watch TV nowadays, I am struck by a few things. One is the bewildering array of choices that the typical consumer now faces. HD (High Definition) televisions have now given way to UHD (Ultra High Definition) sets, with even clearer resolution and detail. Television sets are nowadays larger, flatter, and "smarter" than ever before, but also increasingly more affordable to the average consumer, and in many ways the lines between a television set and a personal computer are becoming ever more blurred. The notion of a home space for TV viewing being transformed into a "home theater" is not all that far-fetched. TV sets today also often have such features as 3D viewing, built-in WIFI, smart TV Internet platforms, and webcams. The array of technical offerings now available are such that many are predicting the eventual end of the widespread subscription to ever-more expensive cable or dish TV packages, as consumers seek out alternative content sources such as Google/YouTube, Hulu Plus, and on-demand pay services such as Amazon and Netflix. Various cellular phone service providers like Sprint, Verizon, and Virgin Mobile want to get in on the act by offering apps and data plans that allow their customers to consume media content in ways that they might have once done through a membership in (now defunct) Blockbuster Videos. And interestingly, just as some consumers of recorded music have returned to collecting and listening to records on vinyl, some TV users are returning to using TV antennas to receive broadcast signals on their sets. The choices are truly wide-ranging.

Experientially, watching TV nowadays means that one is likely multi-tasking and partaking in a more decentralized activity than were the TV audiences of the twentieth century. Watching a marathon of selected shows—everything from *Breaking Bad* or *The Walking Dead* to *Top Chef* or *Curb Your Enthusiasm*—on a video streaming service, means that one can spend a day or a weekend diving headfirst into an entire season of a show. The notion of a "TV season" or a standardized 30-minute-based time frame for shows is coming to seem increasingly quaint, or less orderly and predictable than it once was. Providing a less centralized set of choices to consumers may also mean that consumers are able to increasingly pursue a much wider range of content options; while many will likely choose the more familiar options, others will likely peruse a wide range of options and some will probably pursue the most obscurely quirky. We see this already in the large number of examples of YouTube videos that have gone viral, much to just about everyone's surprise.

As was the case in the mid-1980s, I may be somewhat behind the curve at the moment, but I remain very interested in future possibilities. I still own a non–flat screen TV, a 27-inch Sharp television that I purchased in early 2001—and it seemed rather state of the art at the time. It seems anything but, nowadays, and while I am still in the window-shopping phase of determining its best possible replacement, it is soon to be replaced by something newer. I am looking toward soon cutting my cable and setting up a different and hopefully better way of receiving audiovisual content. And if anything, I find myself even more immersed in the Internet than I was when I began with it some 20 years ago. So while I certainly do not think of myself as an early adopter of technology, I do believe in staying open to new ideas, including the idea of technology. In short, I am like millions of others my age or close to me in age; we were not born into a digital world, but having immigrated into it, we are more or less assimilating into it to the best of our abilities.

As I reflect on the progression of styles of watching TV and how it has changed over time, there are many features of this change that stand out. Some of these are technical and others more content-related. Technological changes have given modern televisions greater capacities those of the past. High-definition broadcasting is now a norm and goes hand in hand with the demand for LCD and plasma TVs. Some TVs allow for 3D imagery; others for "picture-in-picture," which allows the viewer to watch two channels at once. Some TVs allow for Internet or

Wi-Fi connectivity. In fact, how TVs connect with the world—that is, the number and types of inputs for connecting to other devices—is now a variable. And along with this, TV watchers increasingly want to replicate the movie theater experience at home, hooking their TV sets up to enhanced, external sound systems and arranging their large flat-screens in front of carefully arranged specialty furniture created for maximum comfort. Yet, while such flat screen sets have gotten larger, flatter and more technically sophisticated, watching TV has at the same time become a more mobile activity, as individuals bring their smart phones and tablets with them virtually everywhere, placing themselves in a position to watch TV content in a wide range of settings and on a variety of possible screens.

And as the act of watching TV has been technically freed up from the need to be stationary, one final conclusion that one might draw is that TV watching has shifted away from a social to a more individualized—perhaps one might even say atomized—experience. Perhaps we are moving away from the notion that "mass audiences" are even possible, given the wide variations in both content and context for TV viewing.

Thomas Conroy teaches in the Department of Sociology at Lehman College—City University of New York, and studies topics broadly related to everyday life cultural practices. He is the editor of *Food and Everyday Life* (Lexington Press, 2014). He teaches courses on research methods, the sociology of culture, the sociology of youth, and the sociology of food and nutrition. He received his Ph.D. in sociology from Boston University.

References

Lyotard, Jean-François, Geoffrey Bennington, and Brian Massumi. 1984. *The Postmodern Condition: A Report on Knowledge*. Minneapolis, MN: University of Minnesota Press.

Thompson, Robert J. 2014. "Television in the United States." in *Encyclopedia Brittanica online*. Retrieved from http://www.britannica.com/EBchecked/topic/1513870/Television-in-the-United-States/283635/The-era-of-the-miniseries.

2

WATCHING REALITY TELEVISION

Tony E. Adams

In this chapter you describe the experience of watching reality television. You focus on watching one reality television series—*Here Comes Honey Boo Boo*—and think about the ways your experience connects with this text. You examine the values and practices represented in this series, as well as moments when personal and televisual experiences merge. You demonstrate how watching reality television can be an exercise in identification and an experience that incites an "assemblage of disparate forms and realms of life" (Stewart 2007: 21).

*

You begin by thinking about the embodied experiences of watching television. With Langsdorf (1994: 102–103), you agree that "many of the voluntary and involuntary responses characteristic of embodied experience"—responses such as "muscle tension" and "fear"—occur while watching TV, yet you know, "cognitively," that you do not share the same "spatiotemporal contexts" of the televized content. Here, like Langsdorf, you note the "curious disjuncture" between "cognitive activity" and "sensory, affective, and kinesthetic-tactile activities," as these activities, while watching, are "evoked by cognitive activity other than your own"—that is, evoked by actors, producers, and editors. Chvasta and Fassett (2003: 217) make a similar observation about the "immediacy" of watching: "The images on the screen are right there with us, time and again," they write. "The action feels as though we are watching 'the real' unfold, that we are co-present with the bodies projected on the screen."

You then think about the embodied experiences of watching *reality* television—a genre of programming characterized by "grand productions" of "banal interactions" (Fox 2013: 190–191), "unscripted" yet "carefully crafted and contrived" situations involving "people who are not professional actors" (Dubrofsky 2011: 10); intimate glimpses into the "everyday, domestic, and backstage regions of ordinary individuals' lives" (Cavalcante 2014: 41). Using a mixture of unscripted yet contrived backstage portrayals of sometimes grand, sometimes banal events and people, reality television programming makes it easy for you to "project [yourself] into their situations and decide whether [you] would behave similarly" (Chvasta and Fassett 2003: 215). Or in the words of Langsdorf (1994: 103): Your "cognitive activity" and your "sensory, affective, and kinesthetic-tactile activities" may align as the people and situations on screen could be, and could happen to, you.

*

The reality television programs you tend to watch align with the identities and lifestyles which you desire, appreciate, find most intriguing, or are most familiar (identification). A competitive edge and desire for travel might lead you to *The Amazing Race, American Ninja Warrior*, or *Survivor*; an interest in health and weight loss might lead you to *The Biggest Loser*; a desire for love and marriage might lead you to *The Bachelor, Flavor of Love*, or the *Million Dollar Matchmaker*; an intrigue with social conflict and living with strangers might lead you to *The Real World* or *Big Brother*; and a fascination with celebrities and material excess might lead you to *Keeping Up with the Kardashians* and *The Real Housewives*. Given your rural upbringing, you find yourself watching *Here Comes Honey Boo Boo*—a reality television series with which you identify.

Here Comes Honey Boo Boo started on The Learning Channel (TLC) in 2012. A spin-off series from the reality series *Toddlers and Tiaras* and set in McIntryre, Georgia (United States), the show portrays some of the family life of Alana ("Honey Boo Boo"); her parents, June and Sugarbear; her three sisters, Lauren ("Pumpkin"), Jessica ("Chubbs"), and Anna ("Chickadee"); and Kaitlyn, her niece (Anna's child).

Although plenty of watchers support the series (see Cavalcante 2014; Friedman 2014), there has been much criticism of the series and the family. For example, in "The Psych Approach," an opinion-editorial in the *New York Times*, Brooks calls the family a "train wreck working-class family" and classifies the series as a popular text that shows how "social dysfunction can ruin lives." Similarly, Miller (2013) analyzes the program in terms of unintelligent, crude, violent, and unhealthy behaviors.

*

You dislike these critiques—they feel personal—and think about your profile as a reality television watcher. You were born in 1979 in a conservative, and economically depressed factory and farming town of approximately 30,000 people. You lived in this impoverished town for the first 20 years of your life. You were not surprised by a 2014 report from the U.S. Bureau of Economic Analysis designating the town as the "cheapest place to live" in the entire United States (Bomkamp 2014). Your family life consists of many secrets and betrayals, hoarding behaviors, and unnerving silences about physical health and mental illnesses. But you also have fond memories of childhood and do your best to appreciate this complicated family.

As an only child living in a rural setting, you remember that, as a child, your best friend was a stick. You spent much time outdoors, playing in the sand, fighting off monsters, talking to yourself while hiding in a variety of self-made clubhouses. After it rained, you would sometimes splash in post-rain puddles, and, if it rained enough, you would swim in the ditch next to the road. Barefoot and careless, you would wade around for minutes and maybe even hours. Later that evening, your body would itch from an abundance of chigger bites.

These experiences inform how you watch *Here Comes Honey Boo Boo*. In one episode, you see members of the family swim in a body of water with a "contaminated water" sign posted nearby; in other episodes, you watch family members splash in post-rain puddles. In these moments on the screen, you identify with the family and ruminate on the barefoot and careless moments of youth. You think fondly of those moments and wonder if you could ever return to living a "simpler," more imaginative existence.

*

A neighbor, and one of your dad's employees at his rural bar and grill, appreciated the ditch for another reason: the space served as a source of food. Often post-rain, she would go to the ditch and hunt for crayfish. She would collect them, boil them, make a casserole, and bring the dish to your dad's restaurant for everyone to share. With the crayfish-heads still attached, sticking and staring out of the casserole, you would take them, crack the skulls with your mouth, and suck out the guts.

After moving away from this rural setting, you started to distance yourself from such a "disgusting," rural past. But watching *Here Comes Honey Boo Boo* has encouraged you to reclaim and reframe your past—especially memories of the ditch as a space for entertainment and food. You find yourself judging the past less and assume that critics of *Here Comes Honey Boo Boo* do not know about the mundane pleasures of random and "contaminated" water areas or the foods these areas harvest.

*

Reflecting on childhood eating habits also encourages you to think about the raced and classed characteristics of food, nourishment, and health. On *Here Comes Honey Boo Boo*, you watch many discussions of finding and eating "road kill"—an animal killed by traffic—as long as the animal has not been dead for too long (more than three hours). In one episode, you even see a dead raccoon with its paws still attached; family members say the paws are necessary insignia to indicate that the dead animal is a raccoon, not a cat. In another episode, you watch Pumpkin participate in a contest requiring her to dunk her head in a tub of water and use her mouth to collect (severed) pigs' feet. In another episode you watch the family make "sketti"—pasta with butter and ketchup sauce and remember that your family also used to eat sketti. And in another episode, you watch the family eat as much food as they can at a local restaurant and remember numerous, enjoyable family visits to all-you-can-eat buffets.

While watching, you think of Boylorn's (2013: 182) research about the raced and classed aspects of food: "Black country families have an acquired taste," she writes.

> In many ways our cultural heritage is tied to class circumstances. We make do with what other people don't want. We eat the parts of the pig that everyone else throws away. Pig's feet, ears, jaws, snout, brains, and chittlins are fried or boiled and drowned in vinegar and

hot sauce, a delicacy only prepared for special occasions. Fixing chittlins was a time-consuming labor of love generally saved for Thanksgiving and Christmas. My grandmother would spend hours "cleaning" the pork intestines before she cooked them. I never understood how with that much meticulous cleaning they still smelled like shit. It only took them about an hour to cook, but it would take all day to the get the smell out of the house. But little or nothing, we never perished for lack of food. If you were hungry, my grandmother was Jesus, feeding the multitude with loaves and fishes. Everyone always left full.

You think about people who criticize the eating habits of the *Here Comes Honey Boo Boo* family,[1] and you want to call these critics classist, racist, elitist, and privileged, especially if they can avoid eating crayfish from the ditch, road kill, and sketti, and especially if they can avoid cleaning pork intestines and living in a house that smells like shit.

*

Many episodes of *Here Comes Honey Boo Boo* show Sugar Bear (the father) chewing tobacco. June (the mother) tells Sugar Bear to "take the dip out" before he kisses her. You remember the male baseball players in high school religion class who would chew tobacco during every class. When the teacher—a Catholic priest—would turn his back, the boys would spit their tobacco-spit on the steam heater in the back of the room. Even though the mixture of spit, tobacco, and heat created a terrible smell, the priest never caught them in the act.

As Sugar Bear removes the dip, you see images of his rotted and rotting, brown-stained teeth, and you think about teeth, smiles, and social class: "When you smile," Hodges (2014: 3) writes, "you are letting us know who you are and where you come from—what sort of advantages you do and do not have."

You recall a recent dentist visit when you asked the hygienist if she cleans the teeth of patients who chew. She said that in Chicago chew is rare, at least for her clients—the people who have the time and money to visit a dentist. She also said she encountered more chew while working as a hygienist in rural Michigan.

You then think not only of Sugar Bear in rural Georgia but also of your uncle in rural Illinois who chews tobacco throughout the day, spitting in a glass or a bottle and sometimes even swallowing the spit. He no longer has many teeth but seems to take pleasure in a constant mouthful of tobacco.

You also think about who chews: even though your father has owned a rural bar for decades—a place where alcohol and chew freely flow—you have never met a woman who chews. As a gay man who has met many other gay men, you have only ever met two gay men who chewed—one in Tampa, Florida, and one in Nashville, Tennessee. The Nashville gay man wanted to kiss but you politely and adamantly refused his advance; it would have felt like kissing Sugar Bear, or your uncle. But in this refusal, you cannot help but feel like the elitist and privileged snob you never wanted to be—a snob trapped by biases in support of straight and white teeth (Hodges 2014; Myers 2008).

*

On camera, Honey Boo Boo's family seems full of love and support. You rarely see any drama—no thrills, no suspense, and no intense conflict, just images of the family getting on and along together. Sugar Bear and June often say that their girls need to focus on themselves rather than worry about dating. They frequently discuss sex and sexual practices, as well as June's hesitation to marry Sugar Bear—even though they had been a couple for eight years, June said that she did not need the term "marriage" to legitimate their relationship. One of the daughters has been in an interracial relationship for nearly two years, and then there is gay Uncle Poodle, and Honey Boo Boo saying that everyone is "a little bit gay." June also says, "no matter what, I think my child does good," and Sugar Bear remarks, "I'm happiest when I'm home with the girls."

Whereas you admire this love and support, you also feel envious of such progressive attitudes and the well-cultivated representation of unconditional love; you did not experience these attitudes or this love from your family, especially after coming out as gay. In these moments while watching, you dis-identify with the series.

*

Stewart (2007) characterizes reality television as a kind of "trauma TV" consisting of "vicious spectacles of pain and dysfunction," television in which the "camera busts in on intimate dramas of whole families addicted to sniffing paint right out of the can" (105). But with *Here Comes Honey Boo Boo*, you do not watch much pain or dysfunction—unless dysfunction is defined as unsanitary swimming habits, inexpensive and lower class food choices, (the appearance of) unconditional love, or the choice to chew tobacco.

Although you worry about the family being exploited and judged by audiences, you hope that they are financially compensated and protected in their outside-of-reality-television life. You also hope that the appearance of love and support is sincere and felt by family members. As you watch, you recognize that your past has made you who you are: you may no longer splash in post-rain puddles or catch crayfish from the ditch or chew tobacco, but you try to judge your past less. You are also reminded of the joys of childhood, feel envy toward the portrayed abundance of family love and support, and feel less lonely and peculiar about your family's behaviors, especially when you watch others celebrate rural life. And so now, when you hear critics criticize Honey Boo Boo and her family, you become defensive; you take this criticism personally, as it could be directed at you.

You conclude by wondering if watchers who dis-identify with the series offer the harshest critiques, while those who identify with the series offer different, more complicated and supportive responses. You do not have any reservations critiquing *The Amazing Race, American Ninja Warrior*, or *Survivor*; or *The Biggest Loser*; or *The Bachelor, Flavor of Love*, or the *Million Dollar Matchmaker*, or *The Real World* or *Big Brother*; or the Kardashians or the Housewives—but you also do not relate to these texts. Instead, you identify most with *Here Comes Honey Boo Boo*, as it incites an "assemblage of disparate forms and realms of [your] life" (Stewart 2007: 21).

*

One week after completing a draft of this essay, news stories emerge about Mama June being seen with Mark McDaniel, a former boyfriend who was recently released from prison for child molestation and who may have sexually assaulted Anna, Mama June's oldest daughter. Supposedly, Mama June and Sugar Bear separate as well. Even though TLC has an entire unaired season of the series, the network immediately cancels the show.

You worry about the negative media coverage of Mama June and the former boyfriend, Sugar Bear and the children, the child molestation and sexual assault; you worry that the family—your TV family—is falling apart. You try to watch more television in search of clarification, eager for the news sources to be incorrect. If the sources are correct, you hope the family stays secure, strong. You wish them well, though they have now inconvenienced you; you must search for another program—and another family—to watch.

Tony E. Adams is an Associate Professor and Chair of the Department of Communication, Media and Theatre at Northeastern Illinois University. He attended private Catholic school from ages four to eighteen, worked as a bartender at Yellowstone National Park, and as a teller supervisor at a bank; he has been a vegetarian since 1998. He studies and teaches about interpersonal and family communication; autoethnography; qualitative research; communication theory; and sex, gender, and sexuality. He has published 4 books and more than 50 articles, book chapters, and reviews in these areas.

Note

1. Miller (2013) writes, "In one episode, June, otherwise known as 'Mama,' clocked in at over 300 pounds. Rather than seeming concerned for their health, the characters made minimal efforts to change their eating and lifestyle habits."

References

Bomkamp, Samantha. 2014, May 29. "Danville, Ill., the cheapest place to live in the U.S." *Chicago Tribune*. Retrieved from http://my.chicagotribune.com/#section/-1/article/p2p-80346236/.

Boylorn, Robin M. 2013. "'Sit With Your Legs Closed!' and Other Sayin's From My Childhood." In Stacy Holman Jones, Tony E. Adams and Carolyn Ellis (Eds.), *Handbook of Autoethnography*. Walnut Creek, CA: Left Coast Press, 173–185.

Brooks, David. 2012, September 28. "The Psych Approach." *New York Times*. Retrieved from http://www.nytimes.com/2012/09/28/opinion/brooks-the-psych-approach.html.

Cavalcante, André. 2014. "You better 'Redneckognize'!: Deploying the Discourses of Realness, Social Defiance, and Happiness to Defend *Here Comes Honey Boo Boo* on Facebook." In Alison F. Slade, Amber J. Narro, and Barton P. Buchanan (Eds.), *Reality Television: Oddities of Culture*. Landham, MD: Lexington Books, 39–58.

Chvasta, Marcy R. and Deanna L. Fassett. 2003. "Traveling the Terrain of Screened Realities: Our Reality, Our Television." In Matthew J. Smith and Andrew F. Wood (Eds.), *Survivor Lessons: Essays on Communication and Reality Television*. Jefferson, NC: McFarland, 213–224.

Dubrofsky, Rachel E. 2011. *The Surveillance of Women on Reality Television: Watching* The Bachelor *and* The Bachelorette. Lanham, MD: Lexington.

Fox, Ragan. 2013. "'You are Not Allowed to Talk about Production': Narratization On (and Off) the Set of CBS's *Big Brother*." *Critical Studies in Media Communication 30*: 189–208.

Friedman, May. 2014. "Here Comes a Lot of Judgment: *Honey Boo Boo* as a Site of Reclamation and Resistance." *Journal of Popular Television 2*: 77–95.

Hodges, Nathan. 2015. "The American Dental Dream." *Health Communication 30:* 943–950. Retrieved from DOI:10.1080/10410236.2014.914621.

Langsdorf, Lenore. 1994. "'I Like to Watch:' Analyzing a Participation-and-Denial Phenomenon." *Human Studies 17*: 81–108.

Miller, Ariel. 2013. "The Construction of Southern Identity Through Reality TV: A Content Analysis of *Here Comes Honey Boo Boo, Duck Dynasty* and *Buckwild*." *Elon Journal of Undergraduate Research in Communications 4*(2): 1–5.

Myers, W. Benjamin. 2008. "Straight and White: Talking With My Mouth Full." *Qualitative Inquiry 14*: 160–171.

Stewart, Kathleen. 2007. *Ordinary Affects*. Durham, NC: Duke University Press.

CHARLES EDGLEY

3

WATCHING DRUG COMMERCIALS

Charles Edgley

Man must be everyday, or he must not be at all.
—Henri Lefebvre

Turn on television and you'll likely find yourself watching programs sponsored at least in part by drug companies. Big pharma's slick and compelling ads permeate television as they cover the entire gamut of human ills, real and imaginary, the distinction itself making no sense in the everyday world of how we view them. In drug ads, it seems, if you think you're sick, you're sick—although, as the ads purr, you "should always check with your doctor." These commercials are such a firmly planted feature of popular culture that even occasional viewers know their format by heart. We interact with and interpret these cultural tropes from the standpoint of what Schütz calls "the natural attitude" (Schütz 1962). In other words, we see them through a "veil of familiarity" (Mitchell 2006) or a semiotic "code" (Baudrillard 1994). They are examples of what de Certeau (2011) called "the practice of everyday life." But far from being helpless victims of a mass media juggernaut, we "do" them rather than simply consume what the industry has offered us and, as we shall see, our doings are often designed to blunt their power.

As I watched dozens of drug commercials in preparation for writing this essay, I was reminded of Thomas Szasz's (2007) ideas about the "medicalization of everyday life" where all of life's problems have been transformed into diseases. A Cymbalta ad asks the viewer to "imagine the day with less pain" as it shows an assortment of limping, knee- and back-grabbing wretches writhing in agony. But one "non-narcotic" pill later they emerge from their cocoon of suffering smiling, laughing and ready to take on the day. Am I one of those? Not usually, but on those days when I am, I find myself reaching for one of their products even when I know better.

Symbolic creatures that we are, such ads are among the best known parables of our culture. (Postman 1987) Their power lies in the fact that they are not thought of as either parables or stories. The allegory of drug ads goes roughly like this: (1) begin with a description of an intractable medical problem superimposed over helpless sufferers; (2) follow with the revelation of an impressive pharmacopeia offered up as a solution; (3) end with a depiction of a grateful and now-cured former victims, their life pharmacologically restored as if by some inscrutable magic. In the narrative of this prescription drug utopia, life is seen as a steady parade of diseases all of which can be ameliorated by a chemical substance. Unlike former campaigns against recreational drugs that told us to "just say no", drug companies urge us to "just say 'yes' to drugs—their drugs" (see Devaney 2014). Drugs taken on one's own are the paradigm of "drug-abuse" whereas drugs taken under the supervision of a doctor are the standard of proper drug "use." So in the logic of drug commercials we accept this medical paternalism without thought or protest even though prescription drugs are far more likely to be "abused" than are illegal drugs. As I watch I can't help but notice that that law firms often run their ads, virtually in tandem, seeking clients injured by the same drugs. One hand washes the other.

I'm trying to watch television, but I keep getting interrupted by what seems like an unending procession of drug ads. Can't sleep? With the prescription sleep aid Lunesta, I will finally be "ready for bed." Soothing words purr their message of pharmacological bliss: "We know a place where tossing and turning have given way to sleeping; where sleepless nights have given way to restful sleep." The words are shown over a video of a diaphanous bright green Luna moth hovering dreamily over a cityscape. The rheumatoid arthritis drug Embrel hits the jackpot with its celebrity endorsement from pro golfer Phil Mickelson who emphasizes how the drug has helped him with the "little things"—family, friends and kid's soccer games. The fact that these narratives are almost wholly fictional is beside the point. I know this, but they draw me in anyway, perhaps in the same way that soap operas do.

Everyday life in America is saturated with these inducements to buy,[1] pitched to a public that is always suffering from something. If you don't think so, the job of the ads is to put doubts in your mind. Acid reflux, gout, social anxiety disorder, hemorrhoids, upset stomach, rashes, and phobias all have symptoms which are common to most everyone at some time, and the ads are ready to offer us remedies for the numerous diseases to which hypermodern citizens are said to be subject.

"Natural" Alternatives

Like the price, the safety and effectiveness of prescription drugs have come under scrutiny.[2] Alternate treatments, home remedies, and over-the-counter nostrums have developed an expanded market of their own, hyping their healing powers with the same zeal as prescription drugs. Worried about listlessness? Why not try the *Twelve-Day Liver Detox* program? Fearful of prescription pain killers? Try acupuncture or chiropractic adjustments. Do you think that the 45 million prescriptions doled out yearly for cholesterol-lowering drugs might be a problem? Oats, garlic, and red wine might just be the answer, because "a study shows that these substances lower cholesterol as well as statin drugs."[3]

Don't like those numbers? Try Hawthorne berries. Battling acid reflux? It's the fad disease of the new millennium. Try the purple pill. But if you're worried about the possible link between Prilosec and esophageal cancer, slippery elm lozenges are a "natural" alternative. One might note that cyanide is also "all natural", but these ads are unsurprisingly vague about what constitutes "natural" and why it is better than conventional pharmacology. But, as Postman's aforementioned parables remind us, ads are not to be examined literally—or even rationally—but emotionally and metaphorically, and so such questions are inappropriate.

The Disclaimer Masquerade

The 1969 FDA requirement that drug advertisements include a comprehensive list of side effects did not constitute a serious problem as long as drug ads were primarily limited to print media. But in the 1980s when television became the preferred medium of direct-to-consumer advertising, space limitations became overwhelming, especially with the large number of side effects associated with many drugs. Hence, the drug companies rolled out a series of maneuvers designed to avoid or minimize this requirement. This is why voice-overs talk so rapidly. Imagine this disclaimer for the smoking cessation drug Chantix rattled off at fast-forward speed:

> Some people have had changes in behavior, hostility, agitation, depressed mood, suicidal thoughts or actions while using CHANTIX to help them quit smoking. Some people had these symptoms when they began taking CHANTIX, and others developed them after several weeks of treatment or after stopping CHANTIX. If you, your family, or caregiver notice agitation, hostility, depression, or changes in behavior, thinking, or mood that are not typical for you, or you develop suicidal thoughts or actions, anxiety, panic, aggression, anger, mania, abnormal sensations, hallucinations, paranoia, or confusion, stop taking CHANTIX and call your doctor right away. Also tell your doctor about any history of depression or other mental health problems before taking CHANTIX, as these symptoms may worsen while taking CHANTIX. (Standard disclaimer found in Chantix ads).

I watch and listen with a sense of wonderment coupled with amusement. Couldn't this entire litany of symptoms be associated with quitting smoking itself and not with taking the drug? The format of disclaimers has become an occasion for comedy, both for the public and probably for the drug companies themselves. Written by lawyers to comply minimally with regulations the drug companies would like to avoid altogether, they are a masquerade of seriousness not to be taken seriously at all. It works. I find myself laughing and ignoring them at the same time.

Erectile Dysfunction: Adventures in Hyperland

Sex has traditionally been used to sell products, but in the hyperreal world of biotechnology, sex does not sell products so much as the product produces new forms of sex. Viagra has become the poster child for lifestyle drugs that transcend the real and propel us into the domain of what Eco (1986) and later Baudrillard (1996) call the "hyperreal." They figure heavily in television commercials, and these ads have undergone a major transformation since Pfizer discovered the drug quite by accident and began marketing it in 1998 as a treatment for the new disease of "erectile dysfunction," defined as the inability to get or keep an erection. The first Viagra ads were targeted at males and urged them to "have the talk" with their doctor. This followed the general premise of direct-to-consumer marketing which was that since doctors write the prescriptions, the first conversation needed to be with them. But more recently Viagra ads have targeted women ("the other victim" of ED) who urge their men to fix this problem. An alluring and seemingly aroused female with a British accent lounges on a bed and speaks softly into a close camera which serves to emphasize the intimacy of the occasion: "So guys, it's just you and your honey. The setting is perfect. But then erectile dysfunction happens *again*," she says before following the script which encourages men to ask their doctor about Viagra. "Plenty of guys have this issue—not just getting an erection, but keeping it" (YouTube 2014).

Television ads for Viagra and its imitators Cialis and Levitra play on a dream of eternal phallic perfection (Croissant 2008) coupled with a sexual body unable to achieve this goal without pharmacological assistance. Failure to achieve the preferred norm—penetrative sex on demand (Croissant 2008)—is seen not as a moral failing or even a cause for alarm, but as an easily remedied mechanical breakdown akin to a flat tire. How did we get to this new place with a phenomenon as old as sex? Part of the answer is that simulacra are never faithful representations of reality.

Since there is no unmediated reality to be faithful to but only simulations of it, they can never be "accurate" or "inaccurate" (Croissant 2008). Reality-based critiques are simply irrelevant to the procession of simulacra that constitute ads for Viagra. In this new hyperreal world of sexuality, age, disability, fatigue, or anything else that intervenes to prevent the delivery of flaccid flesh at a time when turgidity is called for are no longer excuses for the inability to perform. Moreover, with its longer-lasting effective performance window, Cialis commercials alter the traditional gender balance of sexual power by urging men to take the drug so they can "be ready when she is." The old non-pharmaceutical world of sex forced women to "be ready when he was." But now in the new hyperworld of lifestyle drugs she's in charge. When his socialized penis fails to perform, a pharmacological solution is readily available. Just as Viagra revolutionized the making of pornography by eliminating male down-time (Faludi 1995), Cialis leveled the gender playing field in the bedroom by removing male excuses for failure to perform.

Conclusions on the Everyday Life of Producing Drug Ad Culture

In spite of the sheer volume of everyday human interactions responsible for the kind of dramatic productions we have observed in this essay, the conventional way social scientists have analyzed advertising (including drug ads) is to move from cultural products to their presumed effects on the consuming public. Human beings are seen, as Garfinkel's ethnomethodology famously maintained, as "cultural dopes" reflecting and reproducing society without being aware of what they're doing (Garfinkel 1967: 68). But popular culture does not come about this way. Instead, it arises as an interactive accomplishment. If people do nothing—absurd on the face of it—nothing happens that can be called "popular culture." Moreover, as de Certeau maintains (2011), the strategies and tactics used by advertisers to impose themselves on consumers are often met by counter-tactics which resist their manipulation. An advertiser may stage all the talk and visual imagery their hired image makers can summon, but in the end, it is the consumer whose actions or inactions, determines the fate of a product.

In this sense, ads are always a buyer's market. Meaning and action are paramount and the annals of advertising are filled with products that didn't make it because the public used such counter-tactics to reject the inducements of its ads. As I think about this, I'm heartened by the old joke among marketers about the CEO of a dog food company who pours millions into an award-winning ad campaign, yet sales remain disappointingly flat. He summons his underlings to account for the failure. "Since the ads are so good, why aren't sales better?" he asks. "Only one problem, boss," says a subordinate: "The dogs won't eat it." We may be forced to consume, but the way we do so determines our relationship to the objects of consumption and thus their fate in the marketplace. De Certeau takes us further by wanting to know what consumers make of what they absorb, receive, and pay for and what they do with it? Drug ads are just this kind of product we are obliged to consume by virtue of our desire to watch television, but: *"It is always good to remind ourselves that we mustn't take people for fools"* (De Certeau 1984: 176).

The active ways in which people relate to drug commercials underscores that we most certainly are not fools. Viewers use numerous tactics to blunt the force of ads. Among them are objective analysis, *satire, and irony* as we get on with our lives even as the ads try to reduce us to cultural dopes and consuming fools. In my case, and no doubt because of my profession, analysis offers a foil. Finding that most ads ripped out their natural context and placed into an analytical one become funny, I laugh at them, reducing their effectiveness. So the consumer is not as passive as we thought and can even be wholly unmanageable (Gabriel and Lange 1995). I sigh with relief. I'm a human being after all.

Charles Edgley teaches for the Department of Sociology and Anthropology at the University of Arkansas at Little Rock where he moved after a long career at Oklahoma State University. He has written, edited, or revised eight books, as well as publishing numerous articles within the symbolic interactionist tradition. He has written extensively on both sexuality and the health and fitness movement. His has recently contributed a chapter to Thomas S. Weinberg and Staci Newmahr's book *Selves, Symbols, and Sexuality: An Interactionist Anthology* (Sage Publications, 2015). Dr. Edgley also edited a recent collection of original essays on dramaturgy for the Ashgate *Interaction Currents* series entitled *The Drama of Social Life: A Dramaturgical Handbook* (Ashgate, 2013). In addition, he is the editor of *Life as Theater: A Dramaturgical Sourcebook* (with the late Dennis Brissett; AldineTransaction, 1990), a book that has become a standard reference in dramaturgical social psychology. Dr. Edgley also co-edits, with Jeffrey Nash, the *Journal of Contemporary Ethnography* (Sage Publications).

Notes

1. Only two countries have legalized direct-to-consumer prescription drug advertising: the United States and New Zealand. What we have said here about the saturation of drug ads cannot be said about other countries.

2. Johns Hopkins' Bloomberg School of Public Health regularly publishes studies of this problem through their Center for Drug Safety and Effectiveness. See http://www.jhsph.edu/research/centers-and-institutes/center-for-drug-safety-and-effectiveness/.

3. Ads for supplements and other forms of alternative medicine are filled with this kind of data of dredging: "In a study ..." For a full debunking of this kind of misuse of statistics, see Best, 2012.

References

Baudrillard, Jean. 1994. *Simulacra and Simulation* (trans. Sheila Glaser). Ann Arbor, MI: University of Michigan Press.

Best, Joel. 2012. *Damned Lies and Statistics: Untangling Numbers From the Media, Politicians, and Activists*. Berkeley, CA: University of California Press.

Croissant, Jennifer L. 2006. "The New Sexual Technobody: Viagra in the Hyperreal World." *Sexualities* 9(3): 333–344.

De Certeau, Michel. 1984. *The Practice of Everyday Life*. Berkeley, CA: University of California Press.

De Certeau, Michel. 2011. *The Practice of Everyday Life*. Berkeley, CA: University of California Press.

Devaney, Erik. 2014. "Say 'Yes' to Drugs? The History of Pharmaceutical Marketing" [blog post]. Retrieved from http://blog.hubspot.com/marketing/pharmaceutical-marketing-history.

Eco, Umberto. 1986. *Travels in Hyperreality*. New York, NY: Harcourt Brace Jovanovich.

Faludi, Susan. 1995. "The Money Shot." *The New Yorker* (October 30): 64–70.

Gabriel, Yiannis and Tim Yang. 1995. *The Unmanageable Consumer: Contemporary Consumption and its Fragmentation*. London, UK: Sage Publications.

Garfinkel, Harold. 1967. *Studies in Ethnomethodology*. Englewood Cliffs, N.J.: Prentice-Hall.

Mitchell, W.J.T. 2006. *What do Pictures Want?: The Lives and Loves of Images*. Chicago, IL: University of Chicago Press.

Postman, Neil. 1986. *Amusing Ourselves to Death*. London, UK: William Heinemann Ltd.

Schütz, Alfred. 1967. *Phenomenology of the Social World*. Evanston, IL: Northwestern University Press.

Szasz, Thomas. 2007. *The Medicalization of Everyday Life*. Syracuse, NY: Syracuse University Press.

YouTube. 2014, September 30. "Viagra Targets Women for the First Time." [TV Commercial]. Retrieved from https://www.youtube.com/watch?v=L_ETKkt2r80.

YouTube. n.d. "Pretendarin Drug Ad Parody." Retrieved from https://www.youtube.com/watch?v=tvFh84SGksQ.

4

USING MOBILE PHONES[1]

Christopher J. Schneider

> Everyone has a phone in their pocket. Just a few years ago nobody had *their* phone. It was just *the* phone.
>
> —Louis CK (emphasis original)

Louis CK's astute observation that everyone has a phone in his or her pocket might be amended to something like *everyone* has a phone *everywhere*—pockets or not! I am reminded of this norm as I walk into the men's locker room at my local gym after a good workout. I am sweaty and thirsty and looking forward to a dip in the hot tub. A sign reminds all those that enter that, should anyone in the locker room use their mobile phone, membership will be revoked. The shared assumption of course is that those holding their mobile phones are assumed to be documenting—in the form of pictures or even video (gasp!) the blatant (and not so sexy) nudity around.

It is at this time that I remember that I have left my phone in my car to ensure a workout free from distraction. My mobile phone serves as an extra appendage that connects me to the outside world. But no need for me to worry about having the sudden urge to use my phone to check my email and be confused for a pervert! Men's locker rooms can be strange places often with shared (and mostly unspoken) "rules" of conduct against wandering eyes. The "no mobile phone" sign peaks my curiosity prompting my eyes to wander, forgetting briefly about the context in which my eyes are wandering. As I walk to the back to change into my swim trunks I find myself looking around to see if anyone has the balls to actually be on their mobile phones. I see no phones, but also some things that cannot be unseen.

Mobile phones have privatized public spaces (e.g., listening to people annoyingly yell into their phones that they have arrived the second a plane lands) and have publicized private spaces (e.g., communicating with others by using these devices everywhere, even when going to the bathroom, see Waskul, this volume).

Now, "mobile phone," used in reference to the various devices that permeate our culture (and apparently gym locker rooms), is somewhat of a misnomer. Even versions such as "smart phone" or "camera phone" are not entirely accurate. Phone, short for telephone, has its root in the Greek word *phōnē*, meaning speech sound. The intended purpose and function of a telephone was to make and receive calls—to connect us verbally, or as the Bell Telephone television advertisements of the 1970s reminded consumers, to "reach out and touch someone far away—give 'em a call."

To be sure, use of a mobile phone can and still does involve speaking to others, but how we use these devices to "touch someone far away" is much more than just "giving 'em a call." In fact, speaking on mobile phones has largely become a secondary feature of the device, where users now surf the Web, listen to music, send and receive pictures, watch and make "domestic" videos (see Vannini, this volume), as well as communicate via text messages, email and on social media platforms (see Newmahr, this volume). In fact, the average number of voice minutes used has decreased and so has time spent *actually* speaking on mobile phones (Worthham 2010). Many of us now spend more time speaking to (or at) our mobile phones by using applications like voice to text, or speaking to artificial intelligence (AI) voice assistants like "Siri" (for iPhone) or "Jeannie" (for Android) as two examples.

There are many facets to using a mobile phone (far too many it turns out to explore in a short essay including, listening to music and playing games—both topics explored elsewhere in this volume). This short essay explores my own use of and interest in the mobile phone, circa 1998, to present day. I wish to provide readers with a brief social and historical technological synopsis as well as a biographical account of what I do (and have done) with my mobile phone as well as touch upon the feelings associated with these processes, which, collectively, help detail some of the "common sense-meanings" (Douglas 1970) of mobile phone communication.

The Telephone

A rusty city limits sign just down the road from where I live in southern Ontario, Canada, reads: "Brantford—The Telephone City." The invention of the telephone by engineer Alexander Graham Bell occurred on July 26, 1874, not very far from where I write this essay. The Bell Homestead, as it is referred to around Brantford (as the literal place where the telephone was invented), is a national historical site and is one of Ontario's oldest home museums, having opened in 1910.

Communication and information technologies bring together social activities and collective experiences (Couch 1984), but also, shared perspectives (Altheide 1995). Perhaps, no other single communication and information technology has shaped our lives (and popular culture!) in a more profound manner than the telephone, and later, it's now distant[2] mobile cousin—which is far more "mobile" than it is "phone." The mobile phone might be thought of as a "super-artifact" one that has profoundly contributed to "the most important social change since the industrial revolution: the mediated communication order" (Altheide 2014: ix). But let us not get ahead of ourselves. I will get to this shortly.

Telephone technology developed throughout the course of the twentieth century. Iterations of these technological advancements permitted—to varying degrees—live person-to-person verbal contact thereby "enhancing social structures" across vast geographical locales (Couch, Maines, and Chen 1996: 166). This technology developed over the last 100 years, however, these characteristics were nowhere as dramatic as to render the speaking use of the technology as a secondary feature.

Some of these earlier characteristics are preserved in the popular culture canon of yesteryear. One might briefly consider the "party line telephone" service. Multiple subscribers (i.e., users) shared this service; perhaps best represented in the 1959 Hollywood film *Pillow Talk*.

However, until the advent of mobile phone technology all telephone communication was tied to a specific time and place (and early mobile phones or "car phones" as they were called for a brief time were restricted to use in fixed locations, albeit, mobile locations). Another early exception might include "airplane phones." These devices were usually installed on the back of each seat on most commercial airplanes and unlike car phones were available to the public. A credit card was required to use the phone should a passenger wish to call someone in flight assuming they were willing to pay the exorbitant rates.[3] These devices are relics on older airplanes (like cigarette ashtrays) and remain largely forgotten by most people who are likely more familiar with the "airplane mode" setting on their mobile phone. In most circumstances, before the introduction of cordless home phones, users were quite literally tethered by way of a telephone cord to the wall, and later restricted by a cord tethered to their car or airplane seat.

I cannot recall (without checking my call history) the last time that I *actually* spoke on my mobile phone. Mobile phones have extended telephone use, a once largely private affair, into the public realm. A more recent development includes the use of mobile phones as socially significant devices for the display of communicative performance in daily life.

Altheide (1995: 7) observed that "one's competence is often judged by communicative performance, but this performance increasingly involves the direct or indirect manipulation of information technology and communication formats." Such performances, however, are not simply limited to the technological use of the device itself, but increasingly include, use of the device in *public settings* providing a whole host of potential performance blunders. Many of these have become the fodder of the Internet and news media. Consider, for instance, a 2013 *Telegraph* headline that read: "Woman busy texting walks straight into freezing cold canal in Birmingham." In another, similar circumstance, it was reported that a text-messaging shopper that walked into a mall water fountain planned to take mall employees to court for laughing at her public gaffe. Never before have we been so near (connected) yet so far (disconnected) from one another in daily life. To paraphrase Simmel, we have become "e-strangers" (Wolff 1950).

My First Mobile Phone

Where did it all begin? I got my first mobile phone a Motorola MicroTAC model sometime in 1998. It was grey in color, one of those clunky brick flip phones with a pull up antenna. I felt like James Bond. The numeric buttons glowed green and orange and the crude screen (by today's standards) only displayed the digits that were dialed which had to be pressed hard to register. This was difficult to do while driving and, while certainly dangerous, few laws restricted this activity at the time. The primary function was as a *phone* that was mobile so it made sense to me to use the phone while driving.

While versions of these devices had been around more or less since the 1980s, they were prohibitively costly, so few people had them. The expansion of these devices into daily life can be directly linked to the reduction of cost, which is the only reason why I got one. I mean, who the hell really needed a "mobile phone" anyway? Short answer: *very few people*, and I was certainly not one of them, perhaps someone like the Prime Minister, or someone equally as important needed one? But hey, I vividly recall that Zack Morris from the teen sitcom *Saved By the Bell* had one and he used it to order pizza from his high school classroom! Sweet! For a brief time it was rare to see a mobile phone on television or in the movies. Now these devices serve as central props in Hollywood films, in popular television shows, and even in cartoons! A June 2011 episode of popular children's program *Sesame Street* titled "Oscar Calls Too Much on His New Cell Phone" demonstrates the point. Nevertheless, an August 18, 1989 *Globe and Mail* article (Canada's national newspaper of record) hit the nail right on the head when reporting on the expansion of mobile phone technology: "It all depends on getting the cost of buying and using cellular phones low enough so that people who don't really need them will buy them" (Globe and Mail 1989).

In the late 1990s, mobile phones were, relatively speaking, inexpensive, however, using them as phones as they were intended remained *very* expensive. This was at a time when using a mobile phone was usually nothing other than a silly novelty (certainly not a millennial generation birthright!). I can distinctly remember calling a friend at his home from his doorstep and shocking the hell out of him when I told him that I was standing in front of his house. We giggled on the phone together like children. Turns out that this was some of the most expensive laughter ever at 1.50 dollars per minute. I learned as many other early users of mobile phones had before me that when I used the phone to call people, while infrequent, to every few seconds pull it away from my ear to look at the digital timer on the phone so that I could hang up at 59 seconds so that the call would only cost me $1.50 and not a penny more. Anger ensued when trying to get off of the phone only to hit 1:01 on the timer and add another $1.50 to the call that was probably not necessary in the first place.

Ringtones

Just as mobile phones were limited in terms of their functionality as "phones," so too were the ringing sounds that these devices emitted to indicate an incoming call. For the first few decades, mobile phones were largely indicators of social status.[4] Now most people in the Western world have a mobile phone. Statistics Canada data indicate that 81% of Canadian households have an active mobile phone (Statistics Canada 2014). Mobile phones have become largely indicators of cultural status. In some discernible ways, this shift can be linked to advancements in mobile phone technology, where production practices (i.e., individuals making ringtones) and consumption practices (i.e., individual broadcasts of selected ringtones) further reshape everyday actions, meanings of what people do and how they feel about it, and changes in communication. This can include the use of mobile phone ringtones as "identity management devices" (Schneider 2009: 35).

"Ringtone" officially entered the lexicon in 2006 when the word was added to the Merriam-Webster dictionary as "the sound made by a cell phone to signal an incoming call." These sounds included snippets of popular music recordings such as those on the Billboard Top 100 chart. In the fall of 2006, I began employment as a substitute high school teacher. In this environment I observed the use of ringtones as hyperauditory "tie-signs" (Goffman 1971) relating to one's identity. One student told me, "I think some of the songs people choose as ringtones or just as what they listen to in general can describe them in a lot of ways." These students were using ringtones to help manage their presentation of self (Goffman 1959).

Just as speaking on mobile phones was pricey, so too was the initial cost of ringtones (e.g., the 30-second snippets of popular songs could cost as much as $3.99 each). It was around this time in my life (circa 2006–2008) that I had great fun learning how to make ringtones myself to avoid the cost of purchasing them, and then changing these tones (or *tone-shifting*) on my mobile phone to reflect my mood, or choosing tones suitable for a particular social environment.

One of my first ringtones was the song "Cult" by thrash metal band Slayer. The song was released on June 6, 2006 (06/06/06). It was an arduous process to create this and other ringtones. The song had to be converted to a special format and then imported into editing software on a computer. Sitting in front of the screen I had to painstakingly watch the wave sounds while listening to find the exact audio clip that I wanted to preserve as my ringtone. Once completed the song had to be exported to an external drive and uploaded into a mobile phone capable of playing ringtones (most mobile phones available today have this option as a stock feature).

But Slayer was just a single tone. I wanted *many* ringtones as I could set each tone to specify each incoming caller. Next, I set Willie Nelson's "On the Road Again" to play when my father called (he was then a long-haul truck driver). This played every time that he called me from the road on his mobile phone until his retirement. Anytime I hear this song I think of my father (and my phone ringing!). I spent a lot of subsequent time making and carefully selecting tones to ring when specific people called my mobile phone: girlfriend, friends, etc. Turns out I got pretty good at it as some of these very same people asked me to custom-make them ringtones for their mobile phones. But then something unexpected happened: *people stopped calling*. People began to use their mobile devices less as phones for calling others in lieu of other forms of communication like mobile text messaging.

Text Messaging

I am sitting on the couch alongside my spouse when her phone text message tone indicates that her friend Kelly has messaged her. I know this because my spouse has assigned a duck "quack" tone to Kelly and she "quacks" at my spouse all of the time (and quacks at me by virtue of my proximity to my spouse). This time her text message is asking whether my spouse can provide some concrete feedback on a research paper Kelly is working on. They text back and forth for the next hour or so which makes me feel like I am at a pond with annoying hungry ducks rather than on my couch trying to watch some television. "Why don't you just call Kelly", I ask. My spouse tells me, "it is quicker and easier this way." Quicker? Easier? Text messaging, or "texting" as users refer to it, has become *the* way to communicate using mobile phones because *actually* phoning someone now takes too much time. It is worth noting that during this "mobile" encounter both people were in fact stationary, my spouse was on the couch, and Kelly was at her home. The daily use of mobile phones occurs in many stationary contexts (in bed, on the toilet), and not only when we are mobile. In these ways, the device itself has become less "mobile" and less "phone."

Texting allows people to avoid some of the subtle (but necessary) social nuances of daily interaction. Consider phone greetings. When phoning another person the usual pleasantries still apply: "Hello" and/ or "How are you?" The person on the other end will respond in similar fashion: "Fine, how are you?" The vocal gesture remains a "significant symbol" that elicits a vocal response in kind (Mead 1934). This can take as little a few seconds or even perhaps upwards of a several minutes. The omnipresence of mobile phones that possess the ability to access information immediately in many mundane circumstances (e.g., in the bedroom or at the mall) seem to have exacerbated our sense of immediacy at the interaction level. This might include "text-speak," an emergent communication form where the rules of grammar mostly do not apply. Text-speak can include acronyms such as YOLO short for "you only live once," which has become the subject of much ridicule in popular culture. As an example, YOLO was once referred to on a Jack Black Twitter parody account as "carpe diem for stupid people." Text-speak can also include missing letters and numbers in place of words (e.g., cul8r for "see you later." This form of mostly text-driven communication on mobile phones will be largely unfamiliar to many "digital immigrants" (Prensky 2001). Sometimes students will even use text-speak to communicate with their professors since it is often faster and easier. This has driven a few of my colleagues crazy trying to decipher sentences of text-speak sent from student mobile phones to university email addresses. Mobile phone devices are also used increasingly for sexual purposes (see Waskul 2014; see also Montemurro, this volume, for a discussion of sex).

It is faster and far easier; it turns out, to send a text message to my spouse as a reminder of a prearranged movie date ("see you at the theater at 9 p.m.") than to call her (we avoid the use of text-speak when we text message each other). Should I opt to phone her (and she most certainly sees that it is me calling on her mobile phone display) and she was to answer "Hello!" and my reply was simply, "see you at the theater at 9 p.m." followed by me abruptly ending the call, I would no doubt be sleeping in the backyard that evening! However, it remains certain that sleeping in the yard for an evening will be more quickly forgotten than my mobile-free experience in the gym locker room.

Christopher J. Schneider is Associate Professor of Sociology at Brandon University, Manitoba. His most recent books include, *The Public Sociology Debate: Ethics and Engagement* (co-edited with Ariane Hanemaayer; University of British Columbia Press, 2014) and *Qualitative Media Analysis, 2nd ed.* (co-authored with David Altheide; Sage Publications, 2013). Schneider has received awards for his teaching, research, and service. Recent recognition includes a 2013 *Distinguished Academics Award* from the Confederation of University Faculty Associations of British Columbia. His research and commentary have been featured in hundreds of news reports across North America, including the *New York Times* and CBC's *The National*.

Notes

1. This essay has benefited from helpful and playful comments and conversations with many others including, Ariane Hanemaayer, Phillip Vannini, and Dennis D. Waskul.
2. Contemporary mobile phones—sometimes referred to as "smartphones"—bear little resemblance and functional relevance to the telephone. It is unlikely that Alexander Graham Bell himself would recognize these devices. Indeed, modern mobile phones are much more like pocket computers in terms of functionality and usage than their historic counterparts, landline telephones.
3. Airplane phones were introduced on Air Canada flights in 1987. These devices allowed passengers to call anywhere in Canada or the continental United States at a cost of $10 for the first three minutes and $2.50 for each additional minute (Financial Post, 1987).
4. Consider that in 1985, the cost of a handheld Bell mobile phone was nearly $6,500, and this did not include use of the phone itself (Horgan 1985).

References

Altheide, David L. 1995. *An Ecology of Communication*. Hawthorne, NY: Aldine de Gruyter.

Altheide, David. 2014. *Media Edge: Media Logic and Social Reality*. New York, NY: Peter Lang USA.

Couch, Carl. 1984. *Constructing Civilizations*. Greenwhich, CT: Jai Press.

Couch, Carl, David R. Maines, and Shing-Ling Chen. 1996. *Information Technologies and Social Orders*. Hawthorne, NY: Aldine de Gruyter.

Douglas, Jack D. (Ed.). 1970. *Understanding Everyday Life: Toward the Reconstruction of Sociological Knowledge*. Chicago, IL: Aldine Publishing Co.

Financial Post. 1987, June 8. "Please Call Home Airplane Phones." *Financial Post* (Toronto, ON). Sec. 1: 1.

Globe and Mail. 1989, August 18. "The Ring of Success." Toronto *Globe and Mail*.

Goffman, Erving. 1959. *The Presentation of Self in Everyday Life*. New York, NY: Anchor Books.

Goffman, Erving. 1971. *Relations in Public: Microstudies of the Public Order*. New York, NY: Basic Books.

Horgan, Denys. 1985, May 9. "Telephone Innovation Could Ring Only for Rich." *Globe and Mail*.

Mead, George H. 1934. *Mind, Self and Society*. Chicago, IL: University of Chicago Press.

Prensky, Marc. 2001. "Digital Natives, Digital Immigrants." *On the Horizon 9*(5). Retrieved from http://www.marcprensky.com/writing/Prensky%20%20Digital%20Natives,%20 Digital%20Immigrants%20-%20Part1.pdf.

Schneider, Christopher J. 2009. "The Music Ringtone as an Identity Management Device." *Studies in Symbolic Interaction 33*: 35–45.

Waskul, Dennis D. 2014. "Techno-Sexuality: The Sexual Pragmatists of the Technological Age." In Thomas S. Weinberg and Staci Newmahr (Eds.), *Selves, Symbols, and Sexualities: An Interactionist Anthology*. Thousand Oaks, CA: Sage Publications, 89–107.

Wolff, Kurt H. (Ed., trans.). 1950. *The Sociology of Georg Simmel*. Glencoe, IL: Free Press.

Wortham, Jenna. 2010, May 13. "Cellphones Now Used More for Data Than for Calls." *New York Times*. Retrieved from http://www.nytimes.com/2010/05/14technology/personaltech/14talk.html?_r=0.

5

SHARING AND WAITING ON FACEBOOK

Staci Newmahr

While walking to the parking lot after a fabulous concert recently, I tried to upload a video clip to Facebook on my iPhone. It wouldn't upload. I stopped walking. I tweaked my settings a bit and tried again. No dice. Frustrated, I quickened my pace, intending to figure it out when I got to the car. In the car, I tried again. It just hung there. I spent 10 frustrated minutes trying to get it to work, decimating my post-concert bliss as I obsessively tried to get my video clip onto Facebook. By the time I accepted defeat and began driving, my adrenaline high had dissipated. I was antsy to get home to my much more reliable desktop.

Only a year before, my hour-long drive home would have been an extension of the pleasure of the concert. Now it took me nearly half of that drive to shake off my disappointment at having been denied the satisfaction of sharing a video clip of the concert at precisely the moment at which I had felt inspired to do so. When did the moments of my life become so intertwined with a desire to share them on Facebook? How had I allowed that to happen? Was this sort of thing going on with other people also? Was it happening with Twitter users too?

I started asking around. This was not a "study" in any systematic or scientific sense; I asked my Facebook friends and talked to acquaintances and students about their uses of Facebook. This essay is a set of reflections on some of the themes that emerged from these conversations.

Show-and-Tell: The Act of Sharing

People post on Facebook to share a wide range of information: major personal news, minor details about their days, feelings and moods, political views, and reactions to various kinds of entertainment and news items. Psychologists have explored possible motivations for posting on Facebook, including self-presentation, wanting to feel a sense of belonging (Nadkarni and Hofmann 2012), and expressing a "true self" (Seidman 2014). For some people, the appeal is in the sharing itself (as it was for me in the anecdote above). Whatever the motivation, Facebook is a forum in which adults can revisit the show-and-tell of their kindergarten days—but every day, all day long.

The significance of the temporal aspect of Facebooking is tricky, since it is not always clear whether people are sharing something immediate, or whether they've been thinking about these things for days and just decided to post. However, the information being shared relates to events that have either just occurred of just transpired. It is as if we want to feel that we are present in the poster's everyday moment. In their work on digital representation, Bolter and Grusin posit that we, in effect, sublimate our desires for immediacy, to live fully in our moments, through our media use: "Instead of trying to be in the presence of the objects of representation, we then define immediacy as being in the presence of media" (1999: 236).

Sometimes, perhaps out of an impulse to "come clean" about a time lag, a Facebooker clarifies, as in "I meant to post this earlier, but never got to it." These confessions simultaneously threaten the team performance (Goffman 1959) of the immediacy of Facebook, as the goal of immersion in Facebook life is—like all virtual reality—for the feeling of mediation to disappear into the "real" (Bolter and Grusin 1999). However, such status updates simultaneously bolster the authenticity of the solo performance. The confession that the status update I am sharing is actually several hours old is a stage whisper—a wink to the audience—and the audience therefore concludes that I am more trustworthy than the other actors.

Recently, while waiting in line at a coffee shop, I caught myself formulating a Facebook post in my head about the coffee shop. I was not merely reflecting on the coffee shop; I was thinking about performing my reflections. The incredulous exclamation, "I was *just* thinking of posting that on Facebook!" is another example. The speaker does not find coincidence in that she was *thinking* of the very same matter, but that she was thinking of *posting* about the very same matter.

The use of Facebook can decrease the distance between the experience and the desire to share the experience. Before Facebook (and Twitter), the closest approximation was to have an experience and then think, "I can't wait to tell people about this!" But the necessity of the waiting at least meant that there was a "this" and then an impulse to share. Desires to post an update to Facebook do not require an event or even a separate recognition of a thought that we *then*, a moment later, want to share. Instead, these frames suggest that at least some of us are *thinking* in terms of our sharing. I suspect that most Facebook users have had an impulse to post something on Facebook and then decided, for one reason or another, that it did not warrant sharing. We simply had a "thought" that felt an awful lot like a Facebook post.

Twenty years ago, during those moments in which we excitedly anticipated our own disclosures, many of us were really thinking, "I can't wait to tell *[so-and-so]* about this!" Or perhaps the occurrence was so unbelievable that we wanted to tell *someone*—anyone—and we looked around, excitedly, for a person with whom to share this experience. I can remember this feeling vividly, but it now feels like a relic of a former world. There is no need to glance around for someone with whom to share what just happened.

These links are situated in and mediated by particular technologies even beyond social media. The people to whom I spoke—younger people who generally use Facebook on their phones—said that they often post immediately, when the inspiration strikes, but that they do not experience posting things on Facebook as an interruption. When I asked one if he had ever felt antsy waiting to post something, replied: "What makes you wait? I can pull it out and post something in under a minute, I'd imagine. Tap the app, write a status, send. Back to 'living.'"

Another said that while she could recall "a few standout moments where [I'm posting] something and I feel like everything must stop until I get it posted," she did not generally interrupt what she was already doing in order to post (I suspect that this sense is at least partly generational, for proficiency with one's smart phone, a lack of concern with which Facebook friends see which posts, and an unlimited data plan seem to me to be prerequisites for a life in which one posts to Facebook without breaking one's stride).

Perhaps because of my age and social group, I have seen a person exclaim, "I'm gonna post this on Facebook when I get home!" as often as I've seen someone whip out a phone and announce that they are tweeting or posting about this *right now*. I've seen both countless times. Either way, the experiences of moments appear to be intertwining with felt desires to share those moments. One friend commented that after she really "feels a need" to post something and does, she "usually feel(s) a sort of relief, I guess. Like I got that out there and now I can move on."

Anticipatory Excitements

I was inspired to write this essay by observations (and recognitions) of desires to post on Facebook and tweet on Twitter. I was primarily interested in the pre-posting emotional state. When I started talking to people about their social media use, several people did not find anything remarkable or interesting about their pre-posting states, but located the moment of the posting as when the fun begins. For them, what was most relevant was not the impulse to share, but that the sharing was, simultaneously, with hundreds (or more) of people. They spoke of an anticipatory excitement between the posting and the responses from others. Some of them view their post as starting a conversation; a twenty-first-century take on waiting for the "postman" weeks after mailing letters to hundreds of people: "It feels like I've just contributed. It feels like I've reached out to others. I sometimes feel like I have initiated contact with others, and I'm anticipating a response, which is exciting."

In particular, several people said they eagerly awaited comments from their Facebook friends. One said, "I like to see other people's reactions and responses ..." Another said that responses to status updates were "fulfilling," and that he would not post if he knew the status would garner no responses. Everyone with whom I spoke—a very small, (very) convenient "sample"—remarked that they posted in order to feel noticed, which they can only feel once someone responds. Once the status is sent, the waiting for acknowledgement begins. If it doesn't come, this can feel deflating. As one person told me: "If I post something and hope/expect for a response and I don't get one, I feel kinda crappy. I feel like no one cares, or no one pays attention to me … any response … is better than no response because I know someone took a minute to notice me."

Another person thought she would not be especially bothered by a status update going unnoticed, but then mused, "But I think my statuses and pictures are typically things that I know I'd get comments/likes for." This is similar to the motivation of at least some Twitter users to tweet what they think their friends or followers "might find interesting or have an opinion on" (Marwick and boyd 2011: 118). On Facebook, where posts are not public, where friends are more consciously and carefully chosen, and where status updates are not limited to 140 characters, the posting also triggers a state of eager anticipation of feedback from others.

Was it Good for You? (Chasing the Likes)

Other people told me, quite unabashedly, that they posted on Facebook in order to generate "likes." As one friend put it, Facebook posts are often about, "Let's get a bunch of likes from people I like with this amusing little anecdote." These people checked back to count likes, or else had their notifications set up to alert them when someone "likes" their comments. The same friend admitted that she thinks that "I should post this" really means "a lot of people will tell me that they enjoy this." Another person confessed, "I also would say I look for validation on some things. I want other people to like (literally and the button) what I do." As one person put it, "the "like" is the head nod of 'Yup, I agree. You're awesome.'"

The space to ask and quickly receive public approval, from multiple people, further contributes to the intertwining of the experience with the desire to share. Facebook becomes the stage on which we deliver the impressive soliloquy; hitting the send button dims the house lights and cues the audience to applaud. Posting on Facebook draws out the anticipation, however, as we wait to find out whether our audience members will applaud at all … and then watch them do so one by one.

Knowing and Being Known: Access and Intimacy

I am always astounded when people tell me that they do not have their Facebook friends assigned to different "lists." Everything they post is visible to all of their Facebook friends. I could not use Facebook this way. My Facebook friend list includes colleagues I barely know, family members, students, the kid who sat next to me in third grade, my very best friends, ex-lovers, current lovers, friendly acquaintances, and, at any given moment, one or two people I am no longer sure I actually know. I can think of almost nothing that I would want to share with *all* of these people. I have never posted on Facebook without consciously choosing the specific people to which that particular content will be visible. For me, audience matters. My Facebook has multiple regions (Goffman 1959), and as I select who can see which status update, I shift my frontstage to my backstage (Goffman 1959), and vice versa. I am mystified when people tell me that it is of no consequence to them if their bosses or neighbors or coworkers know how cold their houses are, or what they ate for lunch, or what their children are for Halloween. They, it appears to me, have redefined the "personal" to exclude the mundane.

Yet the mundane is quite personal. When I asked people whether their relationships have grown closer as a result of Facebook friendship, the examples and stories came readily and enthusiastically. And I have my own: in fact, not too long ago, I marveled with a colleague-turned-friend about how much closer we felt as a result of Facebook. The key in all of these stories is the access to the mundane aspects of each other's lives.[1] Some studies have found that updating Facebook statuses increases feelings of connectedness among Facebook friends (Grieve, Indian, Witteveen, Tolan, and Marrington 2013; Köbler, Riedl, Vetter, Leimeister, and Krcmar 2010).

Cohabitation often characterizes relationships as "intimate" precisely because of access to the mundane. The details of our everyday lives are either considered too banal to share, or else they simply get lost in the business of the more "important" aspects of our lives. People who know what our children are for Halloween and how cold we keep our house *know* us better, regardless of whether we deem that information private. The mundane bits that are shared on Facebook—the location of your favorite lunch spot this month, the transcript of the argument your children had this morning, what your boss said when she didn't give you the raise—come together to paint a richer and fuller portrait of you, one that can only be seen and appreciated by the people who have access. The culmination of this "ambient awareness" (Ito 2005) can be an ability to "sense the rhythms of [people's] lives in a way [we] never [had] before" (Thompson 2008), leading people to feel "a type of ESP." (Thompson 2008: n.p.).

The connective power of ambient awareness works the same way intimacy always does: by gaining and granting access to aspects of lives that we feel are normally protected, we construct feelings of intimacy (Newmahr 2011). The more you share on Facebook, the more access your Facebook friends have to your everyday life and over time, one would expect, the less you feel "known" to others. A friend told me that she is closer to people she sees every day now that they are Facebook friends: "I feel like it sometimes solidifies or gives a boost to our already existing real-world relationship ... because I only see them at school, so then they're entering my non-school world by interacting on Facebook."

Face-to-face conversations that begin with "I saw your post on Facebook" (which I overhear dozens of times in any given week), are, on the surface, follow-ups, often with the intention of checking in or clarifying or expressing support or appreciation. But this is intimation, in all senses of the word: it begins a conversation while subtly laying claim to a particular intimacy; a reminder and in some cases an announcement of access to certain knowledge. It is a reminder of a connection we have in another space, and when said in front of others, it is a claim to some knowledge of this person that the others may not have [I have even heard conversations in which one person says he posted something on Facebook, and another replies (usually indignantly) "I know; I 'liked' it!"]. Perhaps even more often, people in face-to-face interaction forego segue and refer immediately to the *content* of the Facebook status, "as if picking up a conversation in the middle" (Thompson 2008: n.p.).

Facebook and Twitter have impacted everyday life on multiple levels. These technologies have changed how we feel our moments and what meanings we make of them, our definitions and frames for social interaction and approval, our conceptualizations of private/public, and the intersections between privacy and intimacy.

As I sit in a Buffalo cafe and type this essay, a woman in her fifties speaks to her friends at the table beside me.

> "Someone posted on Facebook today, this thing about the top 13 places to have chicken wings ..."
>
> "Oh, I saw that too!" one replies.
>
> The third woman says nothing. It seems she might not be on Facebook.

Then, after a beat, she says, "We only get chicken wings when someone is visiting from out of town," whereupon the other two engage in a series of comments intended to convince all parties that they, too, only eat chicken wings when visitors are interested. Twenty-five minutes later, the woman who initially brought up the Facebook list makes a reservation for the three of them at said restaurant for the following Friday.

The interpersonal satisfactions of Facebook are nothing new: approval, support, validation, intimacies and expanded social networks, possibilities and outcomes. The excitements, though, are different: They are digital arousals and textual anticipations. Social media have changed not only what we do in our everyday lives but also how we experience each moment and how we talk about them. They have become part of our everyday lives, not only habitually, but by reshaping the social and temporal relationships among occurrences, desires, and gratifications; in short, by fusing our "reality" with its mediation.

Staci Newmahr is Associate Editor of *Symbolic Interaction* and Assistant Professor of Sociology at the State University of New York, Buffalo. She is the author of *Playing on the Edge: Sadomasochism, Risk and Intimacy* (Indiana University Press, 2011) and co-editor of *Selves, Symbols and Sexualities* (with Thomas Weinberg; Sage Publications, 2014). Newmahr is interested in the intersections of gender, eroticism, and risk. She is currently thinking and writing about modes, maps, and expressions of the erotic in the digital era.

Note

1. For a thorough discussion of the ways in which electronic mediations of communication have impacted social behavior, see Myrowitz (1986).

References

Bolter, Jay David and Richard Grusin. 1999. *Remediation: Understanding New Media*. Cambridge, MA: MIT Press.

Goffman, Erving. 1959. *The Presentation of Self in Everyday Life*. New York, NY: Anchor Books.

Grieve, Rachel, M. Indian, K. Witteveen, G. A. Tolan, and J. Marrington. 2013. "Face-to-Face or Facebook: Can Social Connectedness Be Derived Online?" *Computers in Human Behavior 29*(3): 604–609.

Ito, Mizuko. 2005. "Introduction." In Mizuko Ito, Daisuke Okabi, and Misa Masuda (Eds.), *Personal, Portable, Pedestrian: Mobile Phones in Japanese Life*. Cambridge, MA: MIT Press.

Köbler, F., C. Riedl, C. Vetter, J.M. Leimeister, and H. Krcmar. 2010. "Social Connectedness on Facebook—An Explorative Study on Status Message Usage" In Proceedings of the Sixteenth Americas Conference on Information Systems (AMCIS), Lima, Peru, paper 247.

Marwick, Alice and danah boyd. 2011. "I Tweet Honestly, I Tweet Passionately: Twitter Users, Context Collapse, and the Imagined Audience." *New Media & Society 13*(1): 114–133.

Nadkarni, Ashwini and Stefan G. Hofmann. 2012. "Why Do People Use Facebook?" *Personality and Individual Differences 52*(3): 243–249.

Newmahr, Staci. 2011. *Playing on the Edge: Sadomasochism, Risk and Intimacy*. Bloomington, IN: Indiana University Press.

Seidman, Gwendolyn. 2014. "Expressing the 'True Self' on Facebook." *Computers in Human Behavior 31*: 367–372 .

Thompson, Clive. 2008, September 7. "Brave New World of Digital Intimacy." *New York Times Magazine*. Retrieved from http://www.nytimes.com/2008/09/07/magazine/07awareness-t.html?pagewanted =all&_r=0.

6

READING
Michael Schwalbe

Drew and I liked to ask questions that made our Lutheran grade school teachers squirm. One time when we were being instructed on the grave importance of adhering to a fine point of Wisconsin Synod Lutheran doctrine, Drew asked if this meant that Missouri Synod Lutherans, who believed something else, were going to hell. I once asked how it was possible for scientists to be wrong about evolution and the age of the earth—only about 6,000 years, according to our teachers—and yet be able to make vaccines and send rockets into space. Drew and I tried to outdo each other in appearing to ask such questions in all innocence.

In that cramped intellectual space it somehow happened that a few science fiction novels ended up on the seventh-grade bookshelf. I don't remember which books they were, but when I read them, I remember thinking that someone had slipped up. The stories in those books put into question much of the religious dogma we were being fed. Our seventh-grade teacher that year—a youngish, energetic woman—had been hired to replace a teacher who had died suddenly. We were surprised when she wasn't hired back the next year. I wonder now if failing to properly monitor the classroom library was one of her mistakes.

Of course Drew and I gravitated to those novels; we read them all and sought more. We were in our early teens by then, and we had started to frequent Chet's Used Books and Magic Shop, which was on the corner down the street from Drew's house. We ignored the magic tricks that Chet sold to the weirdo kids who were interested in that sort of stuff. For us, the boxes and piles of cheap paperbacks in the science fiction room were the magic. Even better, Chet traded two science fiction paperbacks for one Western novel. Which is why my dad's Zane Grey and Louis L'Amour novels disappeared soon after he read them and put them away.

One of the books I found at Chet's was Robert Heinlein's 1964 novel *Farnham's Freehold*.[1] The blurb on the front cover of the paperback edition calls it "the novel that begins where *On the Beach* left off—the dramatic story of what happens to a middle-class American family who survive World War III." I was 8 years old when the book was published, and probably 15 or 16 when I found it. I read it first, then shared it with Drew.

The novel's protagonist is Hugh Farnham, a 50-ish white suburbanite, general contractor, and former navy officer. His family members think him paranoid about the prospect of a nuclear war between the United States and the Soviet Union. But when the attack comes, early in the book, they gladly take refuge in Farnham's impregnable, well-stocked bomb shelter. They are rocked by two blasts, which Farnham interprets as the Soviet first strike and, 45 minutes later, a counterstrike after U.S. retaliation. Just when it seems they have survived the exchange, they are hit by a third blast—"the biggest slam of all."

When Farnham and his family emerge from the shelter, they expect to find a ravaged, radioactive landscape. They are astonished to see green hills, healthy trees, clear streams, and abundant wildlife. After some brief speculation about how far the shelter has been thrown or whether they are in another dimension, they set the mystery aside and, under Farnham's forceful leadership, begin scrabbling to survive. In this first part of the novel most of the drama arises out of dysfunctional family dynamics.

Duke, Farnham's adult son, is headstrong and resists his father. The two almost come to violence. Farnham's wife, Grace, is a former beauty gone to fat and alcoholism. In the post-blast encampment, she refuses to accept that the world has changed and sinks into dementia. Karen, the home-from-college daughter, is cooperative and upbeat, generally siding with her father. She is also, unbeknownst to the others, pregnant.

Barbara, Karen's sorority sister, is visiting when the attacks occur and joins the family in the shelter. She and Hugh Farnham become sexually involved. Then there is Joseph, the family's black "houseboy." Joseph is young and smart (he's studying to be an accountant), shows forbearance in the face of subtle and overt racism, and is Hugh Farnham's loyal right-hand man.

With hard work and ingenuity, the group manages to provide for itself in what seems like an unpeopled Eden. One day, while hunting, Duke and Hugh realize that the landscape in which the bomb shelter now sits is the same landscape in which it was built. Although the surface of things has changed, the hills, valleys, and mountains are the same. The shelter hasn't been thrown any physical distance at all. Only later, after months have passed and powerful, silently levitating aircraft appear, do members of the group discover that the third blast sent them 2,000 years into the future.

The world in which Farnham and company now find themselves is technologically far ahead of twentieth-century America. It is also ruled by dark-skinned people—mainly Africans and other southern hemisphere survivors of the nuclear war that obliterated North America and Europe. Whites are kept as slaves and bred for small stature and servility. When Farnham's crew is discovered by the authorities, they are assumed to be escaped slaves poaching on royal land. If not for the presence of Joseph, who is seen as a member of the chosen race, Farnham and family would have been killed on the spot.

Members of Farnham's group are taken in and treated as objects of curiosity by the local prefect, who, as it turns out, is a scholar of ancient languages. Members of the group adapt more or less well to their new circumstances. Hugh learns the new language, teaches the prefect, Ponse, how to play contract bridge, and becomes Ponse's historian and translator of ancient English texts. For this he is elevated to the status of upper servant, nearly on par with the household's chief domestic. Joseph thrives, becoming Ponse's protégé and enjoying considerable privileges as a member of the Chosen. Hugh's daughter, Karen, dies in childbirth and is out of the picture. Duke is uncooperative at first, but later agrees to help his father translate in exchange for better treatment. Farnham's wife, Grace, now living in drug-induced bliss, becomes a decorative object in Ponse's household. Barbara—impregnated by Hugh and having given birth to twin boys—is relegated to "slut quarters" with the other breeding and bed-warming white women.

This new world, for all its scientific and technological prowess, is hierarchical, authoritarian, and obsessed with status. It is also unabashedly racist and sexist. And while there is superficial civility, order is maintained by force. Those in power carry electronic whips that are used to inflict intense pain when subordinates do not obey quickly enough. Male slaves and menials are castrated ("tempered") if they are not needed for breeding. The topper, as Hugh is shocked to discover after settling into his new life, is cannibalism. Some slaves are bred for slaughter and consumption by the elite.

Hugh communicates in code with Barbara via his assigned bed-warmer. He and Barbara plot to escape with their twins and live in a mountain community of runaway slaves. Duke, who has been tempered and is now living docilely as his mother's companion in Ponse's household, has no desire to leave. The escape is thwarted, but in the attempt Hugh accidentally kills Memtok, Ponse's chief of staff. After being caught, Hugh and Barbara expect to be executed. To their surprise, Ponse gives them the choice to stay and serve him—though Hugh will have to be tempered—or, given how much trouble they're likely to cause, participate in a time-travel experiment that could send them back to the twentieth century. Hugh and Barbara are amazed to learn that this is even a possibility (Ponse explains that he simply ordered his scientists, under threat of the whip, to figure out how to do it). Though going back means returning to a world on the brink of nuclear war, they don't hesitate to opt for freedom. Joseph decides to stay and get rich running Ponse's business schemes. He says he prefers being a member of the Chosen to being black in twentieth-century America.

The experiment works. Hugh and Barbara end up back in the town where the story began, a short time before the bombing starts. They briefly observe themselves in Hugh's house, before taking Barbara's car from the driveway and trying to get as far from the blast zone as they can. As they head for the mountains, they notice that the car has a manual transmission, not the automatic transmission Barbara remembers. This suggests to them that subtle changes have occurred and that it is possible to create a future different from the one they saw. They survive the blasts by taking shelter in an old mine, and then carry on as rugged post-apocalypse freeholders and entrepreneurs.

*

For Drew and me, *Farnham's Freehold* was a resource for humor; it became part of our idioculture. We identified neighborhood girls as candidates for bedwarmer status, and neighborhood bullies as being in need of tempering or a touch of the whip. The nickname of the character Memtok—when he was at stud—"One-Shot Memtok," suggested "No-Shot Drew." It was the kind of juvenile humor typical of American boys in their early teens. But there was something else about the novel that intrigued us: the future world it described was one in which blacks were naturally assumed to be superior to the whites over whom they ruled. I don't recall joking about this, perhaps because Heinlein made it so plausible as to be scary.

Heinlein inverted the racial order that we took for granted. We had grown up on the all-white south side of Milwaukee in the 1960s. As far as we could see, white supremacy was a fact just about everywhere but on the basketball court. And at the time, having been immersed in an ideology of white superiority, that supremacy seemed justified. The casually used racist language that was all around us and a vast supply of racist jokes about black inferiority reinforced it all. Heinlein's novel unsettled it.

One thing I learned from reading *Farnham's Freehold*—and I can't say what Drew learned from it; our conversations weren't *that* serious, and we haven't been in touch for a long time—is that deeply entrenched social arrangements, ones that are taken for granted as reflecting the natural order of things, are not inevitable but contingent; that things could have been, and could be, different. Other works of science fiction affirmed that lesson; it's a premise of the genre. But Heinlein's novel, by challenging my ingrained and previously unexamined racist assumptions, gave me a jolt. Yes, whites are in charge *now*, it occurred to me, but that's an accident of history, not a result of natural superiority. Things *could* be different.

But while Heinlein puts people of color on top and shows them to be efficient and smart (they outwit Hugh, who is no slouch, at every turn), he also shows them as having simply turned the tables on whites, whom they enslave and keep illiterate. He also portrays the Chosen as having created an undemocratic, repressive, quasi-tribalist social order. And then there is the cannibalism. This could be read as implying that dark-skinned people are innately primitive and brutal, qualities that will always show through a high-tech veneer. I don't recall if this is how I interpreted the story. Perhaps I did, since it would have been a way to maintain belief in the superiority of "white" civilization. At that time, neither the slaughter of World War I trench warfare nor the horrors of Auschwitz were present in my mind as counterexamples.

Rereading the book in 2014 corroborated some memories and qualified others. This time I was struck by the sexism of Heinlein's imagined future world—in which women are reduced to decorative or sexually servile functions—and by his portrayal of even the most admirable female characters—Hugh's love interest, Barbara—as largely helpless without men. My guess is that Heinlein would have said that his female characters, perhaps with the exception of Grace, are strong because they are sexually liberated. He might also have said that in his imagined future world familial wealth and power flow from uncle to oldest nephew, making the oldest sister a revered figure in the kinship system. Still, in Heinlein's novel women are squeamish, exercise no power, need men's protection, rarely initiate action, and constantly seek men's approval. It's not that I missed all this 45 years ago. I just didn't see the problem.

On rereading the novel I was also struck by its unabashed libertarian politics and Cold War anti-communism. The Soviets are portrayed as naked aggressors in the nuclear war that launches the story. Farnham, an ex-navy officer (as was Heinlein), wants to survive the war in part to help give the Soviets hell when they invade. Heinlein also has Farnham say that he doesn't "regret a megaton" of massive U.S. retaliation. There is no doubt, in the context of the novel, that the communists are the enemies not only of the United States but of freedom as well. From the standpoint of 2014—after Vietnam, after Afghanistan, after Iraq, after decades of U.S. support for pro-capitalist dictators around the globe—Farnham's faith in the U.S. as a force for freedom in the world seems dangerously naive.

On the other hand, I found Farnham's libertarianism appealing when it condemns politicians who blithely speak of nuclear war as winnable; when it denounces elites who presume to know what's best for everyone else; and when it skewers liberals who pay lip service to racial equality but won't give up any class privilege to achieve it. Considering what Heinlein has Farnham say about these matters, I can now see the anti-racist message in the book. The problem of oppression, Heinlein implies, does not originate in moral failings specific to any racial group. It originates in the desires of some people to deny freedom to others, desires that can be found in human beings of all kinds. Heinlein offers slavery as the paradigm case, and it is of course the case that resonates most strongly with U.S. history. What Heinlein doesn't see is that the same problem is inherent in capitalism.

In the early 1970s, had I cared about Heinlein's politics, I could have taken the bus downtown to the Milwaukee Public Library, enlisted the aid of a reference librarian, and spent hours digging. In 2014, I googled. After rereading the book once, I did a web search and learned that Heinlein was indeed a self-identified libertarian, though with conservative leanings underpinned by his patriotism, love of martial virtues, and anti-communism. When I reread the book a second time, I was primed to see these elements. Hugh Farnham's voice echoes Heinlein's. My point: even bracketing the changes *I've* gone through since first reading Heinlein's novel, how I experienced it over 40 years later was altered by today's commonplace technology. That's science fiction come true.

Once upon a time, *Farnham's Freehold* led me to think about the constructedness of the social world. It showed me how behavior hinges on the meanings people attach to things, including skin color. It suggested to me that such meanings can change radically over time. For a boy steeped in a culture that did not encourage sociological thinking, this was no small awakening. It was one thing to be clever and spot contradictions in the doctrine proffered by my grade school teachers. It was another thing to begin to understand where doctrines come from, how people use them, and why they need them.

Another lesson I took from my first experience of reading Heinlein's novel, a lesson that became clear in retrospect, is that reading can change not only minds but lives. Whatever else their limitations, my grade school teachers knew this; it's why they made us read the Bible—they wanted us to be *formed* by what we found there. And no doubt they worried about how the worldly texts we encountered outside school might corrupt us. Their understandings of the forces at work in shaping us and shaping our behavior were too simple. Yet they knew an important truth about reading: it can be enormously consequential and potentially dangerous.

Today, I sometimes joke with my students by referring to course readings as "sacred texts." They laugh because it sounds absurd to attach a religious label to academic books and articles. I suppose it also sounds funny to call our texts *sacred*, given that I often criticize those texts. But I am reverent about reading. It's the transformative power of reading that I want students to discover (if they haven't already) and learn to find their way back to again and again—through whatever book, essay, or poem is the right one at the right time. An encounter with this power is the closest thing to a sacrament that a teacher has to offer.

Michael Schwalbe is Professor of Sociology at North Carolina State University. He is the author of *Unlocking the Iron Cage: The Men's Movement, Gender Politics, and American Culture*; *The Sociologically Examined Life*; *Remembering Reet and Shine: Two Black Men, One Struggle*; *Rigging the Game: How Inequality Is Reproduced in Everyday Life*; and *Manhood Acts: Gender and the Practices of Domination*.

Note

1. Heinlein, Robert A. 1964. *Farnham's Freehold*. New York, NY: G. P. Putnam's Sons.

7

MAKING VIDEO

Phillip Vannini

The timeworn boardwalk handrail is something to behold in its obvious shortage of aesthetic pretense. And yet the crumbly cedar beam dramatically struggles to bear the burden of its own water-soaked weight and dips in its middle with a deep, heavy inward hump. It is late in the afternoon and we'd rather be making camp before the impending nightfall than still be slogging through ankle-deep mud for another pair of miles. The cloud cover is getting thicker and everybody in the group is reaching into their waning energy reserves to quicken their pace. And yet, the strangely asymmetrical structural form cast by the aging beam—bathed in the crisp, light contrast afforded by the overcast sky and the surrounding verdant foliage—frames the depth of the forest field in a dark, haunting, unmissable way. I simply can't resist. "Hold on guys, I need to record this," I holler at my friends.

Recording video is not like pointing and shooting a still picture with a camera phone. Good DSLR video-shooting cameras are cumbersome and can't be easily worn around your neck all day—especially on a treacherous trail. So they are regularly put away and need to be first unsheathed from their protective packs before every use. Once the camera body and correct lens are readied attention must then be turned to your own body. First you need to secure your bodily balance well enough to hold a motionless pose. This may require a few different kinetic adjustments—or better yet the assembly of a tripod mount. Then you need to work with your ears by switching on your external microphone and checking and adjusting your recording levels. Is there too much wind? What direction is the sound coming from? Are you breathing too loudly? Next you need to record a handful of different shots in order to have a wider range of choices during the editing process: a still frame, then some lateral movement of the camera. Maybe left, then right. Or slowly up, then down. It's also always ideal to record an establishing shot followed by something closer up. And if the shot is particularly important you also want to play back the footage to make sure you ...

"FOR FUCK'S SAKE, PHILLIP, LET'S GO!!"

*

This is an essay about the practice of turning an outdoor adventure into a video—or, more broadly, about the challenges of turning everyday situations into a media product meant for distant people's enjoyment. At the most basic level I wish to outline how shooting outdoor adventure videos is not as easy as it looks from the finished products. Dealing with the time-consuming character of video recording and with the ways a camera's presence alters the definition of a social situation—as described in the opening passage—are only some of the difficulties this practice demands. At a deeper level I argue that at a time when the production of photographic self-portraiture ("selfies") and camera-phone videos seems nearly instantaneous, elementary, and ubiquitous, mastering the difficulties of adventure video recording stands as a mark of media literacy distinction and ostentatious skill performance. As a matter of fact, adventure video creators craft their visual products to distance themselves from the masses of amateur camera-wielding consumers. Their performance of skill can teach us a great deal about the creation of a media product, the turning of everyday life situations into media culture fit for niche consumption, and about the significance of video as a technology for chronicling mundane existence.

Please Wait While Your Video is Being Rendered

Ever since the advent of affordable "camcorders" in the late 1980s, amateur filmmaking and home video-recording have become commonplace practices. Relatedly, camcorders, camera phones, and higher-end DSLRs[1]—whether they are used for recording weddings, holidays, or kids' birthday parties, school recitals, or sports games—are now fully domesticated household technologies (Strangelove 2010). Academics worldwide have found plenty of interesting material in all of this, especially in the way amateur video shooting and sharing has counter-hegemonically chipped away at the authority of expert systems (Gauntlett 2011) and at the power of news ownership, production, and distribution (Burgess and Greene 2009; Snickars and Vonderau 2010; Strangelove 2010).

But just as we live in an era of citizen journalism and social media–driven social movements, we also live in an epoch of mediated adventure. Vimeo, YouTube, Blip, Photobucket, Archive, and dozens of video-sharing websites—not to mention thousands of personal webpages and social media platforms—nowadays feature countless videos depicting the backcountry exploits of trekkers, climbers, skiers, snowboarders, kayakers, sky- and ocean-divers, surfers, mountain bikers, and many other types of outdoor enthusiasts no longer satisfied with just having a fun day outdoors, but rather keen on chronicling their adventures via increasingly sophisticated HD video technologies. Vimeo alone, for example, features about thousands of videos under the "Sports" and "Travel" category.

As is typical of Vimeo—in contrast for example to YouTube—many of these videos are shot by "professional consumers:" individuals who straddle an increasingly blurred line between amateurs, serious leisure practitioners, and professionals (for more, see Buckingham and Willett 2009; Burgess and Greene 2009). Many of these videos are even high quality enough to be also shown at "outdoor" or "mountain" film festivals worldwide (see Muller 2010). But why, exactly, is this happening? Why is a good day outdoors no longer enough? Why must it be turned into a sleek video production, compelling enough to score 10,000 web views and reap festival awards? Fascinated by this phenomenon, a year ago I began a small ethnographic project focused on such artistically inclined outdoor enthusiasts, together with graduate assistant Lindsay Marie Stewart. And just like everyone else, we made a video about it. The trailer of the upcoming film can be viewed at https://vimeo.com/100785999 as a companion to this chapter.

At the same time Lindsay began editing the footage she had collected, a group of friends and I made a plan to embark on a six-day trekking expedition into the coastal forests and beaches of British Columbia. By the time we left in the spring of 2014, I had read so much about the practice of recording and editing video—though I had never actually done it on my own—that I simply couldn't pass up the opportunity to give it a try. I ended up shooting a second video—later in the summer of 2014—about my climb up Mt. Fuji, in Japan (https://vimeo.com/101804153). What I discovered in the process was that producing these videos was actually much more difficult than any of the outdoor activities themselves. The technical and conceptual difficulties I encountered taught me a great deal about both the recording, editing, and sharing technologies I used, as well as about making media culture in general terms.

Now, if you log on to YouTube, you'll get the impression that making a good video is as easy as pressing REC. Millions of clips await playback, rating, and commenting. But watch carefully a few of those and you'll come to the realization that most of them are, to speak candidly, absolute garbage. Sure, they may be useful in teaching you how to mount snow chains on your car's tires or how to improve your ab crunch technique, but let us face it: the quality of their recordings is so poor that you'd lose face by having your name associated with them. The sound is often barely audible, the editing lazy, the colors dull, and the light was never even given the time of the day. The low quality of the vastest majority of amateur recordings allows us to understand the nature of adventure videos found on Vimeo. Let me explain.

According to Erving Goffman (1959), human beings are keenly aware of their expressiveness. For Goffman day-to-day conduct is a careful performance carried out for the sake of casting and managing impressions before specific audiences. Goffman never wrote about the phenomenon of recording one's own performance through video, but from his dramaturgical perspective it is quite easy to view actions such as adventure video making as a mediated attempt to convey information about the self. And the information, in this case, is rich and varied. Adventure videos convey impressions about their makers' cultural taste, character, and subcultural identity, for example. But first and foremost, in my experience, they clearly express their *skills*. And there are two sets of important skills clearly being performed in amateur adventure videos: the physical ones pertaining to the outdoor activities depicted on video and the aesthetic/technical ones related to the production of such films.

As mentioned, the ostentatious *performance of skill* in the context of adventure video making is something that we must understand in the broader context of video making and sharing. Typically, home video filmmakers and their subjects are the exact antinomy of the perfectly executed and accurately scripted action featured in Hollywood movies and much TV programming. Think of the goofy blooper material typical of *America's Funniest Home Videos*, for example. Or think of dreadful holiday videos, or your uncle's unedited footage from your little nephew's birthday party, or the red-neck character of backyard wrestling matches, or the crass vulgarity of stunt "dumbass" videos, or even the anyone-can-do-it nature of homemade porn. What all these homemade videos connote—regardless of their precise content—is that shooting video and uploading it on the Web is easy, and even a complete idiot can do it (as *The Complete Idiot's Guide to Digital Video* articulates).

It is precisely in contrast to this "low-brow" attitude to filming that the "middle-brow" (Bourdieu 1996) practice of creating adventure videos must be understood (see Muller 2010). In *Photography: A Middle-Brow Art*, sociologist Pierre Bourdieu (1996) argues that the practice of taking aesthetically sensitive photographs serves to demarcate personal and social boundaries. Photography is not the same as the more traditional high-brow art of painting and sculpture, but it still works in delineating group membership, social capital, aesthetic and intellectual ambitions, identity, and the will to break away from lower-brow expressions. The same argument can be easily extended to the makers of adventure videos—as Lindsay and I learned from our athlete/artist informants' words—and more broadly to the making of amateur videos that make a conscious attempt to stand out from the mass (see Buckingham and Willett 2009).

Ethnographer Patricia Lange obtained these same insights by researching youths who create videos for YouTube as a way of expressing their technological literacy and "technical identity." As she writes, "when young people express themselves through video and socialize with family and friends, they are building on a long tradition of media sharing [...]. Having an online presence and sharing one's message through media are key aspects of being a socially connected young person" (Lange 2014: 9). Managing others' impressions of oneself as a skilled and competent person is a characteristic common to all of us. In fact, the practice of distinction of my skills and technological literacy is something that is meaningful, even to this not-so-young person.

There is an overwhelming amount of academic research available on the content of YouTube and other video-sharing platforms and on its alleged social and cultural consequences. However, this is often research conducted by way of watching video, not making it. Very few scholars have the time or inclination to learn about video by making some. Learning how to shoot video, therefore, was for me from the very beginning an ostentatious performance of skill display. It was also important to me to be capable of doing something that few of my friends and colleagues knew how to do. And to be candid, as Buckingham and Willett (2009) have also found, the opinions of the "community of practice," comprised of adventure videos mattered a great deal to me. But more importantly, in the process of completing my first lessons about making videos, I acquired skills that convinced me that our adventure-video-making informants' words were true: producing video is very complex, and the challenge is a key part of its appeal.

Now, I could outline many of these technical challenges—from applying the rule of thirds to my shots to the trickiness of mastering manual focus, or from choosing the right transitions between clips to finding the right soundtrack for a video—but instead I want to highlight a unique challenge that strikes right at the core of the subject matter of this book. As Dennis and I have outlined in our introductory chapter, media culture and everyday life are profoundly interwoven. Yet, at times, the dynamics of everyday life and the demands of media production do not align well. We might call these situations *subworld alignment failures*. Let me outline what I mean.

Making a video about my adventures required spending a great deal of time getting the right shots. There were two types of shots I needed: action shots and landscape b-roll. B-roll required keeping my eyes open to appealing features of the places I walked through: interesting rock formations, panoramas, vegetation, and, yes, even strange-looking handrails. Recording physical action instead required at least two things. First, it meant sticking my camera in my friends' faces while they were trying to climb ladders, walk over suspension bridges, or otherwise chill out on the beach and have fun. Second, it necessitated mounting an action camera (a GoPro Hero 3) on my own body to get great point-of-view shots and letting it run as long as the battery allowed. And all of this had clear interpersonal consequences.

A heightened sensitivity to landscape meant being constantly busy looking for something to capture on camera. This caused me to slow down my pace considerably, which at times unnerved my friends and at other times caused me to break my pace, lose my rhythm, and get tired of being always "on"—rather than just enjoying the moment. Yet, the first thing good documentary filmmakers will tell you is that unless your camera is rolling all the time, you will miss the moment you want to have on film. This prompted me to realize that as discreet and as considerate of others as you can be, filming an adventure you undertake with friends will inevitably result in a clash of *subworlds*.

Social phenomenologist Alfred Schütz argued that multiple subworlds constantly operate in our mundane existence (1982). The most basic division between these subworlds operates on the basis of who is present. "Consociates" are people who share with us a community, time, and space in virtue of their presence. In contrast, there are distant others such as contemporaries (who could potentially become consociates in the future), predecessors, and successors who are not immediately present. When you are in the midst of an outdoor leisure activity you are automatically concerned with your consociates. But turning a camera on for the sake of sharing the moment with distant others alters the subworld in operation, and suddenly there are two *Umwelten* jostling with one another for dominance, which can cause confusion and conflict amid those present.

So, while the consociates' subworld in the context of an outdoor adventure feels encompassing, enveloping, and captivating—what we might call an experience of "flow" (Csikszentmihalyi 1990)—the subworld brought about by the presence of cameras alerts one to being reflexive, self-conscious, and guarded (or conversely, at times, histrionic) in front of the lens and microphone. At times this is fun. But at times it can be very annoying. Schütz (1982) himself remarked on the frequent possibility of social situations becoming intertwined and causing social tensions. Shooting an adventure video will inevitably cause some of this tension. You may be able to continue getting along with your friends by choosing the right moments for recording, using the camera in a way that will be sensitive to the subworld of consociates, and repairing instances where infractions occur. Continuing to get along with your friends requires the performance of very important technical *and social* skills (incidentally, it is precisely because my West Coast Trail video was never meant for *your* consumption, but rather only for mine and my friends' and friends' families' consumption, that you're not going to be given a link to it!).

In conclusion, watching and making adventure videos are deeply interwoven activities, at times painfully so. It is by watching adventure videos that amateur filmmakers learn the tricks of the trade and become inspired to go have fun in the great outdoors with a camera. It is by watching and then producing such videos that communities of practice are made and re-made. And it is such extended networks of practitioners/connoisseurs that end up building and enforcing the high aesthetic standards that separate adventure filmmakers from the rest of homemade video recorders. In turn, these high standards become the middle-brow testing grounds for the ostentatious performance of adventure filmmakers' skills worldwide. And no doubt also the testing grounds of many groups of friends turned unwittingly into film subjects who sometimes, without a doubt, would rather be just friends simply hanging out! As communication technologies and the corresponding production skills continue to become more pervasive in everyday life year after year, more and more of our media culture will inevitably be so deeply interwoven with our everyday life. But whether this will be a testament to our growing ability to produce popular culture on our own and truly for ourselves or a testament to our waning capacity to just "be" in the flow of the moment with our consociates is something that remains to be seen.

Phillip Vannini is Canada Research Chair in Public Ethnography and Professor of Communication and Culture at Royal Roads University

(British Columbia). He is the author and editor of 12 books; he has also served as editor of two book series, including Ashgate's *Interactionist Currents*. He is the co-author of *Understanding Society Through Popular Music* (Routledge, 2008) and was a contributor to *Material Culture and Technology in Everyday Life: Ethnographic Approaches* (Peter Lang: 2009). The rest of his scholarship has addressed numerous aspects of popular culture and everyday life issues, including camping, eating, drinking, traveling, building, consuming, body modification, and experiencing the weather.

Note

1. It is interesting to note how each of these technologies seems to have spawned genres and markets uniquely its own. What GoPros and high-sensor video DSLRs are to HD adventure videos, camera phones are to citizen journalism, and camcorders are/were to family videos.

References

Bourdieu, Pierre. 1996. *Photography: A Middle-Brow Art* (trans. Shaun Whiteside). Stanford, CA: Stanford University Press.

Buckingham, David and Rebekah Willett. 2009. *Video Cultures: Media Technology and Everyday Creativity*. Basingstoke, UK: Palgrave Macmillan.

Burgess, Jean and Joshua Greene. 2009. *YouTube: Online Video and Participatory Culture*. Cambridge, UK and New York, NY: Polity Press.

Csikszentmihalyi, Mihaly. 1990. *Flow: The Psychology of Optimal Experience*. New York, NY: HarperCollins.

Gauntlett, David. 2011. *Making is Connecting. The Social Meaning of Creativity, from DIY and Knitting, to YouTube and Web 2.0*. Cambridge, UK: Polity Press.

Goffman, Erving. 1959. *The Presentation of Self in Everyday Life*. New York, NY: Anchor Books.

Lange, Patricia. 2014. *Kids in YouTube: Technical Identities and Digital Literacies*. Walnut Creek, CA: Left Coast Press.

Muller, Eggo. 2010. "Where Quality Matters." In Pelle Snickars and Patrick Vonderau (Eds.) *The YouTube Reader*. Stockholm, Sweden: National Library of Sweden, 126–129.

Schütz, Alfred. 1972. *The Problem of Social Reality*. New York, NY: Springer-Verlag.

Snickars, Pelle and Patrick Vonderau (Eds.). 2010. *The YouTube Reader*. Stockholm, Sweden: National Library of Sweden.

Strangelove, Michael. 2010. *Watching YouTube: Extraordinary Videos by Ordinary People*. Toronto, ON: University of Toronto Press.

8

SHARING SELFIES[1]

Uschi Klein

"Do you take selfies?" A friend asked me this recently while we were discussing photography, and I have to confess the question caught me by surprise. As a photographer, conversations around the medium are hardly unusual for me, but the assumption that I too might be taking photos of myself with a camera phone and posting them on Social Networking Sites (SNS), such as Instagram, Flickr, or Facebook, struck me as a little strange, embarrassing even. Bourdieu (1984) might understand my reaction as a form of cultural or professional "distinction;" however, the rise of the selfie phenomenon in recent years suggests many others don't share my reluctance. Photography has long stopped being the preserve of an elite, but its place within social networking culture has changed amateur practice too. No longer called upon only for special occasions, popular photography—epitomized by the selfie—has rapidly become a cultural practice of the everyday.

A quick hashtag search on Instagram using the word "selfie" reveals countless variations of the term; from #selfietime to #selfiegame, #selfieoverload and #selfielove, people appear to be creative in formulating new hashtags containing the word selfie and adding their own images (often simultaneously) to different online pools of millions of selfies (at the time of writing #selfie alone has 217,932,440 posts on Instagram, and the number is growing steadily). The everyday creativity of the form is expressed both textually and visually, as exemplified in one image in #selfiegame: the black-and-white image is composed of three different representations of a man's head and shoulders lying on the grass. While each variation takes up one-third of the frame, the man's gaze is always straight at the camera, yet his facial expressions vary in each portrayal. This montage of different versions in one image (rather than three individual selfie images) suggests a desire for visual originality that matches the textual creativity of #selfiegame.

And selfies are a global phenomenon, or at least a phenomenon of the global city. In 2014, the research project Selfiecity surveyed the multitude of selfies in five cities around the world (Bangkok, Berlin, Moscow, New York, and São Paulo) (Selfiecity 2014). Selecting 120,000 images from a total of 656,000 collected on Instagram, the project found that fewer actual selfies are taken than people assume (approximately 4% of the image sample). While 4% might seem low, bearing in mind that selfies are "photographs that one has taken of oneself" (Oxford Dictionary), not images of other people, food, or animals, this still represents a significant volume of images.

The selfie is also a gendered form. In each of the cities, more posted selfies are of women. Bangkok at 55% was the lowest, while 82% of selfies in Moscow were of women. Many of these images show their subjects posing with tilted heads, which might call for a more detailed study and comparison to Erving Goffman's (1959; 1979) classic study of the performance of gender in advertising, but mostly we find an abundance of selfies illustrating people smiling. With millions of selfies on SNS, people seem to have a strong desire to share their selfies with friends and followers, otherwise why take them in the first place?

Selfies are a compelling and proliferating phenomenon in our contemporary popular and visual culture, raising important questions around the notion of photographic time, the visual performance of the self (Goffman 1959; 1979), the shifting boundaries of privacy, and their wider impact on other social and cultural fields, in which people engage with everyday practices when they share selfies on SNS. These questions are crucial because selfies embrace all those aspects. Taken in fleeting moments and quickly shared in everyday life, they relate to the lived experiences that are "composed of various social fields of practice that are articulated, codified and normalized ... in different ways ... each combining time and space in a unique way" (Burkitt 2010: 211). Selfies function to share the present moment with others on SNS.

So what is it about self-representation in our contemporary visual and popular culture that so many people are drawn to and that leads to the assumption that *everyone* who has a camera phone or who shows the slightest interest in photography is taking and sharing selfies online? In the following essay, I explore the notions of self-representation, online sharing, and the boundaries of privacy and online relationships. But, to better understand the cultural form of selfies and how they are shared via SNS, I want first to recall the history of photographic self-portraits.[2]

Are Selfies Really so New?

Selfies are ubiquitous and abundant. People appear to love representing themselves visually in contemporary popular culture. Self-representation in the form of photographic self-portraits is not, however, a new idea or a new cultural practice, even though the word "selfie" only made it into the Oxford Dictionary in 2013. One of the earliest forms of photographic "self-portrait" was the *carte-de-visite*, invented in 1854 by Parisian photographer André-Adolphe Disdéri, and which subsequently took off as a "global phenomenon, being produced in huge numbers on every continent" (Batchen 2009: 81). Although often made in professional photographic studios or by professional photographers in the homes of sitters, the *carte-de-visite* bears comparison to the selfie. This distinctive photographic format was actively shared and exchanged with family and friends who often stored them in family albums. It was the beginning of a photographic era that was characterised by mass reproduction, consumption, and active use. Photography was not simply a means of making images but a significant cultural practice and a substantial arena of commercial enterprise. *Cartes-de-visite* were products of repetition and difference. They were multiples, printed and reproduced almost identically in the thousands, putting the authenticity of the original into question and establishing reproducibility as photography's most distinctive, and disruptive, feature (Benjamin 1968).

While this multiplicity and easy reproduction was the primary selling point and success for the *carte-de-visite* (Batchen 2009), Walter Benjamin argues that "[e]ven the most perfect reproduction ... is lacking in one element: its presence in time and space, its unique existence at the place where it happens to be" (1968: 214). In other words, the reproduction of *cartes*, no matter how identical they were, replaced the uniqueness (or authenticity) and present moment of the single image for the plurality of copies that were now widely distributed and became an accepted form of commodity. They were collected in albums, consumed, shared, exchanged, and discussed with friends and family. *Cartes* enabled people to re-create relationship structures "that overcame time and space, class and gender" (Batchen 2009: 91). Indeed, *cartes* facilitated the production of visual connections in albums, linking people who might otherwise have not been associated, arguably making *cartes* the predecessor of Instagram.

As I hope this brief account has indicated, practices of self-representation, the sharing of photographs and their use within social relationships, were firmly established within the history of photography before the arrival of the selfie.

What Makes a Selfie?

Examining a selfie at random, I am confronted by a woman who glances at the camera but does not smile. A close-up of her cropped head in the top left corner of the image depicts half her face, nose, left eye and eyebrow. Her medium ash brown hair fills the right side, and a yellow scarf covers the bottom of the image. There is no discernible context and the effect of the closeness of the camera to its subject creates a strange and rather unflattering distortion to the image. (It is interesting how rapidly these distortions, which would once have been regarded as a photographic mistake, have come to be an accepted part of the selfie aesthetic.) In another, the black-and-white image displays a medium close-up of a woman's head and shoulders. Her shoulder-length hair frames her face in the center of the image. She smiles lightly and her eyes look straight at the camera. Both these images are self-representations of women, uploaded as #selfies on Instagram. As Nancy Thumim argues, however, "[u]biquitous self-representations may look alike, but analysis of the various dimensions of mediation process shaping their production and display highlights the important distinction between them" (2012: 5). Indeed, the previously described selfies are different from each other as the women perform their selves in individual ways. Even within these tight visual limits, according to Martin Hand, "people are finding other ways to make their photos feel like *their own*" (2012: 91, italics in original). He claims that people increasingly resort to originality and creativity "in the face of ubiquity" to find novel ways to own an image as they are on a "quest to be original" (2012: 91–92), which at the same time prompts reflection on the cultural valuing of this novelty and creativity.

Mediated self-representation is not something that people do on their own. Rather, Thumim observes, participatory online communities are undergoing a continuous struggle "to make spaces for more democratic media production" (2012: 5). SNS facilitate self-representation as a condition of participation in Web 2.0, or the other way around; in order to participate in social media people must represent their selves. People's experience of the everyday is individual and unique to them, therefore it is crucial that they have choices about which facet of their selves they want to represent and how to represent them (Rivière 2005).

It is not an unusual idea that individuals make a presentation of their self to others. As proposed by Goffman (1959), each individual has various selves. Like a Russian doll, they are concealed inside each other and presented to others and the outside world according to the structure of social life. Thus, individuals perform their selfies to influence others. Depending on their roles, relationships, and statuses those performances are restricted by social and cultural norms. Performances are also idealized. As individuals are capable of experiencing pride and shame, they present their self in the best possible way while they safeguard their self against embarrassment.

The millions of mediated selfies on SNS may look alike to the casual eye, but their role is not simply to visually present one's self to the world; selfies allow individuals to actively participate in the world. Sharing selfies enables individuals both to visually perform their self and engage in a cultural form and everyday practice that facilitates their participation in an online community with which they can share their present experiences and moments. Pierre Bourdieu termed this idea "habitus" (1984). According to his ideas, moving across and between cultural fields shapes people's habitus and helps make sense of the different relationships individuals develop between social structures (such as

SNS) and everyday practices (like sharing selfies). So selfies are not randomly posted. People choose what part of their selves they want to represent and how to present it before selecting the appropriate hashtag on Instagram.

Who Looks at Selfies?

Contemporary technological advances in popular and digital culture increase the use of SNS. Writers across disciplines observe that people create more digital photographs out of a perceived need to share them (Gómez-Cruz and Meyer 2012; Hand 2012; Murray 2013). Indeed, the fusion of the mobile phone and digital photography enables users to share their selfies widely and, subsequently, for these selfies to be re-shared with others—often in seemingly arbitrary ways, and "in real time" (Gómez-Cruz and Meyer 2012: 214). Visual self-representation has become ubiquitous, "an extension of the way in which one sees oneself, and it gives value to communicating with other people [in the present]" (Rivière 2005: 173). According to Geoffrey Batchen, "photography is predominantly a vernacular practice and has always been a global experience" (2008: 126). Indeed, photography is about sharing and interpersonal communication, which are both central to participation. Selfies are often shared without formal permission, maintaining a cycle of production, consumption, and distribution—friends and followers on SNS actively share selfies with their friends and followers and so on. Daniel Rubinstein and Katrina Sluis maintain that the exposure of the private snapshot has increased to such an extent that "snapshot photography ... is both ubiquitous and hidden" (2008: 10). Yet when the unstated codes and conventions that shape this cultural practice are breached, as in the recent example of selfies made at the Sydney gun siege in December 2014 (McAteer 2014), they can be quickly subject to public exposure and censure.

In this light, perhaps it seems necessary to consider how contemporary selfie images shift socially agreed-upon ideas of the private moment and the boundaries of privacy. Digital technologies have blurred the boundaries between public and private communication on SNS, as selfies are shared in an online space whose "publicness" differs according to

individual privacy settings. Sharing selfies is self-generated and voluntary; it is not merely the social media institutions that frame, approve,
or heavily regulate them. Selfies are self-sponsored and self-circulated,
which is how they have become so ubiquitous (Thumim 2012). However, as research suggests, privacy is important to users of SNS (Marwick
and boyd 2014), so instead of paying attention to the issue of whether
SNS is private or not, users should "take as given that social networking
is not a private activity, and consequently that self-representations that
are produced in the process of social networking are also not private"
(Thumim 2012: 148).

Selfies and Online Social Worlds

Digital technologies are increasingly changing the way individuals act
in their everyday lives, enabling new activities and the formation of new
communities (Barton and Lee 2012). To share selfies is to participate
and collaborate in an online world and to interact as a member of an
online community—sometimes by textually commenting on selfies,
sometimes by sharing them with others. Furthermore, the cultural practice of creating and sharing selfies, no matter how original or mundane
they are, asserts new identities through the performance of online selves
in interaction with others and in the present moment. This interaction
is a two-way practice, as one connects and relates to the world in different ways. While identity and self-expression have always been crucial
to self-representation, and are particularly salient practices for teenagers
and young people (Davis 2011), digital technologies have increased the
proliferation of identity creation and the speed in which relationships
and friendships develop online. In other words, the practice of selfies
emphasizes the individual experience of seeing ourselves as part of the
world, yet the relationships and connections we create and maintain
with others by sharing selfies is no less important as part of our popular
and visual culture.

Indeed, writers broadly agree that sharing and exchanging personal
photographs, including selfies, is fundamental to maintaining off- and
online relationships (Davis 2011; Gye 2007). As the mobile phone is no
longer limited to merely transmitting voice and includes other functions
such as photography, it enriches communication. Selfies communicate

and establish both a visual presence and photographic communication that functions to maintain contact without the content that is being exchanged being particularly meaningful. Thus, selfies are a form of relationship-focused, rather than task-oriented, communication, where the content that is being exchanged is less important than the maintenance of mutual presence (Villi 2012). Sharing selfies is therefore part of many people's daily lives and the fact that they are widely shared, even without consent, may simply contribute to being part of a wider network and increase the chances of online connectivity. This also means that identity has become fluid and multi-faceted as people move from one social context, using their selfies across different platforms and for different reasons.

Borrowing the linguistic term of contextual redundancy (Wit and Gillette 1999), others also argue that the concepts of repetition and ritualization are endemic to the genre of self-representation, otherwise we would not see the vast number of selfies on SNS that are taken at different times of the day or week—yes, the following hashtags do also exist on Instagram: #selfiemonday, #selfietuesday, #selfiewednesday, #selfiemorning ... You get the idea.

In conclusion, the selfie phenomenon is more complex than it first appears and it is not necessarily driven by self-absorption and self-love, or representative of a narcissistic turn in contemporary popular culture. The impulse to be creative and original when taking selfies indicates a strong desire to connect with others in a variety of ways and to share experiences in real time. Photography is about communication, which serves to maintain contact and relationships with others. Moreover, selfies are a condition of active online participation. They are shared, networked, and connected visual reflections of everyday life. Those reflections help to maintain and expand social connections as selfies are shared and re-shared. Thus, they move from personal and private to public spheres. The proliferation of selfies is contributing to the visual landscape of contemporary popular culture. Even those of us who don't take selfies cannot stay aloof, in one way or another we are likely to be part of the production, consumption, and distribution of them, as even the British monarch found out (BBC 2014).

Uschi Klein is a doctoral candidate at the University of Brighton (UK) and works as a photographer in London. Her undergraduate degree was in linguistics and media studies, after which she received a master's degree in photography. Her research interests include the relationships between photography, visual culture, representation, identity, and visual research methods. Her current research project is a participatory, image-based study that explores the everyday photographic practices of young people with autism spectrum disorders.

Notes

1. I wish to thank Darren Newbury for his comments and suggestions during the writing of this essay.
2. See Jeffrey (1981), Wells (2009), and Rosenblum (2008) for a more comprehensive historical overview and discussion of photography.

References

Barton, David and Carmen K.M. Lee. 2012. "Redefining Vernacular Literacies in the Age of Web 2.0." *Applied Linguistics 33*(3): 282–298.

Batchen, Geoffrey. 2008. "Snapshots." *Photographies 1*(2): 121–142.

Batchen, Geoffrey. 2009. "Dreams of Ordinary Life: *Cartes-de-Visite* and the Bourgeois Imagination." In J.J. Long, Andrea Noble and Edward Welch (Eds.), *Photography: Theoretical Snapshots*. Abington, UK and New York, NY: Routledge, 80–97.

Benjamin, Walter. 1999. "The Work of Art in the Age of Mechanical Reproduction." In Hannah Arendt (Ed.), *Illuminations: Essays and Reflections*. London, UK: Pimlico, 211–244.

Bourdieu, Pierre. 1984. *Distinction: A Social Critique of the Judgement of Taste* (trans. Richard Nice). London, UK: Routledge & Kegan Paul.

BBC. 2014, July 24. "Glascow 2014: Queen 'Photobombs' Hockey Players' Selfie." *BBC [Sport]*. Retrieved from http://www.bbc.co.uk/sport/0/commonwealth-games/28464014.

Burkitt, Ian. 2010. "The Time and Space of Everyday Life." *Cultural Studies 18*(2–3): 211–227.

Davis, Katie. 2011. "Tensions of Identity in a Networked Era: Young People's Perspectives on the Risks and Rewards of Online Self-Expression." *New Media & Society 14*(4): 634–651.

Goffman, Erving. 1959. *The Presentation of Self in Everyday Life*. New York, NY: Anchor Books.

Goffman, Erving. 1979. *Gender Advertisements*. New York, NY: Harper & Row.

Gómez-Cruz, Edgar and Eric T. Meyer. 2012. "Creation and Control in the Photographic Process: iPhones and the Emerging Fifth Moment of Photography." *Photographies 5*(2): 203–221.

Gye, Lisa. 2007. "Picture this: The Impact of Mobile Camera Phones on Personal Photographic Practices." *Continuum: Journal of Media & Cultural Studies 21*(2): 279–288.

Hand, Martin. 2012. *Ubiquitous Photography*, Cambridge, UK: Polity Press.

Jeffrey, Ian. 1981. *Photography: A Concise History*, London, UK: Thames and Hudson.

Lister, Martin. 2013. *The Photographic Image in Digital Culture*. Abington, UK and New York, NY: Routledge, 165–182.

Marwick, Alice E. and danah boyd. 2014. "Networked Privacy: How Teenagers Negotiate Context in Social Media." *New Media & Society 16*(7): 1051–1067.

McAteer, Ollie. 2014, December 14. "Sydney Siege: People Are Taking Selfies Just Metres Away From Hostage Case." *Metro.co.uk*. Retrieved from http://metro.co.uk/2014/12/15/sydney-siege-people-are-taking-selfies-just-metres-away-from-hostage-cafe-4987447/.

Murray, Susan. 2013. "New Media and Vernacular Photography: Revisiting Flickr." In M. Lister (Ed.), The Photographic Image in Digital Culture. Abington, UK and New York, NY: Routledge, 165–182.

Oxford Dictionary. No date. Selfie. http://www.oxforddictionaries.com/definition/english/selfie. Accessed September 29, 2015.

Rivière, Carole. 2006. "Mobile Camera Phones: A New Form of 'Being Together' in Daily Interpersonal Communication." In R. Ling and Per E. Pedersen, *Mobile Communication: Re-negotiation of the Social Sphere*. London, UK: Springer, 167–185.

Rosenblum, Naomi. 2008. *A World History of Photography* (4th ed.), New York, NY: Abbeville Press.

Rubinstein, Daniel and Katrina Sluis. 2008. "A Life More Photographic." *Photographies 1*(1): 9–28.

SelfieCity. 2014. SelfieCity. http://selfiecity.net/. Accessed September 29, 2015.

Thumim, Nancy. 2012. *Self-Representation and Digital Culture*, Basingstoke, UK: Palgrave Macmillan.

Villi, Mikko. 2012. "Visual Chitchat: The Use of Camera Phones in Visual Interpersonal Communication." *Interactions: Studies in Communication and Culture 3*(1): 39–54.

Wells, Liz. 2009. *Photography: A Critical Introduction* (4th ed.). London, UK and New York, NY: Routledge.

Wit, Ernst-Jan, C. and Marie Gillette. 1999. "What is Linguistic Redundancy?" (Technical Report, University of Chicago). Retrieved from http://www.math.rug.nl/~ernst/linguistics/redundancy3.pdf.

9
PLAYING MUSIC
Simon Gottschalk

To play a wrong note is insignificant; to play without passion is inexcusable.
—Beethoven

"You must be a guitar player," said Joni with a mischievous smile, leaning back in her office chair.

"How can you tell?" I asked, completely surprised.

"The fingertips on your left hand; they're hard and blistered. That's typical."

I looked at them and chuckled. Why would she notice that?

Taking place many years ago, this conversation introduces a short discussion of *embodiment* and *improvisation* in hypermodern music performance. More precisely, I use the video game *Guitar Hero* as an exemplar to discuss the elective affinities between virtual guitar playing and a certain sensibility or "structure of feeling" characterizing everyday life and psyche in the hypermodern moment.[1] Of course, there are countless other aspects of musical performance I could have selected, but as I hope to convey in the following paragraphs, embodiment and improvisation seem especially pertinent.

The study of musical forms should be of utmost interest to sociologists. If—like language and mathematics—music is universal, Plato, Max Weber, John Dewey, Theodor Adorno, Howard Becker, cultural studies scholars, and many others too numerous to mention have proposed incisive insights about the reciprocal relations between musical forms and societal conditions. As Vannini and Waskul (2006: 6) also remark, "by discerning how musical esthetics emerges out of music-making, we should be able to craft understandings of how esthetic dynamics inform the constitution of meaning (i.e., semiosis) in contexts well beyond music proper." The same obtains for the sociological study of games. Huizinga (1971), Caillois (2001), and Barthes (1972), for example, provide a wealth of insights into their social and cultural significance. Here, I focus especially on what *Guitar Hero* articulates about music.

As is customary in musical improvisation sessions, let us first attune to each other. The purpose of this paper is not to join the chorus of critics who deride *Guitar Hero* because the game is "fake" and because playing it has little in common with playing a real guitar. In her research with *Guitar Hero* gamers, Miller (2009) found that her respondents indeed understand the difference between the two very well, and several add that "being like a real guitar" was never the purpose of the game anyway. So, while I do believe that there are significant differences between playing *Guitar Hero* and playing a real guitar (and while I do not hide my preference for the latter), I do not want to dismiss the game simply because it fails to meet purist and orthodox criteria of what "real" music-playing should be like.

Further, I am not suggesting that the characteristics of *Guitar Hero* I discuss here are found in all or even most forms of music performed in the hypermodern moment—far from it. My purpose here is to critically examine the elective affinities between the logic of this game and the hypermodern sensibility, especially around issues of embodiment and improvisation.

Digital and Tactile Contacts

In hypermodernity, technologies of the body take over, which results in the ever-greater objectivization and externalization of the body.

(Varga 2005: 209)

The digital screen—the emblem of the hypermodern era—destabilizes and recodes the connections between our senses and those that have traditionally linked body/mind, time/space, private/public, present/absent, self/others, simulated/real, ephemeral/eternal, and human/machine. This

recoding occurs at an accelerated pace, thanks partly to the rapid mul-
tiplication of technologies of computer-mediated communication that
induce new immersive experiences of embodiment. For example, email,
Twitter, Facebook, and other text-based platforms enable us to experience virtual omnipresence—the extraordinary ability to manifest on
countless screens any passing thought, need, or emotion from wherever,
whenever, and to whomever. While this ability is now taken-for-granted,
it is unique in human history and psychology.

Among those new technologies that seem to materialize faster than
anyone can really synthesize or predict, recent decades have witnessed
the proliferation of ever-more sophisticated video games, and among
those *Guitar Hero* has been named by a few "tech" journalists as one
of the most influential technological devices of the early twenty-first
century (see *Advertising Age* 2009; Sauer 2009; Stuart 2009). Miller
(2009: 397) explains the game in the following manner:

> To play a song, a *Guitar Hero* guitarist must read the on-screen
> notation, simultaneously pressing a particular fret button with
> the left hand and a strum bar with the right hand ... The player
> functions as the gatekeeper for prerecorded material; correct fret-
> ting/strumming allows each note to make its way from the game
> console to the speakers. If the player misses a note, that note
> drops out of the audio playback ... At the borders of the stream-
> ing notation track, animated avatars perform the song in a rock
> club or arena. Frenetic camera angles and stage effects add to the
> excitement ...

Guitar Hero has also been the topic of several academic articles and
book chapters that discuss its different facets from a multiplicity of perspectives (see, for example, Arsenault 2008; Svec 2008; Tanenbaum and
Bizzocchi 2009). Those texts that elaborate on the embodied experiences induced by the game have typically focused on players' ability to
hit plastic keys and to squeeze the whammy bar in time, and to their
body movements, such as raising their pseudo-guitar in the air, swaying,
jumping, performing stereotypical rock star poses, and other relatively
simple gestures.

Although quite interesting, it seems that this game-based view of embodiment is not unlike *Guitar Hero's* approach to playing guitar. In other words, while hitting plastic keys at the right time and performing a number of stereotypical body gestures evidently constitute a certain type of embodiment, plucking, picking, bending, hammering, strumming, muting, pinching, bouncing, or pulling off real steel taut guitar strings is quite another. At the simplest mathematical level, compare the *Guitar Hero* five uniform keys, strum bar and whammy bar with a real guitar. The latter has six strings, each of a different width and resistance. This means that each string will have a very different feel and sound depending on how one touches it, whether one touches it on the 3rd or the 23rd fret, and whether one touches it with the fingertip or the fingernail, with the thumb or the the the palm, with a plastic pick or a Pyrex bottleneck, with a Zippo lighter or with a violin bow. Thus, given 6 strings times 23 frets, there are—at minimum—138 different kinds of tactile contact with the strings and thus of sound. And that's just with *one* kind of touching. On a virtual guitar, however, this infinite number of permutations has been simplified and reduced to a very standardized and uniform sort of contact.

In addition, while playing a real instrument typically mobilizes the sense of touch and hearing (think about outstanding blind musicians such as Ray Charles, Stevie Wonder, Blind Willie Johnson, or Jeff Healey), virtual guitar playing mobilizes eye-hand coordination and completely recombines the connections between mind, eyes, ears, fingers, and sound. This recombination is further complicated because the relationships between different notes on a virtual guitar have nothing to do with mathematical relationships—and *possibilities*—across notes, frets, and strings on a real guitar. More worrisome, as some of Tanenbaum and Bizzocchi's respondents remark, "understanding how the real-world playing of the song 'actually goes' can *interfere* with success in the game-world playing of the song" (2008: 133). As Miller concludes, the *Guitar Hero* experience is schizophonic: "the performing body is almost entirely severed from the musical sound [it produces]" (401).[2]

To go back to the fingertips story, while *Guitar Hero* gamers can most certainly also develop blisters, those marks left by the repeated hitting on plastic keys attest to a very different sort of embodied engagement with one's instrument—and music performance more generally—than shown by deep grooves sliced by years of steel guitar strings vibrating into the digital skin. This remark does not seek to glorify the latter as more authentic. It simply invites reflection about what both experiences might teach–about music, embodied performance, and the performing self.

Collaborative Emergence and Individualistic Performance

> It's louder than words, this thing that we do, louder than words
> the way it unfurls.
> —Pink Floyd, "Louder than Words" (*The Endless River*)

"Let's try playing Radiohead's *House of Cards* in a reggae style," I suggest to members of our jam band. I strum the first chords, hope the others will follow, and hope it's going to "work." It should, though. For years now, we've been improvising on practically anything we set our mind to.

The defining principle of the jam genre is, of course, the central place given to improvisations in the songs we play. The way we look at it, a song is not a rigid text we have to faithfully reproduce, but a structure— a launching pad from which we can improvise and explore the many different musical landscapes that reveal themselves through our very act of playing together. Sometimes, the jams are memorable and the songs gracefully soar to delightful places. At other times, the songs derail and crash like a screeching train wreck. Sometimes, we have an audience, sometimes we do not, or are not sure if anyone is going to show up. Sometimes we record our session, sometimes we do not. We never really know what is going to happen.

Beyond the obvious aesthetic and social pleasures it enables, a musical improvisation is a useful metaphor for other sociological purposes as well. As Sawyer reminds us (2000: 184):

> In fact, everyday conversation is also a collective improvisation … Like jazz, conversations are sometimes less creative, and "larger social organizations" determine how free we are to improvise. In many situations we will use clichés and follow culturally shared

scripts for conversation. But in the many everyday situations where no script is specified ... most of us can rise to the occasion and engage in emergent, improvised behavior. This phenomenon remains a puzzle for social scientists—the tension between pre-existing structure and interactional creativity is at the core of many contemporary social theories ... In this sense, improvisation is a critical issue for the social sciences, and the study of everyday social life faces the same key issues as the study of improvisation.

In addition to those improvisational aptitudes we all deploy in everyday conversations, musical improvisation is intimately related to other interactional skills as well. In the "Etiquette of Improvisation" (2000), Becker suggests that successful musical improvisation sessions require not only musical skills and "keeping time," but also the musicians' ability to *listen* to each other, to give fellow musicians time and space to develop their musical lines, to be attentive to where they are moving the music, to decide whether and how to join, and to hear other potential paths in the musical terrain they are tracing. As he puts it (2000: 172):

> The players thus develop a collective direction that characteristically— as though the participants had all read Émile Durkheim—feels larger than any of them, as though it had a life of its own. It feels as though, instead of them playing the music, the music, Zen-like, is playing them.

Then, of course, the musicians also interact with an active and unpredictable audience, and as Becker reminds us, their relationships to various audiences will shape the boundaries of improvisational freedom and creative élan.

Considering those complex dynamics, it is not difficult to understand the intense pleasure that musicians can experience when an improvisation session works well, when they communicate with each other and the audience *through* their instruments and the "collaborative emergence" they create (Sawyer 2000). The "collaborative" part is important.

In an ensemble improvisation, we can't identify the creativity of the performance with any single performer; the performance is collaboratively created. Although each member of the group contributes creative material, a musician's contributions only make sense in terms of the way they are heard, absorbed, and elaborated on by the other musicians. The performance that results emerges from the interactions of the group.

(Sawyer 2000: 182)

On *Guitar Hero*, these potentialities have all but disappeared. First, the room for improvisation is severely curtailed as what counts here is not creativity and exploration, but the timely execution of simple orders signaled by rapidly cascading visual stimuli. Second, while playing music with others necessitates the cultivation of both complex musical and interactional skills, *Guitar Hero* reduces a mutually attuning conversation to digitally encoded and self-centered monologues celebrating the individual player whose participation is limited to following on-screen instructions, whose skills are measured by accumulated virtual bonus points, whose rewards include a camp version of "Feeling Like a Rock Star" (Miller 2009), and who never has to interact with anyone. Of course, *Guitar Hero* is meant to be a solitary game and not an instrument with which to compose and play music with others. At the same time, by equating *Guitar Hero* with playing guitar, the game reframes the meaning of music—its creative, embodied, and collaborative dimensions. This reframing is not innocent.

Calliope.mp3

Anyone can play guitar and they won't be a nothing any more.
—Radiohead, "Anyone Can Play Guitar"
(from *Pablo Honey*)

From creation to reception, the practices surrounding music both inform and articulate "the organization of self, mode of attention and engagement with the world" (Vannini and Waskul 2006: 16). As a highly entertaining virtual training ground for the young—and especially male—citizens of contemporary society, the sound of *Guitar Hero* echoes distinctly hypermodern principles or riffs: (1) Rigidly encoded interaction with intelligent machines rather than collaboration with others; (2) Response time to on-screen instructions rather than creativity and reflection; (3) "Conformist perfectionism" (Miller 2009: 414) rather than improvisation and risk-taking; (4) Visual decoding rather than attentive listening; (5) Clicking rather than touching; (6) A binary logic rather than nuance, ambiguity, and uncertainty; and, above all, (7) The absolute necessity of a high-tech device without which performing anything is becoming increasingly unthinkable.

Because these riffs are not confined to the screen of this particular game and others like it, and because they seem to increasingly encode our participation in many other settings and institutions of hypermodern society, they prompt important and rather urgent questions about the fate of our physical memory and the quality of our attunement to others, about our creativity and our willingness to take risks, about our technologically enhanced pleasures and our digitalized self-monitoring, about our de-skilling and our constant "upgrading," and about our self-perceptions and our fantasies.

Of course, *Guitar Hero* is fun! Immensely, narcissistically, and immersively so. After all, that is a main promise of many virtual pleasures in the hypermodern moment. And while playing virtual guitar can doubtlessly bring intense embodied experiences and lead players to the proverbial experience of "flow," I wonder if these pleasures are inspired by Calliope or by another spirit. Or perhaps *Guitar Hero* is her digital manifestation? Ben Azar, a student at the Boston Berklee School of Music in Boston (Zemima 2007), perhaps most succinctly captures the fate of embodiment and improvisation in *Guitar Hero* and, one suspects, in many other scenes of the hypermodern everyday as well. As he puts it, "it is like making love to a rubber doll."

Simon Gottschalk is Professor of Sociology and Humanities Fellow at the University of Nevada, Las Vegas, where he has taught for 22 years. He served as editor of *Symbolic Interaction* from 2003 to 2007, as president of the Society for the Study of Symbolic Interaction in 2011, and is currently an Associate at the *Centre de recherche sur l'individu et la société hypermodernes* (Paris). Co-author of *The Senses in Self, Culture and Society* he has published numerous texts that develop a critical interactionist perspective on topics as varied as youth cultures, hypermodernism, video games, food, speed, Las Vegas, terrorism, postmodern ethnography, ecological identity, psychiatric drugs, mental disorders, sensory social sciences, and virtual interactions.

Notes

1. For more elaborate discussions of the hypermodern term, see Armitage (2001), Ascher (2006), Aubert (2005), Castel (2005), Charles (2009), de Gaulejac (2005), Gottschalk (2009, 2010, forthcoming), Gottschalk and Whitmer (2013), Lippens (1998), Lipovetsky (2006, 2005), Rheaume (2005), and Vannini et al. (2011).
2. This term, schizophonic, refers to "the split between a sound and its source, made possible by recording technology" (Miller 2009: 400).

References

Advertising Age (website). 2009, December 14. "Book of Tens: New Products of the Decade," Retrieved from http://adage.com/article/print-edition/book-tens-products-decade/141032/.

Armitage, John. 2001. "Project(ile)s of Hypermodern(Organ)ization." *Ephemera* 1(2): 131–148.

Arsenault, Dominic. 2008. "*Guitar Hero*: Not Like Playing Guitar at All?" *Loading ...*, Vol. 2(2). http://journals.sfu.ca/loading/index.php/loading/article/viewArticle/32.

Ascher, François. 2005. *Le mangeur hypermoderne: Une figure de l'individu éclectique*. Paris, France: Éditions Odile Jacob.

Aubert, Nicole. 2005. "L'intensité de soi." In Nicole Aubert (Ed.), *L'Individu hypermoderne*. Paris, France: Erès, 73–87.

Aubert, Nicole. 2008. "Les nouvelles quêtes d'éternité." *Études* 2(408): 197–207.

Barthes, Roland. 1972. *Mythologies*. New York, NY: Farrar, Straus & Giroux.

Becker, Howard. 2000. "The Etiquette of Improvisation." *Mind, Culture, and Activity* 7(3): 171–176.

Caillois, Roger. 2001 *Man, Play and Games* (trans. Meyer Barash). Champaign, IL: University of Illinois Press.

Castel, Robert. 2005. "La face cachée de l'individu hypermoderne: L'individu par défaut." In Nicole Aubert (Ed.), *L'Individu hypermoderne*. Paris, France: Erès, 119–128.

Charles, Sebastien. 2009. "For a Humanism Amid Hypermodernity: From a Society of Knowledge to a Critical Knowledge of Society." *Axiomathes* 19: 389–400.

De Gaulejac, Vincent. 2005. "Le sujet manqué: L'individu face aux contradictions de l'hypermodernité." In Nicole Aubert (Ed.), *L'Individu hypermoderne*. Paris, France: Erès, 129–143.

Gottschalk, Simon. 2009. "Hypermodern Consumption and Megalomania: Superlatives in Commercials." *Journal of Consumer Culture* 9(3): 307–327.

Gottschalk, Simon. 2010. "The Presentation of Avatars in Second Life: Self and Interactions in Social Virtual Spaces." *Symbolic Interaction* 33(4): 504–525.

Gottschalk, Simon. Forthcoming. *Interfacework: l'interazione simbolica nell'epoca digitale*. Calimera: Edizioni Kurumuny.

Gottschalk, Simon and Jennifer Whitmer. 2013. "Hypermodern Dramaturgy in Online Encounters." In Charles Edgley (Ed.), *The Drama of Social Life: A Dramaturgical Handbook*. Farmham, UK: Ashgate, 309–334.

Huizinga, Johan. 1971. *Homo Ludens*. Boston, MA : Beacon Press.

Lippens, Ronnie. 1998. "Hypermodernity, Nomadic Subjectivities, and Radical Democracy: Roads Through Ambivalent Clews." *Social Justice 25*(2): 16–43.

Lipovetsky, Gilles. 2005. *Hypermodern Times*. Malden, MA: Polity Press.

Lipovetsky, Gilles. 2006. *Le Bonheur paradoxal: Essai sur la société d'hyperconsommation*. Paris, France: Gallimard.

Miller, Kiri. 2009. "Schizophonic Performance: 'Guitar Hero,' 'Rock Band,' and Virtual Virtuosity." *Journal of the Society for American Music 3*: 395–429.

Rheaume, Jean. 2005. "L'hyperactivité au travail: Entre narcissisme et identité." In Nicole Aubert (Ed.), *L'Individu hypermoderne*. Paris, France: Erès, 89–102.

Sauer, Patrick. 2009. "The Smartest Products of the Decade." *Inc*. 12–21. Retrieved from http://www.inc.com/articles/2009/the-smartest-products.html.

Sawyer, Keith R. 2000. "Improvisational Cultures: Collaborative Emergence and Creativity in Improvisation." *Mind, Culture, and Activity 7*(3): 180–185.

Stuart, Keith. 2009, December 16. "Video Games: the Decade When Playtime Took Over." *The Guardian*. Retrieved from http://www.theguardian.com/technology/games blog/2009/dec/16/games-decade-playtime-took-over.

Svec, Henry Adam. 2008. "Becoming Machinic Virtuosos: *Guitar Hero*, *Rez*, and Multitudinous Aesthetics." *Loading … Vol 2*(2). Retrieved from http://journals.sfu.ca/loading/index.php/loading/article/viewArticle/30.

Tanenbaum, Joshua and Jim Bizzocchi. 2009. "*Rock Band*: A Case Study in the Design of Embodied Interface Experience." In *Sandbox '09: Proceedings of the 2009 ACM SIGGRAPH Symposium on Video Games*. New York, NY: ACM, 127–134. http://josh.thegeekmovement.com/Tanenbaum-Bizzocchi-ICFDG-2009-UnPublished.pdf.

Vannini, Phillip and Dennis D. Waskul. 2006. "Symbolic Interaction as Music: The Esthetic Constitution of Meaning, Self, and Society." *Symbolic Interaction 29*(1): 5–18.

Vannini, Phillip, Dennis D. Waskul, and Simon Gottschalk. 2011. *The Senses in Self, Society, and Culture: A Sociology of the Senses*. New York, NY: Routledge.

Varga, Ivan. 2005. "The Body—The New Sacred? The Body in Hypermodernity." *Current Sociology 53*(2): 209–235.

Zezima, Katie. 2007, July 15 [amended July 17]. "Virtual Frets, Actual Sweat." *New York Times*. Retrieved from http://www.nytimes.com/2007/07/15/fashion/15guitar.html?pagewanted=1&_r=0.

10

SEEING LIVE MUSIC

Emily M. Boyd

Listening to and making music, dancing, rejoicing, and participating in community festivals and events have always been a part of social life. The experience of creative sound production and consumption in our hypermodern world is varied; while we reap the benefits of technology that can connect us to Korean pop or Indian sitars with the click of a mouse, many of us also find ourselves suffering from being force-fed the same repetitive Top 40 hits when in public spaces (Taylor Swift's "Shake it Off" has been following me everywhere for days—a unique paradox given the title!). Attending and participating in live music events and concerts offers a temporary respite from our usual technologically mediated music worlds—an opportunity to see and hear something new, different, and unique that is being created right in front of us. When we see live music, we experience something that is increasingly hard to find: spontaneity.

In this essay, I reflect on over 15 years of regular concert-going experiences, drawing particularly from my recent experiences over the past year. During this time I attended a variety of events, from Midwestern local performances of rock, bluegrass, and folk, to jazz and rock in nearby cities, to stadium-sized events with thousands of people, including Bluegrass, Electronica (EDM), Jamband, Classic and Americana Rock acts.[1] While it's clear that music genres play a big part in constructing the concert environment and shape, I find that even local environments that draw a public crowd also harbor a shared cultural milieu. Seeing live music, whether in intimate spaces or massive fields

with thousands of others, transforms the sound experience into something profoundly different from that of listening to a recording. Both
the sense of community and the actions taken by concert goers and
fans transform passive sound absorption into active crowd participation.
Finally, like most forms of popular culture, concert performances are
shaped by technological advances that impact cultural production and
consumption of the experience of live music.

Meaning Making as Situational

Like most fans of the Grateful Dead and Phish, I've been asked why
in the world someone would want to see so many shows featuring
the same band, year after year. There are a lot of reasons, but the short
answer comes down to, "you've got to see them live." As Carey (1989)
argues, the concept of "communication" can be viewed in two ways: as
the transmission of information, or as fellowship, identity, and unity.
Attending a concert is not simply listening to the transmission of the
notes but instead participating in a unifying ritual of performance.
Small (1998) suggests that another way to frame such experiences is to
consider music as not a thing or a product but as an activity; music or
musicking is something people *do*. Every show is different, and there's
just no comparison to being there to witness and be a part of the creation of the sound. As Blau (2010: 308, emphasis in original) notes,
"Unfolding as it does within a cultural-historical space, performance
becomes *more* ... traffic[king] in values, ideas, norms/normativities—in
manifold meanings."

   In 2006, I went with about 20 friends to the Bonnaroo Music and
Arts Festival in Tennessee. Before this show, I'd listened to The Grateful Dead for years. I never got to see Jerry Garcia (he died when I was
17), but I'd seen various incarnations of the group over the years (The
Dead, Phil and Friends, Bob Weir and Ratdog). I knew what to expect,
and other than the inclusion of the Stones' "Gimmie Shelter" as a cover,
they played a pretty typical setlist.[2] Throwing in a classic rock cover is
pretty standard practice as well.[3] But at that show, the sound was very
different from anything I had ever heard before. It was a product of the
moment: flexible, shaped by the performers onstage and the interactive
environment with fans. Part of it was the weather; it had been crazy hot
all day and thunderstorms had been building up on the horizon. During

the first set the clouds opened up and the crowd responded with cheers, incorporating the energy into dancing and revelry. Together, all of these elements—spatial location, sensation of sound, crowd participation—became part of the musicking situation (Small 1998).

During the second set, winds started picking up as Joan Osborne's vocals went deeper into sultry blues. As they segued into Gimmie Shelter, Joan's voice took on a haunting quality as she sang the first few "ooooh ooooh oohhhs" of the song. The unexpectedness of the song selection, Joan's interpretation of the lyrics, the weather, and the crowd dynamic all coincided to create a unique sound and experience—even listening to recordings of the show now, I literally get goose bumps and involuntary shivers, the energy and experience was that powerful for me.

After the show, we discussed the set while walking back to our campsite, engaging in what Schechner (1988) calls dispersing—the collective recalling and retelling of a performance after its conclusion. I remembered seeing Joan with Phil and Friends two years earlier. I don't recall the details, but I wasn't that impressed. I remember thinking, I'm not sure she's a good fit for the sound. I mentioned this to a friend who also saw this performance (Adams, 2006). She said that Joan reminded her of Donna Jean from the 1970s Grateful Dead lineup. Donna has always been a major divisive point for Deadheads; some of them love her and others get annoyed by her signature Donna "wail" or loud, shrill singing of the chorus. My friend said she really enjoyed the performance, not just because of the way it sounded, but that the addition of Joan to the group allowed her a new opportunity to experience and interpret the sound in new ways. While Joan didn't "speak to me" the first time I saw her with Phil, the second time she blew me away. I'll never hear "Gimmie Shelter" in the same way again.

Concerts as Collective Activity

Going to concerts and seeing live music is also an invitation to join in; not just to absorb the sound but also to become part of the experience. When we participate in such gatherings (Schechner 1988), we are doing what our ancestors have been doing for thousands of years—engaging in ceremonies, theater, rituals, and celebrations that create a sense of solidarity and interconnectedness. In July 2014 I attended the Saturday in the Park music festival in Sioux City, Iowa. This is a free community event, but it's also well known among those who frequent music festivals and shows because it gets some relatively popular headliners, with a nod toward reggae, jam-bands, and mainstream rock. The crowd is therefore reasonably diverse and changes throughout the day.

As my friend and I were walking around, we noticed a sign set up that designated a spot for meeting up with your group if you got disconnected, marked "LOST PEOPLE." At the same time, a concert goer was approaching the same area, dressed rather festively in sparkly blue, short shorts, and a cropped Pokémon t-shirt that revealed at least six inches of navel. I'm not sure if he was wearing a wig or not—he had a head full of mopped, messy hair, a mustache, and aviator glasses. He was also playing with gendered representations of body hair; he had affixed additional hair around his crotch (for a "big bush" effect out of his booty shorts), and had also added underarm hair. We smiled and told him we liked his outfit and I took this picture of him with my friend.

Figure 1

His appearance embodied the festival spirit many people bring to shows; it's is a place to play, a place you can be "weird" and receive positive affirmations from others. Costuming is common—everything from the rather standard and twee floral headbands and gauze butterfly wings, to full-on character costumes (similar to what you'd see at Disney or any other character-based amusement park), crazy glasses and hats, or fancy "party clothes" with sparkles and sequins; it runs the gamut. Some groups of friends make special t-shirts or go with a theme for costumes (e.g., Alice in Wonderland, Star Wars). These practices are significant in that they transform the concertgoer from one who stands and witnesses an event—a passive observer—into one who embraces and embodies a sense of playfulness and inclusion. Turner (1969) suggests that this transformative state can be characterized as *liminal*, or in between statuses—when seeing live music, we are not simply audience members nor are we featured performers; our experience is a hybrid that is communal and shared.

Language is also used to construct collective identity (Becker 1982). Many of the larger festivals create inclusive names for the crowd. At the Telluride Bluegrass Festival, "Festivarians" come to the San Juan mountains to be a part of the bluegrass "reunion"; artists greet the crowd by yelling "Bonnaroo!!" to the audience, with concert goers acknowledging their participation and embodiment of the event by cheering loudly back. Printed show schedules and event fliers remind everyone to "be good family" and look out for one another. Norms of community are stronger in these music environments than in day-to-day settings, including policing behaviors. At the Solstice Outdoor Music Festival in Mankato, Minnesota (a smaller, mostly local event), some kids were playing catch right next to a line of porta-potties and disrupting the queue of attendees waiting to use the facilities. One of the men in line stepped aside and said to them, "Hey, you have all this space (gesturing to the large field on the right), why don't you go over there. Just don't throw that right here." The kids nodded and ran off. I smiled at him and so did a few other people in the line. Within the sense of place and unity that is temporarily constructed at concerts, people are more willing to pitch in and do their part to maintain the scene.

Technological Advances

Seeing live music is a non-tangible, non-material experience, and thankfully there are still some ways to enjoy and participate in music culture without undue commodification. My small Midwestern town, for example, sponsors a free summer concert series on Thursday afternoons in June and Thursday evenings in August, and the performances are well attended by families, college students, and those who live and work nearby. Like most forms of popular culture, technological advances and adaptations are shaping the ways in which people experience sound, even within collective environments. Fans of bands from all kinds of music genres connect online, exchange electronic files of recorded shows, and exchange tickets for upcoming events. As Pattacini (2000: 8) observes, "instead of 'being there,' the traditions and shared experiences are sent pulsing along the wires." Many bands and some festivals now offer live streaming of concerts for those who are unable to physically be in the concert environment. Phish fans jokingly call this "couch tour"— if you've got a job or are otherwise unable to pack up and follow your favorite band on the road for weeks at a time, you can still participate in and experience an entire concert tour from the comfort of your sofa.

This past summer I was unable to make the trek to Telluride, Colorado for the bluegrass festival, but I was able to "be there" in mediated ways; I listened to the live stream on my computer and commented on Facebook that I was enjoying the Yonder Mountain String Band set I was listening to. A friend who was there replied back from the festival, and I was able to ask him questions about the musicians on stage—they had recently gone through a shift in band members, and I wondered who was filling out the lineup. Even though I couldn't physically be a Festivarian that year, I still was able to enjoy the sound and community of the live show from my living room. Technological advances such as these shape the spatial and transitory nature of the concert experience, as Gardner (2004) noted in his study of bluegrass festivals—but with no travel required.

Buying and Selling the Experience

While there are some ways to engage live music without being a consumer, increasing technological opportunities and the absence of constraints have also resulted in new products and capital. As industry analysts are quick to point out, the way music is currently bought and sold has changed considerably over the past two decades. One area that has not suffered, however, is live music revenues. The *Wall Street Journal* (Karp 2014) reports that the concert industry grossed a record-breaking 5.1 billion dollars in 2013, and *Forbes* (Lee 2012) notes that concert ticket sales tripled between 1999 and 2009. The live music industry may also be benefiting from cultural and social shifts in consumption patterns. While capitalism has flourished on the sale of material objects, both through the innovation of new products and marketing strategies like planned obsolescence, *experiences*, not goods, may be the next commodification frontier. A growing body of research suggests that *experiential* purchases, like going out for a gourmet meal or taking a vacation, are more satisfying in the long-term than *material* purchases, like a new phone or furniture (Kumar, Killingsworth, and Gilovich 2014). The choices we make regarding our experiential purchases, such as what concerts we choose to attend, become part of our identity work—activities and physical settings we integrate into our notion of self.

The market stands ready to capitalize on this shift. Music festivals like Bonnaroo and Coachella sell the Woodstock experience to new generations who grew up idealizing the "sex, drugs, and rock 'n' roll" imagery of a massive music festival with little social control. Hypermodern representations of space, time, and even death as in flux and shifting have evolved in the concert arena. For example, in 2012 a hologram of Tupac Shakur, who has been dead since 1996, appeared onstage at the Coachella music festival in California, accompanying Snoop Dogg and Dr. Dre through several of their hits and their collaborations (Kaufman 2012). Over the following week, downloads of the hologram "performing" these songs sold over 30,000 units. This is an example of seduction and simulation (Baudrillard 1983, 1990), as the semiotic or sign value given off from the image replicates reality but is hyperreal.

Adorno and Horkheimer (1993) warn that eventually culture will become so standardized, homogenized, and ubiquitous that it will become meaningless—a concern that is growing among cultural theorists who emphasize that conglomerate ownership of the means of cultural production prefer cookie-cutter artists and sound profiles that are considered safe investments. However, I suggest that live music, festivals, and concerts offer a bright spot for considering the future of cultural production. As I have argued in this essay, live music is a spontaneous construction that integrates musicians as sound producers as well as the audience, sense of place, and community to create unique, interactive experiences. Technological advances offer both the means to sustain this cultural production and defy logistical constraints, as well as creating new "live" frontiers that challenge social constructions of reality. As our sense of community and integration into shared social life is perhaps diminished in the digital age (Keen 2012), the experience of live music continues to offer opportunities to connect with people and sound in innovative ways.

Emily M. Boyd received her Ph.D. in sociology from Florida State University. She is currently Associate Professor of Sociology at Minnesota State University, Mankato. She studies gender, social interaction, and popular culture. Her work has appeared in *Gender & Society*, *Social Psychological Quarterly*, and *Social Science Research*.

Notes

1. Concerts and festivals included: Trampled by Turtles (March, Mankato, MN); River Falls Roots and Bluegrass Festival (April, River Falls, WI); Twin Cities Jazz Fest (May, St Paul, MN); Bob Weir and Ratdog (6/6, University of Minnesota, Minneapolis, MN); Summer Solstice Festival (June, Mankato, MN); Saturday in the Park (7/5, Sioux City, IA), Riversong Music Fest (Huchinson, MN); Paul McCartney (August, Target Field, Minneapolis, MN); Phish 9/29, 9/30, and 9/31, (Memorial Day Weekend, Denver CO); Rock Bend Folk Festival (Sept, St Peter MN); Boats and Bluegrass Festival (Winona, MN); Suwannee Hulaween (October, Spirit of the Suwannee Music Park, Live Oak, FL).
2. The Phil Lesh and Friends show I mention, featuring Joan Osborne (6/18/06), can be streamed through The Internet Archive: https://archive.org/details/phil2006-06-18.schoeps.peluso.35292.sbeok.flac16.
3. Blau (2010) notes that a good setlist can be viewed as an achievement—song selection, song placement, and jamming or improvising in ways that are unexpected and that allow alternative interpretations of the sounds.

References

Adams, Rebecca. 2006. Personal communication.
Adorno, Theodor and Max Horkheimer. 1993. "The Culture Industry: Enlightenment as Mass Deception." In Simon During (Ed.), *The Cultural Studies Reader*. London, UK: Routledge.

Baudrillard, Jean. 1983. *Simulations*. New York, NY: Semiotext(e).

Baudrillard, Jean. 1990. *Seduction*. New York, NY: St. Martin's Press.

Becker, Howard. 1982. *Art Worlds*. Berkeley, CA, University of California Press.

Blau, Jnan A. 2010. "A Phan on Phish: Live Improvised Music in Five Performative Commitments." *Cultural Studies Critical Methodologies 10*(4): 307–319.

Carey, James W. 1989. *Communication as Culture: Essays on Media and Society*. Cambridge, MA: Unwin Hyman Inc.

Gardner, Robert. 2004. *The Portable Community: Mobility and Modernization in Bluegrass Festival Life*. Berkeley, CA: University of California Press.

Karp, Hanna. 2014, January 10. "Concert Industry Hit New Highs in 2013" (blogpost). *Wall Street Journal: Speakeasy*. Accessed November 15, 2014. Retrieved from http://blogs.wsj.com/speakeasy/2014/01/10/concert-industry-hit-new-highs-in-2013/.

Kaufman, Gil. 2012, April 16. "Exclusive: Tupac Coachella Hologram Source Explains How Rapper Resurrected." Accessed November 15, 2014. Retrieved from http://www.mtv.com/news/1683173/tupac-hologram-coachella/.

Keen, Andrew. 2012. *Digital Vertigo: How Today's Online Social Revolution is Dividing, Diminishing and Disorienting Us*. New York, NY: St Martin's Press.

Kumar, Amit, Matthew A. Killingsworth, and Thomas Gilovich. 2014. "Waiting for Merlot: Anticipatory Consumption of Experiemental and Material Purchases." *Psychological Science 25*(10): 1924–1931.

Lee, Timothy B. 2012, January 30. "Why We Shouldn't Worry About the (Alleged) Decline of the Music Industry." *Forbes*. Accessed November 15, 2014. Retrieved from http://www.forbes.com/sites/timothylee/2012/01/30/why-we-shouldnt-worry-about-the-decline-of-the-music-industry/.

Pattacini, Melissa. 2000. "Deadheads Yesterday and Today: An Audience Study." *Popular Music & Society 24*(1): 1–14.

Schechner, Richard. 1988. *Performance Theory*. New York, NY: Routledge.

Turner, Victor. 1969. *The Ritual Process: Structure and Anti-Structure*. Ithaca, NY: Cornell University Press.

11

PLAYING GAMES

J. Patrick Williams

Angwe, if your goal is to ruin my day, you have succeeded.
—Tangles talking to Angwe, both characters in *World of Warcraft*

This is an essay about fun, not-fun, and games. It is not about play in a broad sense, such as when children play "family" or "hospital" or whatever, but rather about playing games and how gameplay is and is not fun. Play involves a relative degree of freedom to make-believe according to the players' interests and interactions on a moment-by-moment basis, while games involve more clearly defined structures, explicitly defined rules, and so on. A basic assumption about playing games is that it is in some way a special activity within everyday life.

> [Gameplay] has its being within a playground marked off beforehand either materially or ideally, deliberately or as a matter of course … The arena, the card-table, the magic circle, the temple, the stage, the screen, the tennis court …, are all in form and function play-grounds, i.e., forbidden spots, isolated, hedged round, hallowed, within which special rules obtain. All are temporary worlds within the ordinary world, dedicated to the performance of an act apart.
>
> (Huizinga 1949: 10)

Games are, in this sense, rituals. Both games and rituals are normal parts of daily life, yet have their own designated spaces, rules that take precedence, and require participants to re-orient themselves to their specificities and peculiarities. Unlike rituals, however, which may be solemn or disturbing, we assume that gameplay is, or at least should be, intrinsically enjoyable.

I am particularly interested in certain kinds of gameplay; the kind you find with card games, board games, role-playing games (RPGs), and video games, some of which have only become popular over the last couple of decades. Playing Monopoly with family or friends; assembling a deck of Pokémon cards or an army of Warhammer 40,000 miniatures to compete in a local tournament; waking up in the middle of the night to join a fight for control of a solar system in EVE Online—if you ask the people that engage in any of these activities why they do it, they will most likely reply first and foremost that it is *fun* (see Fine 1983: 52–53).

Yet when we closely observe the moment by moment experience of gameplay, we find lots of things going on that are not fun frustration, anger, and jealousy, are just a few of the unpleasant emotions that people feel when playing games. Observed more broadly across months or years, people lose sleep, money, even loved ones because of the games they play. So how is it that so many people love playing games when they are equally likely to be *not* fun as to be fun? On the one hand, the fun of gameplay is found in the social activities that comprise it, rather than only the games themselves (Williams, Hendricks, and Winkler 2006). On the other hand, framing gameplay in terms of a "magic circle," divorced from "ordinary life," as Huizinga (1949) has suggested, may encourage an approach to gameplay that ignores its many non-fun aspects. Recognizing that playing games isn't always fun reminds us not to treat games as forms of escape from reality, but rather as significant parts of everyday life.

Fun and Games

In recent years, social scientists have focused on designing specific measures for fun during gameplay. In one study (Read, MacFarlane, and Casey 2002), researchers argued that fun could be measured in terms of three concepts: expectations (if people's expectations are met or surpassed when they play games, then they must be having fun); engagement (if people are engaged with or within a game, then they must be having fun);

and endurability (if people remember positive things about a game, or if they return to it multiple times to play, then they must be having fun).

To test these concepts, I applied them to my recollections of game-play the previous evening, which involved four children aged 4–7 years and me. We played two games of Go Fish and one game of Tsuro. First of all, it was clear that the children expected to have fun. When the three girls entered the apartment, they quickly ran to where I sat on the floor and formed a circle. One girl exclaimed, "Oh, I hope I'm gonna win!" "Me too," said another. As I dealt the cards for Go Fish, the girls instantly began negotiating who would go first. "We'll start with the youngest," I announced, and the fun momentarily fled from everyone except my son, who was the youngest. "Yea, I win!" he yelled, smiling as much because of the deadpan looks on the girls' faces as for getting to go first. Once we started playing, those troubles were forgotten and everyone appeared to have a great time. But at the end of the second game, only two girls, having won one game each, wanted to continue, while the other children refused to play again. This all fits well with the operational definition of expectations: as their expectations of winning weren't met, the enjoyment decreased.

We switched to Tsuro. Two girls had not played this game before and the children immediately engaged with its tokens by arguing over who would get to use which color. Throughout the game, they maintained a focus on all the tokens and cards on the board and within their hands. The oldest of the children seemed to derive pleasure from the mentoring role she was able to adopt because she had played the game previously. Several times she began to snatch cards or tokens from the others while telling them, "No, not like that, you have to …" Fun for her seemed to involve the demonstration of her skill and knowledge in the game as much as playing the game itself.

That the children expressed excitement about the opportunity to play, verbally as well as through smiling, laughing, and wanting to control pieces of the game, suggests that they derived pleasure from the games. They were having fun, but of course fun is comparative rather than absolute. I noticed quite clearly that their fun was neither constant nor even; they had more fun when they were winning (an expectation when playing games) and when they were concentrating on what was going on (engagement). When these aspects of fun were not present, the games became tiresome, even antagonistic. As Tsuro progressed and players started being eliminated, the fun dissipated as their participation waned. With four "losers" at the end and only one winner, the children decided not to play again, thus marking the limit of the game's endurance for this group of players.

The Structure of Fun

Expectation, engagement, and endurability appear to be valid concepts to consider when studying fun. Players, however, rarely recognize them as features of gameplay. Asking my daughter why she wanted to play, she said, "I don't know. It's fun." And when I play games with my adult friends, games are also "just fun." Erving Goffman has suggested that people typically see games along these lines. Games, he writes, "are fun to play, and fun alone is the approved reason for playing them" (Goffman 1961: 17). As a sociologist, however, Goffman was quick to point out that we play games within an existing social order. Games are encounters that "cut us off from serious life by immersing us in a demonstration of its possibilities" (1961: 34).

As discussed earlier, Huizinga (1949: 10) also argued that gameplay occurs both "within the ordinary world" and within a "magic circle," which frames gameplay as "an act apart" from everyday life. What Goffman and Huizinga point out is that games have an imaginary or fantasy aspect that requires players to take on situational identities that are simultaneously similar to and different from everyday life (also see Zurcher 1970). If you and a group of friends play a game—Munchkin, for example—in which only one of you can win, then by definition you are contestants, if not enemies, within the game. In the "ordinary world" everyone is a friend; within the 'magic circle' of a game like Munchkin, nobody truly is. Munchkin players stab their best friends in the back all the time and laugh about it.

This can be an engaging aspect of gameplay that makes it fun—players get to step into unique roles and act in ways that may not normally be available or acceptable. Yet such gameplay is not divorced from everyday life, as I've witnessed when watching a person storm from a room in a rage because her partner tricked and killed her in a game. What this suggests is that gameplay is meaningful beyond the fun players have. Not least, gameplay is meaningful because there are rules involved, and rules both enable and limit what players can do. Rules remain in effect until the game is over, or until players agree to change them. Hopefully, the Munchkin example makes clear that this is just like the rest of life. Rules (and norms, and laws) establish the limits of our abilities and behaviors and thus don't allow everyone to have the same experiences of fun.

Rules are rooted in a game's genre, which shapes the meaning of gameplay and thus players' experiences. Genres tie together the subject matter, setting, visual and aural features, and narrative structure to players' expectations. The fantasy RPG genre, for example, tends to have complex structures that establish players' "horizons of expectation" (Jauss 1982), shaping not only what they expect in a certain kind of game but also what things are supposed to mean (Waskul 2006). Players aren't as likely to become upset when they lose a game of backgammon as when they lose in Diablo III's hardcore mode, where players spend hours, months, even years developing characters that can be permanently destroyed by a single lapse in knowledge or judgment or by some external event like Internet lag or a cat jumping on a keyboard. In RPGs players generally expect to lead their characters on adventures and to be rewarded with gold, experience, and gear that, over time, will make their characters stronger and therefore able to advance into ever more difficult areas of the gameworld. Players are able to engage in such a fantasy when they already expect it and when the game's structure supports it.

When the structure doesn't fit with players' expectations or otherwise negatively influences players' engagement, they tend to find the game not fun. For some, gaining experience and/or advancing within a RPG are key elements of fun, and players often remain engaged because the game offers clearly defined rewards, such as achievements, honorary titles, or rare items. For some fantasy players, whether of a tabletop game like Dungeons and Dragons or a massively multiplayer online game like World of Warcraft, working with a group of friends to raid a dragon's lair for experience points and epic loot is *the* definition of fun. But success doesn't happen overnight—groups may spend a significant amount of time building their characters' skills and equipment to a point where taking on a dragon is even possible.

This of course harkens back not only to the concepts of expectation and engagement but also to that of endurability. The desire to build up one's presence in a gameworld, to win fame or fortune, and to experience the general pleasures associated with playing in a group, draw players back regularly and thus help ensure that the game endures. These ideas apply not only to RPGs but also to games of any genre in which a community of shared meanings is maintained, whether collectible strategy games such as Magic: The Gathering or Warhammer 40,000, traditional board games such as chess, or contemporary multiplayer online games like League of Legends or DoTA 2 (see, e.g., Carter, Gibbs, and Harrop 2014; Fine 2012; Williams 2006).

Some Not-Fun Aspects of Gameplay

In immersive genres in particular, such as massively multiplayer online role-playing games, scholars are building up research on the not-fun elements of gameplay. Hours or months spent managing groups' attempts to achieve difficult feats may become tedious and play may fall into arguing over plans and strategies beforehand, as well as the divvying up of rewards after (Chen 2012). Players report feeling pressure to adapt their offline schedules around things happening online, playing sometimes when they don't want to, and ignoring face-to-face relationships in order to maintain game-based relations (Taylor 2006). Many people have called World of Warcraft "World of Warcrack" to draw attention to the belief that online RPGs seemingly compel players to act in ways similar to drug addicts. Players' level of engagement within, and the endurability of, contemporary online games is closely linked not only to addiction (see Yee 2006a) but also to problems distinguishing the boundary between play and work (Yee 2006b) and to balancing desires to engage in fantasy role-play with real-world management of their own and other players' actions and emotions (Williams, Kirschner, and Suhaimi-Broder 2014).

The latest generation of games has provided other opportunities for players to experience not-fun as well, the clearest example perhaps being a form of play called griefing: "intentional harassment of other players ... which utilizes aspects of the game structure ... to cause distress for other players" (Warner and Raiter 2005: 47). You may have seen the well-known episode of *South Park*, "Make Love, Not Warcraft," in which a powerful player goes around killing relatively helpless players for fun. That episode is a dramatization of gameplay that really happens. Take the case of Angwe, a high-level character who spent months doing this in World of Warcraft. His goal was to kill about 100 other top-level enemy players per day in order to earn points within the game, which translated into status. To achieve this, he prowled around an area filled with low-level enemy players and killed them indiscriminately, hoping that top-level allies would come to their rescue. As long as they came a few at a time, Angwe could earn his legitimate kills with relative ease.

A key aspect of griefing is that so-called griefers do not break the game's design rules; instead, they break the implicit social rules that typically govern player behavior (see Mortensen 2008). Angwe took full advantage of the game's design, to be sure. The name "Angwe" itself suggests a mocking, bullyish way of teasing a child who is angry, and he created a low-level enemy character of his own, ironically named Angwespy, in order to communicate with those he killed. Reading his collected screenshots (search for "Angwe" online), you can almost taste the agony he inflicted on other players through their messages to Angwespy.

> "Can't we make some sort of agreement, so that you can at least stop killing me?"
> "fuck u, I had an hr of time to play with my mates now I cant even get to em ... u sad shit"

As these two messages suggest, Angwe's infamy was rooted in his impingement on prevailing definitions of fun. In the first, a person had to stop playing the game and attempt to engage in negotiations that might allow him to return to having fun. In the second, Angwe's behavior prevented a person from playing with friends, instead reducing his hour of playtime to repeated character death. Angwe's actions enraged so many players that it was eventually featured as the "#1 Most Elaborate Dick Move in Online Gaming History" (see Reddit 2012).

People have certain expectations when they play games; the problem is that not everyone's expectations align. Fun for some players involves negatively impacting other players, which causes grief to the victim. And when players cannot protect themselves from unwanted aggression, their gameplay falls far short of their expectations. Griefing forces them to shift focus away from their current engagement to deal with an immediate threat to their fun. Griefing threatens a game's endurability as well when it causes players to think twice about whether or not to play. In short, fun is very much affected by social processes that transcend the boundary between the game and the rest of life.

Conclusions

Different people are attracted to games for a variety of reasons. Some like to play games for communal reasons, including socializing, collaborating with friends, or developing/maintaining social ties. Some are attracted by the opportunity to compete against and defeat opponents or to gain some kind of objectified hierarchical status within a game or community of players. Others may seek to immerse themselves in an alternative reality, which they may see as a break (or escape) from everyday life. There are very likely other reasons to play games that don't easily fit into any of these categories. Whatever the reason, the point of this essay has been to demonstrate that gameplay, with its roles and rules and interactions, is always very much a part of everyday life. Mead (1934) recognized this nearly a century ago when he wrote, "what goes on in the game goes on in the life of a [person] all the time" (p. 160). The processes and structures of everyday life are built into it. In games, we perform roles, we follow rules, we work with or against people, and we experience highs and lows. Of course we can use games as opportunities to change some of the roles we play and the rules we play by, and this can positively or negatively affect our relations with others and our emotional well-being.

We should not treat games as existing outside of everyday life, although there is increasingly little chance of that. Global consumer culture markets games to us ever more persistently through film, Internet advertising, and cereal boxes. New technologies make games more easily available to us, while social media have facilitated the rapid development of metagaming. Education and work are becoming gamified, while games themselves become more educational and worklike. Meanwhile, mass and social media produce volumes of information daily about the pros and cons of playing games. Is it a game's fault when a person dies of deep-vein thrombosis while playing? Will games save the world? (McGonigal 2011) I'm quite sure that games will persist as contentious cultural objects in the years to come (see Williams and Smith 2007), not least because gameplay is both fun and not fun. We love games, despite being constrained within them, and we seek out opportunities to play despite how rationalized they often are (Mizer, 2014). We continue playing them because they are so much like the rest of everyday life. So while Huizinga suggests we play games because we enjoy them, it is Goffman's sociological point—that we enjoy playing games because of their likeness to everyday life—that seems to be more significant.

J. Patrick Williams is Associate Professor of Sociology at Nanyang Technological University in Singapore, where his research and teaching interests focus on micro-sociology, culture, and new media. He has published research on various aspects of games and gaming, including *Gaming as Culture: Essays in Social Reality, Identity, and Experience in Fantasy Games* (McFarland & Co., 2006) and *The Players' Realm: Studies in Video Games and Gaming* (McFarland & Co., 2007).

References

Carter, Marcus, Martin Gibbs, and Mitchell Harrop. 2014. "Drafting an Army: The Playful Pastime of Warhammer 40,000." *Games and Culture* 9(2): 122–147.

Chen, Mark. 2012. *Leet Noobs: The Life and Death of an Expert Player Group in World of Warcraft*. New York, NY: Peter Lang.

Fine, Gary A. 1983. *Shared Fantasy: Role-Playing Games as Social Worlds*. Chicago, IL: University of Chicago Press.

Fine, Gary A. 2012. "Time to Play: The Temporal Organization of Chess Competition." *Time & Society* 21(3): 395–416.

Goffman, Erving. 1961. *Encounters: Two Studies in the Sociology of Interaction*. Indianapolis, IN: Bobbs-Merrill Educational Publishing.

Huizinga, Johan. 1949. *Homo Ludens: A Study of the Play-Element in Culture*. London, UK: Routledge & Kegan Paul.

Jauss, Hans Robert. 1982. *Aesthetic Experience and Literary Hermeneutics* (trans. Michael Shaw). Minneapolis, MN: University of Minnesota Press.

McGonigal, Jane. 2011. *Reality Is Broken: Why Games Make Us Better and How They Can Change the World*. London, UK: Jonathan Cape.

Mead, George Herbert. 1934. *Mind, Self, and Society*. Chicago, IL: University of Chicago Press.

Mizer, Nicholas. 2014 "The Paladin Ethic and the Spirit of Dungeoneering." *Journal of Popular Culture 47*(6).

Mortensen, Torill E. 2008. "Humans Playing World of Warcraft; or Deviant Strategies?" In Hilde G. Corneliussen and Jill W. Retterg (Eds.), *Digital Culture, Play, and Identity: A World of Warcraft Reader*. Cambridge, MA: MIT Press, 203–223.

Read, Janet, Stuart MacFarlane, and Chris Casey. 2002. "Endurability, Engagement and Expectations: Measuring Children's Fun." *Interaction Design and Children*: Eindhoven, Netherlands: ACM. Retrieved from http://www.chici.org/references/endurability_engagement.pdf.

Taylor, T. L. 2006. *Play Between Worlds: Exploring Online Game Behavior*. Cambridge, MA: MIT Press.

Warner, Dorothy E. and Mike Raiter. 2005. "Social Context in Massively Multiplayer Online Games (MMOGs): Ethical Questions in Shared Space." *International Review of Information Ethics 4*: 46–52.

Waskul, Dennis D. 2006. "The Role-Playing Game and the Game of Role-Playing: The Ludic Self and Everyday Life." in J. Patrick Williams, Sean Q. Hendricks, and W. Keith Winkler (Eds.), *Gaming as Culture: Social Reality, Identity and Experience in Fantasy Games*. Jefferson, NC: McFarland, 19–38.

Williams, J. Patrick. 2006. "Consumption and Authenticity in Collectible Strategy Games Subculture." In J. Patrick Williams, Sean Q. Hendricks, and W. Keith Winkler (Eds.), *Gaming as Culture: Social Reality, Identity and Experience in Fantasy Games*. Jefferson, NC: McFarland, 77–99.

Williams, J. Patrick and Jonas Heide Smith. 2007. "From Moral Panics to Mature Games Research in Action." in J. Patrick Williams and Jonas Heide Smith (Eds.), *The Players' Realm: Studies on the Culture of Video Games and Gaming*. Jefferson, NC: McFarland, 1–15.

Williams, J. Patrick, Sean Q. Hendricks, and W. Keith Winkler (Eds.). 2006. *Gaming as Culture: Social Reality, Identity and Experience in Fantasy Games*. Jefferson, NC: McFarland.

Williams, J. Patrick, David Kirschner and Zahirah binte Suhaimi. 2014. "Structural Roles in Massively Multiplayer Online Games: A Case Study of Guild and Raid Leaders in World of Warcraft." *Studies in Symbolic Interaction 43*: 121–142.

Yee, Nick. 2006a. "Motivations for Play in Online Games." *Cyberpsychology and Behavior 9*(6): 772–775.

Yee, Nick. 2006b. "The Labor of Fun: How Video Games Blur the Boundaries of Work and Play." *Games and Culture 1*(1): 68–71.

Zurcher, Louis A. 1970. "The 'Friendly' Poker Game: A Study of an Ephemeral Role." *Social Forces 49*(2): 173–186.

12

SLEEPING[1]

Carolyn Ellis

Sleep, ah wonderful sleep. A favorite part of my day is plumping my fluffy, duck-down-filled pillow just so, melting into my bed, and letting out a sigh of contentment. Most nights I have no problem falling or staying asleep, and I wake up the next morning refreshed and ready to go.

Not everyone shares in this luxury of trouble-free sleep. The National Sleep Foundation (2005: 18) reports that in 2005, three-quarters of adults said they "had at least one symptom of a sleep problem a few nights a week or more," and that number has increased since 1999. Fewer than one-half of Americans reported sleeping well almost every night in 2005, and that figure held in 2013 for folks in the United States, Germany, Mexico, the United Kingdom, and Canada (National Sleep Foundation 2013). This news is disheartening since in addition to making us feel good, sleep also restores our brains by cleaning out waste, and poor sleep may contribute to brain diseases such as Alzheimer's (Iliff 2014).

Mooallem (2007) points to a heightened awareness of the importance of sleep. He believes sleep is taking its rightful place now beside diet and exercise as good for health. Apparently, what is good for sleep also is good for the economy. Mooallem describes a "sleep racket" worth 20 billion dollars a year that includes sleep clinics, over-the-counter and herbal sleep support, how-to books, and sleep-encouraging gadgets sold in luxury sleep stores. Moreover, sleeping pill prescriptions have been rising dramatically, with 60 million prescriptions being written annually (Mooallem 2007; Rabin 2012). The first study based on person-use (as opposed to those based on sleep aid prescriptions) found that "approximately 4% of adults aged 20 and over reported using a prescription sleep aid in the past month" (Chong, Fryar, and Gu. 2013).

In this essay, I add a personal story and social perspective to the medicalization and commodification of sleep. I focus on my ritualized preparations for slumber, the relational aspects of sleeping, and popular culture messages about what makes a good night's sleep.

Sleep as a Commodity

My partner Art and I bought our king-size Tempur-Pedic foam memory platform bed and mattress around the time we married in 1995. It cost more than 2,000 dollars even then. It was an investment, we felt, given that we planned to spend a great deal of time in bed, one-third of our lives sleeping plus time to lounge and make love. So, we thought, the mattress should be the best we could buy. According to all the commercials and advertisements, the best was Tempur-Pedic. Besides, the material in the bed was originally developed for NASA—it had to be good, right? (Mooallem 2007: 5). Who could resist soft foam that "molded to your body" and "gave you the most comfortable sleep ever?" Tempur-Pedic continues to be a mattress of choice. A full-page ad in a recent edition of our local paper, the *Tampa Bay Times* (October 10, 2014: 12A) promises "all-night comfort—you'll fall asleep faster, stay asleep longer and wake more fully refreshed." But there's a caveat. "Experts have said you should replace your mattress every eight years. Now you can ... INTEREST FREE! Get the world's most highly recommended mattress," the ad blasts. Tempur-Pedic may be the best, but still you will want to buy another one every eight years! I can't help but wonder if this time frame—"eight years"—has anything to do with the myth shown in TV ads for Mattress Firm, which claims that mattresses double in weight every eight years due to accumulated dust, sweat, dead skin, and dust mites (Mattress Firm n.d.)

For just a moment, I wonder if a new bed really would lead to more comfort, deeper sleep and better hygiene. I quickly dismiss the idea since, after all, we protect our mattress with a cover and change the sheets weekly—that has to help with the cleanliness. It's absurd to think about how much a mattress would weigh if the weight really doubled every eight years. Besides, for the most part, my partner Art and I are happy with our 20-year-old Tempur-Pedic, and any complaints we have are due more to our increasing age than to the age of our mattress. We love the quiet: how there is no creaking when one of us rolls over, how the mattress isolates motion so that we do not feel each other tossing and turning, and how it supports our bodies with few pressure points. Art no longer likes the low platform, he says, because with increasing age he finds it harder to get in and out, and bending over hurts his back in the early morning. Bending down doesn't bother my shorter body. But I have been dissatisfied with the heat the mattress tends to hold, especially in the Florida summer, particularly during menopause when I used to wake up covered in sweat. Thankfully, my volcano sweats are over, but still we decided recently to cover the mattress with a thick pad, an "Extra Plush Bamboo Fitted Mattress Topper," which probably defeats some of the memory foam properties but makes the bed softer, cuddlier, and cooler, as well as cleaner.

Reading the literature on sleeping now leads me to wonder if my tendency to wake up in the middle of the night after four hours—especially during menopause—might not reflect age-old sleeping patterns reasserting themselves. In the past, people often slept in two four-hour periods and were involved in activities with others during the several hours in between (Ekirch 2005; Mooallem 2007: 8). Even today, people in much of the world experience sleep as a communal and interactive event, viewing sleep and wakefulness on a continuum with many people in the same room coming and going and drifting in and out of sleep. In contrast, in modern western culture we tend to view sleep and wakefulness as "either/or" and expect sleep to be a "lie down and die," all-night experience (Worthman 2008). That is, unless a newborn baby or a sick child, partner, or pet interferes!

Each night, Art and I and our two dogs, Buddha (an eleven-year-old rat terrier) and Zen (a four-year-old mini-Australian Shepherd) expect to "lie down and die" in the dark for at least eight hours without being disturbed, though we do have our own brand of communal interaction. Once we got tablet computers and a 50-inch flat screen TV for our bedroom, our bed also became more than a place for sleeping, reading, and intimacy; it became our entertainment center, into which we incorporated traditional and social media.

Sleeping Rituals and Social Relationships: A Personal Story

"I'm going to do my teeth," one of us announces to signify it's time to get serious about going to sleep. We usually enter our bedroom between 9:00 and 10:00, after work, exercise, and dinner, in that order. Sometimes we then watch a bit of news, but more often our favorite TV shows, which include movies, *The Daily Show*, and the *Colbert Report*. Once we got our matching iPads in 2011, they took up residence on each side of our bed. Prior to that it was our smart phones. (I now use the Surface Pro 3. I like my technological gadgets.) Sometimes we say we want to read more books at night, but after reading and writing all day, it is easy to escape into junk TV, Facebook, or checking news items online. When we crave more escape, I might play Solitaire or watch silly videos on iTunes, and Art might check sports scores or read stories of interest online.

If you were in our bedroom at night, here is what you most likely would see: both of us would be propped up on two pillows each, TV on, tablets in hand, and the TV clicker between us. We are multitaskers who never watch commercials. No matter what we are doing, Art picks up the clicker to fast forward through commercials. Though I am the technological one in the household, I don't touch the clicker, and I expect Art to keep me entertained with a show I like and to shield me from commercials. He complies. I love him for it.

Looking at our tablets does not mean that we are ignoring each other. Indeed, just the opposite. We treat social media as … well … social. Between shows and sometimes during them, Art and I read to each other from Facebook and other sites. We comment on the lives of our friends. We make fun of different styles of Facebook entries—another baby video, another self-congratulatory pat on the back, another grumpy complaint, an inappropriate message that surely will come back to haunt the person who posted it. The literature on sleeping consistently instructs that one should not engage with social media or use the computer before going to bed. The activity stimulates, researchers say, and the lights, particularly the LED lighting in computers, disrupts melatonin production (National Sleep Foundation 2011; Rabin 2013; Reiney 2011). In contrast, my engagement, especially with Facebook, often lulls me into a place ready for rest.

Actually I've been known to fall asleep with tablet in hand, which wakes me when it suddenly bangs against my face.

Into this scenario eventually will come the announcement about doing our teeth. Immediately then, usually without additional words, we both arise. I go to the bathroom connected to our bedroom and Art goes to the one down the hall. I like separate and private bathroom behavior; so does he. We think it helps to keep the romance alive. We both floss, then use our Oral-B Professional Health Clean cordless electric tooth-brushes and brush for two minutes. I follow this with a Waterpik. Next I clean and put moisturizer on my face and take my vitamins, which are lined up on my counter—calcium, Vitamin D, probiotic, magnesium, and often more. I don't know what Art does then, though he sometimes watches sports in the sunroom while brushing his teeth. We meet back in bed, remove our clothes, and then to induce sleep, we might give Facebook one more shot and/or watch one more segment of *Colbert*. Usually the dogs both get attention as well—kisses and belly rubs.

All this time the dogs have been snoozing and in and out of sleep— they tend to experience sleep on a continuum! But when we return from our nightly bathroom rituals, the dogs know it won't be long before we turn off the light and settle down for serious slumber and our family version of communal sleeping. Once Art is back in bed, our terrier Buddha circles a few times and then plops down beside him, often punctuating the seriousness of this event with a sigh. While Art flips one last time through the TV channels, Zen, our mini-Aussie, takes this opportunity to herd her dozen stuffed animals onto our bed, organizing them into a straight line where they will "sleep" for the night. I make my final adjustments for the night, putting a gel toe spreader between my big toe and calloused second toe and placing my removable retainer in my mouth to keep my teeth straight and correct my bite. After a few minutes of *Colbert*, we both remove our glasses. I plump my pillow just so and pull the covers up to my chin. Art fiddles with his iPad to turn on white noise that will help with his Tinnitus. Once he is assured that the sound is not loud enough to disturb me, he turns off the light and joins me under the covers. It's amazing how many props one needs as one ages—just to get into bed! Immediately, Buddha moves over to curl up near my tummy—sometimes on top and sometimes under the covers, depending on the temperature. We kick some of the stuffed animals off the bed, and Zen coils around our heads for a few last kisses before going to her place in the corner of the room. Art and I spoon for a while with him cuddling me from the back until, in one synchronized move and like a well-oiled machine, we—Art, Buddha, and I—turn over in our motion-isolating bed. Then I cuddle Art, and Buddha snuggles in against my back. Most nights we are asleep in a few minutes.

Of course there are those nights when Art and I plan a "party for two" and then the rituals change. We open a bottle of wine or mix a Sombrero—Kahlua and milk—engage in long, intimate conversation (the best aphrodisiac we know), shoo away the dogs (not always successfully)—dim the lights, and turn on music for the mood. The bedroom is transformed. No iPads or TV on those nights!

No matter the activity though, Art and I are almost always asleep by midnight and awake at 8:00 a.m., a luxury permitted academics and few others, since most people have to be at work as we are waking up. On the weekends, we sometimes stay in bed for an extra hour or two, enjoying the luxury of moving in and out of sleep, dreaming, and a few extra snuggles and turns. When we are ready to wake up—and somehow we both know and agree to the timing—I usually say, "Good morning." Immediately Zen is on the bed, ready for "morning lovin'," though Buddha prefers to pretend she is still sleeping for as long as she can. After some morning talk and laughter—Art, the most cheerful morning person I know, usually awakes singing or joking—we both take showers, go through the morning rituals of teeth brushing, hair combing, and so on. Then I take the dogs outside, get the newspapers that have arrived, make the coffee, and feed the dogs while the coffee is brewing. If it is a weekend, we might read the paper in bed, but whether a weekday or the weekend, the coffee signifies that sleeping is officially done and the day has begun.

Ritual and Social Aspects of Performing Sleep

Most people tend to think of sleeping as an individualized, solitary, and improvisational activity, a time to lose consciousness, withdraw from the social world, and focus on our internal selves. Unless we suffer with a sleep disorder or have a particularly bad night, we don't think much about how we sleep or the rituals that surround our sleeping. But sleep is a social and cultural matter in that the practices associated with how, when, where, and with whom we sleep are accompanied by cultural expectations (Schwartz 1970; Williams 2007: 314). For example, most of us sleep during the same time frame and expect not to be disturbed, though these and other normative patterns of sleeping are affected by historical period, cultural practices, family, and class considerations (Schwartz 1970). A case in point: In families, the presence or absence of small children, available space, and level of authority will affect our expectations of sleep.

Sleeping with another, and preparing to do so, offers a time in the backstage for intimate relationships and contributes to defining our community of close and trusted significant others. As well, sleeping and preparing for sleep are often routinized and ritualized activities, done as much to help *make* us sleepy as they are done *because* we are sleepy. My story shows my partner and me participating in similar rituals every night to prepare for sleep and each morning to designate the break between sleep and wakefulness. The same person turns off the light, adjusts the TV, and we go in tandem to take care of our teeth. In the morning, I take the dogs out and make the coffee. Our actions are so ritualized, they could be "done in our sleep."

As well, all of us are affected by the messages we get from popular culture about what we need for a good night's sleep and how that sleep should take place. We learn from advertisements that the only good sleep is a deep, undisturbed sleep. How could we possibly achieve that without the everyday help of products such as Tempur-Pedic beds, fluffy mattress covers, and soft sheets? And when we have problems sleeping, as we inevitably will, there are products—pills, sleep clinics, apnea machines and other gadgets to help us get that "lie down and die" eight hours of undisturbed slumber we have come to associate with a good night's sleep.

Carolyn Ellis is Distinguished University Professor at the University of South Florida. Her books include *The Ethnographic I: A Methodological Novel about Autoethnography* (Rowman Altamira, 2004); *Revision: Autoethnographic Reflections on Life and Work* (Left Coast Press, 2009);

Music Autoethnographies: Making Autoethnography Sing/Making Music Personal (with Brydie-Leigh Bartlett; Australian Academic Press, 2009); and, most recently, with Tony E. Adams and Stacy Holman Jones, both the *Handbook of Autoethnography* (Left Coast Press, 2013) and *Autoethnography* (in the Understanding Qualitative Research Series; Oxford University Press, 2015). She has published numerous articles and personal stories situated in emotions and interpretive representations of qualitative research, particularly autoethnography. Her current research focuses on collaborative and compassionate interviewing with Holocaust survivors. Carolyn enjoys sleeping with her partner, Art, and their canine companions, Buddha and Zen.

Note

1. Thanks to Art Bochner, Keith Berry, Tony Adams, and Norman Denzin for helpful comments and to Phillip Vannini and Dennis D. Waskul for the opportunity to explore sleeping.

References

Chong, Yinong, Cheryl D. Fryar, and Qiuping Gu. 2013. Prescription Sleep Aid Use Among Adults: United States, 2005–2010. NCHS Data Brief, No. 127 (August). U.S. Department of Health And Human Services, Centers for Disease Control and Prevention, National Center for Health Statistics. Accessed October 10, 2014. Retrieved from http://www.cdc.gov/nchs/data/databriefs/db127.pdf.

Ekirch, A. Roger. 2005. *At Day's Close: Night in Times Past.* New York, NY: W.W. Norton & Co.

Iliff, Jeffrey. 2014, September. [TedTalk video] "One More Reason to Get a Good Night's Sleep." *Temed.* Accesssed October 9, 2014. Retrieved from http://www.ted.com/talks/jeff_iliff_one_more_reason_to_get_a_good_night_s_sleep?

Mattress Firm. No Date. Accessed December 12, 2014. Retrieved from http://www.mattressfirm.com/Sleep-Healthy-Mattress-Replacement-L86.aspx.

Mooallem, Jon. 2007, November 18. "The sleep-industrial complex." *New York Times Magazine.* Retrieved from http://www.nytimes.com/2007/11/18/magazine/18sleep-t.html?pagewanted=all&_r=0.

National Sleep Foundation. 2005. "Sleep in America poll." *National Sleep Foundation*, 1–54. Retrieved from http://sleepfoundation.org/sites/default/files/2005_summary_of_findings.pdf.

National Sleep Foundation. 2011, March 7. "Annual Sleep in America Poll Exploring Connections With Communications Technology Use and Sleep." *National Sleep Foundation.* Accessed November 3, 2014. Retrieved from http://sleepfoundation.org/media-center/press-release/annual-sleep-america-poll-exploring-connections-communications-technology-use-.

National Sleep Foundation. 2013. "International bedroom poll." *National Sleep Foundation.* Retrieved from http://sleepfoundation.org/sleep-polls-data/other-polls/2013-international-bedroom-poll.

Rabin, Roni Caryn. 2012, March 12. "New worries about sleeping pills." *New York Times*. Retrieved from http://well.blogs.nytimes.com/2012/03/12/new-worries-about-sleeping-pills/?_php=true&_type=blogs&_r=0.

Reiney, Patricia. 2011. Not getting enough sleep? Turn off the technology." Accessed November 3, 2014 at http://www.reuters.com/article/2011/03/07/us-sleep-technology-idUSTRE7260RH20110307.

Schwartz, Barry. 1970. "Notes on the Sociology of Sleep." *The Sociological Quarterly 11*: 485–499.

Williams, S. 2007. "The Social Etiquette of Sleep: Some Sociological Reflections and Observations. *Sociology 41*: 313–328.

Worthman, C. M. 2008. "After Dark: The Evolutionary Ecology of Human Sleep". In W.R. Trevathan, E.O. Smith and J.J. McKenna (Eds.), *Perspectives in Evolutionary Medicine*. Oxford, UK: Oxford University Press, 291–313.

13

HAVING SEX

Beth Montemurro

"There are people who I wish I could be like, but I don't think I have it in me. I think like that Angelina Jolie—I think she's very sensual and, you know, and sometimes I think 'God! I just wish I could be like her,' you know?" laments Robin, a 49-year-old administrative assistant. She's been happily married for 28 years. Yet, Robin's never really felt comfortable with her sexuality. Her Catholic upbringing mediated the liberal era of the 1970s, when she came of age. Her parents made it very clear that pre-marital sex was wrong and Robin lived in fear that something terrible would happen if she fooled around with boys. Even after she married, Robin did not feel free to express her sexuality, partly because she does not see herself as sexual in the first place. Robin imagines if she *looked* different, if she had plump pouty lips and large breasts, she might *feel* different. Sex might be better if she was sexier. Watching television, seeing movies, paging through *Cosmopolitan* magazine, perusing the Victoria's Secret catalogue provide Robin and women like her a specific image of "sexy." And so Robin feels inhibited while having sex. She does not know how to "talk dirty" to her husband, but confided she wishes she did. Robin grapples with the image of the sexy woman in popular culture versus who she sees in the mirror. These dueling visions come into play when she has sex.

Robin's comments were echoed in many women I spoke with. Although the image varied—older women talked about Twiggy, Marilyn Monroe, and Diahann Carroll, younger women talked about Victoria's Secret models, Madonna, and Britney Spears, for example—the message was consistent: look sexy to feel and *be* sexy. And even those who identified as feminist—truly believing that all women could and should feel sexually confident regardless of what they look like—noted the influence of popular conceptions of desirability on their private sex lives. Corrine, for instance, 25, a student-life staff member at a college and engaged to be married at the time we met, is a self-defined and proud feminist. In her work, she educates about sexual assault, sexual diversity, body image, and other social issues. She is sure that it is good for women to talk about sex, express sexual desire, and seek sexual gratification. Yet, when she has sex, she sometimes finds herself posing in a particular way so as hide her "problem" spots or look sexy. She notices herself contorting her body and getting distracted by superficial constructions of desirability. She feels self-conscious about stubble on her legs and wonders how her partner is viewing her and if he notices these things while they are having sex.

Popular culture images and ideologies seep into everyday personal sexual expression. Corrine tries to catch herself in these situations and relax, but doing so is not easy. It's hard, she tells me, to unlearn what has been driven home throughout her life. She, like most of the 94 other women between the ages of 20 and 68 whom I interviewed in my study of women's sexuality through the life course (Montemurro 2014), knows what desirable looks like and that desirability is supposed to equal good sex.

Following Sexual Scripts

Simon and Gagnon (1984) introduced the idea of sexual scripting as a way of explaining how sexual behavior is influenced by culture. This is particularly applicable in understanding how popular culture shapes sexualities. Simon and Gagnon (1984) argued that there are three levels of sexual scripts. *Cultural scenarios* are models for behavior that allow individuals to imagine a desired response and expected course of action; *interpersonal scripts* function to govern interaction between individuals in sexualized situations; and *intrapsychic scripts* influence the way individuals mentally process or interpret cultural scenarios. In this essay I focus on the interplay between cultural scenarios from commercial culture and women's intrapsychic scripts. That is, I explore the ways culture influences the way women think about having sex.

The *Cosmo* Effect: Consuming Culture as Learning

Cosmo talked about what you did and you were like "oh!"

Maybe you learned something from it that ... your mother never told you.

—Faith, 52

Because most American women are rarely taught directly about sex, particularly about their own capacity for sexual pleasure or maximizing sexual satisfaction (Waskul, Vannini, and Wiesen 2007), girls and women rely on popular culture to learn how to have sex. Many women I interviewed spoke of *Cosmopolitan* magazine as a source of knowledge. Women looked to *Cosmo* as a guide for tricks to perform in bed. Erin, 22, shared,

> I do remember reading *Cosmo* when I was younger and I wasn't that like sexually experienced and I was like, "Oh my gosh! This is what I need to do!" Not that I would ever act on it but it kind of gave me the confidence to. This was acceptable, this was normal.

Scrutinizing *Cosmo* gave her specific ideas about what sex was and more importantly validated the normality of young women doing it. She studied the pages as if they were instruction manuals so that when the time came for her to have sex, she would be ready.

Other women put tips into practice more readily. Jennifer, 40, explained, with laughter, "I would read *Cosmo* and that was interesting. Then I'd go home and try it out with my husband. I'd go, '*Cosmo* said we should do this.'" Jessica, 38, also used the magazine to get ideas and advice, because she, "liked to hear what other people were doing—like what kind of experimental ideas—like wear the French maid outfit— just little things like that. I'd be like, 'hmmm, maybe I'll try those.' And I did." In all of these cases *Cosmopolitan* magazine puts forth cultural scenarios of sexuality or specific sexual scripts for women to follow. Jessica reads the magazine and learns it's sexy to wear a French maid's outfit, Erin and Jessica mentally try out new techniques and positions as they assess whether or not they could put them into play interpersonally. *Cosmo* also serves as vehicle for conveying interest in sex or sexual experimentation indirectly. Jennifer can say, "*Cosmo* says we should do this," so she does not have to say, "I want to try this," and risk being perceived as hypersexual. *Cosmopolitan* not only provides sexual scripts but also validates the desirability of them. As Erin said, they instill confidence and encourage sexual agency, albeit in a very specific, socially constructed way.

Cosmo may be the most well-read sex primer among the women I interviewed, but it is far from the only source of information. Women born after 1960 benefited from a proliferation of accessible material about sex when they came of age in the 1970s and 1980s. Women shared how Judy Blume's books like *Forever* and *Are You There God? It's Me Margaret* helped them imagine interpersonal sexual scripts. Seeing how characters in these stories navigated sexual decision making and experiences prepared them for what might happen when the time came for them to do so as well.

In addition to showing new ways to have sex, commercial culture also disseminates new cultural scenarios regarding who and what are desirable. Beyond Angelina Jolie and other conventionally sexy celebrities, older women and mothers—two previously desexualized categories of women—can now be read, at times, as sexual (Montemurro and Siefken 2012, 2014; Tally 2007). Films like *American Pie*, *Something's Gotta Give*, and *Hope Springs*, television programs like *Desperate Housewives*, *Modern Family*, and *Cougartown* show mothers and women over the age of 40 as sexually desirable, interested, and available.

Older women told me both implicitly and explicitly how cultural products and images have helped them become more comfortable with their sexuality, particularly among those who divorced and experienced a period of unanticipated sexual self-discovery. "At one point I was seeing a man ... and it was so important to me that I really get to be good at giving blow jobs," Iris, 58, laughed. Married for about 20 years, she divorced in her forties with little sexual experience as her husband had been her only sexual partner. She said, "I wanted to really do like the most fabulous thing ever, and I bought a book about gay men doing that. And so that was helpful to me."

And Regina, 62, implied that seeing movies helped her feel okay about masturbation and continuing sexual desire as a single woman in her sixties. "Well," she said, "you do get shocked when you [still feel turned on]—especially if you don't use something. It's like 'ohhhh, okay.' ... I watched *Mamma Mia* and I went, okay, we can do this," she explained with laughter. Most of the women I interviewed did not mention masturbation at all. But most of those who did, spoke of it indirectly. Regina's reference to *Mamma Mia* is not to tell me about a film she enjoyed—but to mention it as a tool of learning and neutralization. When she sees a 50-something Meryl Streep having sexual flings on screen, Regina acquires information that it is okay to have sexual urges and satisfy them. These images become part of her intrapsychic sexual scripts and help her understand that she can have sex by herself—a very significant piece of information in a culture where women's masturbation and familiarity with their genitals is rarely acknowledged or encouraged (Waskul, Vannini, and Wiesen 2007).

Regina whispered, "A couple days ago I, you know, felt the need. So I took care of that. Since I am so stressed I just need something, and the chocolate wasn't doing it, I went okay," she laughed. "I think it's one of those gifts that we were given, in my mind. ... and I watched—it was a movie ... I was in my forties and it was about women learning how to pleasure themselves." Sexual scripts about women's masturbation often fetishize it as something done for the benefit of a male viewer. Such cultural scenarios continue women's sexual objectification. But, the emergence of women-centered models like those Regina viewed increase women's feelings of sexual self-confidence. They are not just how-to guides, but more importantly they shape intrapsychic scripts that help women feel entitled to sexual pleasure and gratification.

When Oprah Winfrey or Kathie Lee and Hoda on the *Today* show talk about masturbation it becomes even more socially acceptable, which can help women, particularly older, un-partnered women, feel in touch with their sexuality. These celebrity endorsements render self-gratification and sexual experimentation legitimate. This can thus enhance their overall well-being, health, and desire. Joyce, 57, explained,

> It's interesting, because I'm in my fifties and I'm thinking about things that have influenced me a lot, it occurred to me that TV is

responsible for a lot of curiosity or a lot of information distribution
about sexual activity and what's considered to be average, normal
behavior ... Oprah shows—they have doctor shows on. They have—
Dr. Oz tells you that masturbation is great and Dr. Laura Berman
comes on and shows you sexual toys and things like that and you
think "Wow, this is like nothing that ever was on TV before." And I
think that importing that information to people makes them think
differently about their sexuality and what other people are experiencing and maybe they might try things that they wouldn't ordinarily have thought about or tried before.

In the year we turned 40, a handful of girlfriends and I went to New
York City for a celebratory weekend. One of the highlights of the weekend was a *Sex and the City* tour, on which we not only ate cupcakes
from Magnolia Bakery, drank Cosmos, and saw familiar filming sites,
but also visited the Pleasure Chest, a sex toy shop used in an episode
where Charlotte becomes obsessed with her Rabbit Pearl vibrator. We
were given 20 minutes to shop and marvel at the vast array of dildos
and products designed to enhance sex. The existence of the store, the
show, and the tour as elements of everyday life marketed to women illu-
minate a heightened emphasis on women's sexual pleasure and women
as sexual subjects. These sources shape not just behavior but thoughts.
Public figures and commercial institutionalization of sex as everyday
life help neutralize feelings of shame or embarrassment. If Oprah and
Dr. Oz say it's okay, it must be okay. If you can buy tickets for a bus tour
that includes both cupcakes and vibrators, it must be okay. When giving or playing with sex toys becomes standard fare at bachelorette parties or even parties specifically oriented around their sales (Montemurro
2003), women are encouraged to think about how using them might
enhance or alter the way they have sex.

Changing Times, Changing Minds: Point, Click, Climax

Women coming of age in the twenty-first century had even more
resources for not only learning how to have sex, but also for encouraging sexual subjectivity. Sexual subjectivity is possessing confidence
in sexual decision making, in one's body, and in one's sexual desires

(Martin 1996). Changes in the Federal Communications Commission regulations allowed for more sexual content on television and the diminishment of the "family hour" of programming, which restricted both content and advertising (Newson 2011). Programs like the *Love Boat* and *Three's Company*, which seemed progressive at the time with their prominent sexual innuendo, were eclipsed by shows like *Beverly Hills 90210*, *Dawson's Creek*, and *Sex and the City*. On these shows frank discussion of sex among teenagers and unmarried people helped shift attitudes about sex. Women born after 1985 started having sex when doing so before marriage was generally seen as socially acceptable and when people were, at the very least, talking about the fact that most people did so. Furthermore, the multi-modal proliferation of information about political "sex scandals," most famously that of President Clinton, brought private sexual behavior into public light. As Wanda, 64, noted, "When that Monica Lewinsky thing came out, that's when you heard that kids thought that oral sex wasn't really sex. So that changed a lot to make that a news item; it was almost like having instructions in the sacred *National Geographic* or something, you know. They made it okay, that wasn't sex. And our president would say that's not sex, so that was huge."

Chloe, a married 24-year-old college student who hooked up a lot in her teenage years, modeled "sexy" based on what she saw on television. She recalled, "If we would go to a dance, school dance or there was like a teen like dance place somewhere and we would dress as slutty as possible." She cited MTV staples *The Real World* and *Undressed* as introducing her to the concept of oral sex and helping her frame it as not a big deal. She explained, "I think like everyone that watched that show was more provocative, dressed sexier, was more into sex, actually having sex or oral sex or whatever." By watching *Dawson's Creek*, Leeann, 29, learned that it was normal for teenage girls to have sexual feelings and that helped her bridge the topic with her friends. In a way similar to how Jennifer used *Cosmopolitan* magazine to stimulate and validate new sexual activities, Leeann used *Dawson's Creek* as a way of talking about sex, without talking about her own sexuality directly. Popular culture can be valuable to girls and women as a way of making sense of their sexual feelings and desires without having to be forthcoming about them. Girls and women can talk about a sex scene or about the sexual behavior of a television character and in so doing, imagine themselves in that role.

For girls and women in American culture, understanding their own desire is complicated by cultural scenarios that send mixed messages about sexual freedom—telling them that they should at once be hypersexual and innocent (Douglas 1995; Newson 2011; Tolman 2002). Girls and women feel desire, seek sexual pleasure, and enjoy having sex but contend with slut shaming and judgment if they express these desires too strongly or have sex with the wrong partner or at the wrong time (e.g., Armstrong, Hamilton, Armstrong, and Seeley 2014; Thompson 2005; Tolman 2002). These messages are filtered into popular culture and consumed by girls, boys, women, and men who then develop sexual scripts influenced by these mixed messages. So even though commercials for K-Y lubricants and Cialis air on prime-time commercial television, and Herbal Essences shampoo ads suggest it provides a "totally organic experience" (which is not very subtly meant to be read as a "totally orgasmic experience"), girls and women must still contend with judgment for having sex outside of relationships or expressing sexual desire in the wrong contexts (Armstrong, Hamilton, Armstrong, and Seeley 2014; Tolman 2002).

And of course there is the Internet. Adrianna, born in 1970, explained, "I mean porn, for sure … you don't have to show your face, it's very private. And that's definitely made my—made me explore my own sexual parameters a lot, but not in sexual practice in terms of being more promiscuous but in my sexual relationships with people. Like, wow I didn't even know that this could be fun, like wow it turned me on when I was watching it, maybe it would be fun to engage in it." Other women recognized that Internet pornography resulted in more of the same schizophrenic images of women's sexuality and did little to change sexist cultural scenarios and interpersonal sexual scripts. Corrine, 25, commented, "The Internet became bigger when I was in college … So every guy I went to college with was watching Internet porn, incessantly, bless their hearts. So, I think being able to see those images more easily and with less shame was a double-edged sword in the sense that 'Yay! Sexuality is out in the open,' but, 'boo, it's still money shots on women's faces,' and no foreplay, and nothing that I think an actual woman would enjoy sexually."

Popular culture shapes the way women have sex. Sexual scripts are constructed and re-constructed in mass culture. Women consume these cultural scenarios, which influence their intrapsychic scripts and interpersonal scripts. As public dialogue about masturbation, sex toys, desire, pleasure, and women's capacity for sexual gratification spreads through commercial culture and becomes part of everyday life, women's personal desires can be satisfied, their questions answered. The normalization of having and wanting to have sex can change women's ways of thinking, replacing feelings of shame or embarrassment with sexual subjectivity.

Beth Montemurro is an Associate Professor of Sociology at Pennsylvania State University, Abington. Most of her research focuses on constructions of gender and sexualities. She is also the author of *Deserving Desire: Women's Stories of Sexual Evolution* (Rutgers University Press, 2014), *Something Old, Something Bold: Bridal Showers and Bachelorette Parties* (Rutgers University Press, 2006), as well as numerous articles related to sexualities, gender, wedding rituals, and reality television.

References

Armstrong, Elizabeth A., Laura Hamilton, Elizabeth M. Armstrong, and J. Lotus Seeley. 2014. "'Good Girls' Gender, Social Class, and Slut Discourse on Campus." *Social Psychology Quarterly* 77(2): 100–122.

Douglas, Susan. 1995. *Where the Girls Are: Growing Up Female With Mass Media*. New York, NY: Random House.

Martin, Karin A. 1996. *Puberty, Sexuality, and the Self: Girls and Boys at Adolescence*. New York, NY: Routledge.

Montemurro, Beth. 2003. "Sex Symbols: The Bachelorette Party as a Window to Change in Women's Sexual Expression." *Sexuality & Culture* 7(2): 3–29.

Montemurro, Beth. 2014. *Deserving Desire: Women's Stories of Sexual Evolution*. New Brunswick, NJ: Rutgers University Press.

Montemurro, Beth and Jenna M. Siefken. 2012. "MILFs and Matrons: Images and Realities of Mothers' Sexuality." *Sexuality & Culture* 16(4): 366–388.

Montemurro, Beth and Jenna M. Siefken. 2014. "Cougars on the Prowl? New Perceptions of Older Women's Sexuality." *Journal of Aging Studies* 28: 35–43.

Newson, Jennifer Siebel. (producer and director). 2011. *Miss Representation*. (DVD). San Francisco, CA: Girls' Club Entertainment.

Simon, William and John H. Gagnon. 1984. "Sexual Scripts." *Society* 22(1): 53–60.

Tally, Margaret. 2006. "'She Doesn't Let Age Define Her': Sexuality and Motherhood in Recent 'Middle-Age Chick Flicks.'" *Sexuality & Culture* 10(2): 33–55.

Thompson, Sharon. 1995. *Going All the Way: Teenage Girls' Values of Sex, Romance, and Pregnancy.* New York, NY: Hill & Wang.

Tolman, Deborah. 2002. *Dilemmas of Desire: Teenage Girls Talk about Sexuality.* Cambridge, MA: Harvard University Press.

Waskul, Dennis. D., Phillip Vannini, and Desiree Wiesen. 2007. "Women and Their Clitoris: Personal Discovery, Signification, and Use." *Symbolic Interaction* 30(2): 151–174.

14

GOING TO THE BATHROOM

Dennis D. Waskul

For most people, there are few things more profane than going to the bathroom. Likewise, what people really mean by the urgent phrase, "I have to go to the bathroom!" is usually a polite way of announcing an impending "creature release" (Goffman 1963: 69) that are among the most profaning of all human activities. Yet, as some skilled observers of human social and cultural life have illustrated (Cahill 1985; Miner 1955; Weinberg and Williams 2005), the bathroom is a hallowed space, and what we do within it is both highly ritualized and sacred (Durkheim 1915; Goffman 1971). Public bathrooms are a site of many interpersonal "rituals that behaviorally express and sustain the central values of our culture" (Cahill 1985: 44). Private bathrooms are personal "shrines" that are rife with "the powerful influences of ritual and ceremony" that surround the many "charms" of a "magic-ridden people" (Miner 1955: 503; 504; 507). And, indeed, the bathroom is frequented by popular culture too.

For those who conceive of popular culture as primarily the *products* of commercial culture—the television shows that air, the music that is produced, the magazines that are published, the things that are bought and sold at the shopping mall, and so on—then the bathroom is clearly a major market. Who can miss the ways that the hucksters of commercial capitalism colonize public bathrooms to access a captive and target audience—especially above urinals and within toilet stalls? In terms of sheer volume and diversity, the bathroom typically houses more of the products of commercial culture than any other room in our private living space. It is fitting that the kitchen and the bathroom are the two spaces that contain the greatest number of diverse products of consumer culture, considering that one of the central functions of both spaces is at one end of the digestive track or the other. Popular culture heavily seasons that which goes into our body as much as its aroma permeates that which comes out (not to mention all the other things we do in the bathroom).

For those who conceive of popular culture as something that "always emerges from the *collective activity* generated by interlocking networks of cultural creators" (Grazian 2010: 6, emphasis in original) then, once more, the bathroom is a crucial space. Because *Everyone Poops* (Gomi and Stinchecum 2001), bathrooms are a bare necessity for social order, and especially since Thomas Crapper introduced the flushing toilet in the late 1800s. In fact, I would argue that "Where's the bathroom?" is the singularly most common question that people ask in public spaces, and for the same reasons that the most prominent signs in public spaces are frequently those that direct people to them. The half-life of any collective activity is always at least partly at the mercy of the adequate availability of bathrooms—which I recently learned at an outdoor concert for which there were an insufficient number of toilets and I literally "had to go."

For those who conceive of popular culture as the common *doings* of people then, once again, the bathroom is of great significance. It is a sham to call the bathroom a room of "rest," considering all the busy activity that occurs within it—and that certainly includes urination, defecation, flatulation, and vomiting, but also (and just as importantly)—(un)dressing, bathing, showering, brushing teeth, applying make-up, fixing hair, deodorizing, odorizing, and so on. These latter functions are the primary reason why bathrooms are the only spaces (public or private) in which there is almost universally a mirror, for they are "'self-service' repair shops ... [and] individuals often enter ... bathrooms with no apparent purpose other than the management of their personal front" (Cahill 1985: 47). These "doings" in the bathroom are done with the products of popular culture: from toothpaste to toilet paper; from hairspray to toenail polish; from deodorant to perfume; from feminine hygiene products to beard trimmers; from body wash to mouthwash—an enormous collection of artifacts. What we do *with* these material items of popular culture is as important as the items themselves, and especially in the bathroom where our interactions with objects are as much about ritual as hygiene.

And so we arrive more or less where we began: popular culture is infused in all kinds of things (that we do) in the bathroom. For the remainder of this brief essay I highlight those intersections in this most private of space which is, interestingly enough, sometimes the *only* context in which we perform some of the most routine activities of our everyday life.[1]

Politics (and a Good Shit!)

> Here I sit, brokenhearted …
>
> —Author Unknown

"The personal is political," as is often rightly said. Yet I suspect few people in the contemporary western world have considered how the mundane personal act of simply entering a public bathroom is a profound political statement. For at least the last century, public bathrooms are among the singularly most segregated of all public spaces. Until rather recently in the United States, the racial segregation of bathrooms was not only commonplace but a significant civil rights issue (Cooper and Ruth 1999). It wasn't until 1990, with passage of the Americans with Disabilities Act, that handicapped people could expect full and equal access to public accommodations, including bathrooms. Public bathrooms have always been segregated by gender, an issue of great political significance to people who are intersexed, transgender, gender-queer, or otherwise do not identify as male or female. Some bathrooms are also segregated by age so that little boys and girls do not have to do a "number 1" or "2" before the potentially inappropriate audience of adults. Some bathrooms are even segregated by status so those in positions of power and authority do not do their "business" amongst their subordinates. In all of these ways, the simple act of walking into a public bathroom is political: a subtle signification of power, an announcement of prestige, a statement of identity, a taken-for-granted structure of Othering, and most often some combination thereof. Add to this that, once inside the bathroom, many of the common rules of interaction order are also a political a vote in favor of heteronormativity—so, guys, be careful what you are looking at when standing at the urinal!

Whereas the politics of walking into a bathroom are usually unseen to those who have the privilege of being able to use them, the political messages inscribed in the toilet stall are much more apparent. And that should be no surprise in a situation where anonymous authors write to anonymous readers. Yet, the content of what is written on those toilet stalls is just as structured as any other human activity. Pay some attention and you might notice that the content of bathroom graffiti is heavily influenced by its immediate social environment. For example, the bathrooms outside of my campus office often feature ineloquent—although sometimes amusing—political commentary as well as sometimes vile racism, overt sexism, and homophobia.[2] But those bathrooms are surrounded by classrooms where virtually all of our sociology courses are taught in which those subjects are common curricula. Since I seldom get out of my own office and classrooms, I never paid much attention to this until one day I needed to use the bathroom in a building on campus that I seldom visit. Seated in that stall, not only did I notice an absence of political graffiti, but was a bit amused by the mathematical equations that were in its place. While it is tempting to make a derogatory remark about "math nerds" and what qualifies as subversive bathroom humor to them,[3] I suspect the truth is, in fact, unorthodox subversion of another kind: someone figured out a clever way to exploit our micro-political right of privacy when using the toilet to usurp a professor's power in preventing him from cheating on a test. Nonetheless, thinking about the content of bathroom graffiti as emergent from the immediate social environment goes a long way toward understanding why names and initials are so abundant in some bathrooms (typically ones frequented by transitory populations that are literally "on the go," such as rest stops), phone numbers are more common in other locations (typically public facilities, such as parks), and so on.

Even lewd bathroom graffiti is more reflective of and subject to political influences than one might think. Alfred Kinsey (1953) conducted an extensive study of bathroom graffiti and found, unsurprisingly, that 86% of the inscriptions in men's bathrooms were erotic compared to only 25% of the inscriptions in women's bathrooms. Kinsey wisely interpreted this profound difference to be directly related to differing moral codes and social conventions of gender. Twenty-seven years later Farr and Gordon (1975) replicated Kinsey's study and, while also finding the men's room is more prone to erotic inscriptions, the total number of erotic graffiti in women's bathrooms had doubled since Kinsey's study. Confirming Kinsey's conclusions on the moral codes and conventions of gender, Farr and Gordon noted that the change has everything to do with the political advances of women between 1953 and 1975 and that their bathroom graffiti is a reflection of how "women today are much less inhibited" (161). To date no one has replicated Kinsey's study since 1975, but if the theory holds, then the proportion of erotic graffiti in the ladies room should be even more prevalent in the contemporary ladies room. Unfortunately, I'm not allowed to find out for myself. Still, who would have thought that a dirty limerick in the bathroom stall had anything to do with women's liberation?

Buying into the Bathroom

Using Less Never Felt So Good.

—Advertising for Charmin Ultra Soft

In my initial efforts to take stock of bathroom products for sale on the market, I began with a simple distinction between products that we use for health and hygiene (such as soap, toothpaste, and toilet paper) and products that are purely used for vanity (such as cosmetics, cologne, and hairspray). As I began perusing shopping isles, I immediately discovered my own naïveté and was reminded of the risks of creating conceptual frameworks for understanding prior to conducting field work. By means of example, Colgate once successfully marketed its toothpaste with phrases like "Nine out of ten dentists who tried would recommend it!"—a *medical* frame of marketing products to potential consumers. However, in our contemporary era the *seductive* frame has utterly overtaken the medical one, as Vannini and McCright (2004) found in their study of tanning. Judging purely from the products on the market, and especially in how they are marketed, there is no longer any apparent distinction between health, hygiene, and vanity. Allow me to illustrate this narcissism with a few examples.

Of all the consumable items in the bathroom, toilet paper is the most essential. As a testimonial, I'm sure most of us can reflect on a frustrating moment when we were stuck on the toilet because an inconsiderate asshole before us did not replace the empty roll. Or consider how running out of toilet paper at home always requires an urgent trip to the store that cannot wait until the next day. Surely we can poop without toilet paper, but I doubt anyone would disagree that it is a household necessity. So come along with me as I shop for toilet paper!

At my grocery store, toilet paper takes up half an isle where they stock nine different brands for a total of 13 varieties—enough diversity to cater to a wide range of finicky anal wiping preferences. Most brands come in at least two varieties: "Strong" and "Soft" (a difficult choice already!). Charmin ups the ante with both an "Ultra Strong" (featuring two cartoon bears, the larger tugging at the ends of a small strip of toilet paper) and an "Ultra Soft" (now with only one bear who appears to greatly appreciate the feel of toilet paper on her cheek[4]). For those with an anus that is neither that powerful nor that delicate, Charmin also offers "Basic"—but I'm confused; the packaging on "Charmin Basic" boldly claims the product is "3x Stronger!" (than what? I dunno). So how does Charmin "Basic" differ from Charmin "Strong?" Unsure, and without enough information to make a wise commercial choice, I notice "Quilted Northern Ultra Plush" which claims to have "3 silky smooth layers of softness." It's a little perplexing how "softness" can be "layered," but the quilted texture of the toilet paper adds a whole new consideration—but would I prefer Cottonelle's "Clean Ripple Texture" instead? Quilted Northern offers "Ultra Soft & Strong"—effectively resolving my previous dilemma—but Cottonelle offers its "CleanCare" toilet paper that is both "Strong & Absorbent." Now, "Strong" is a good quality in a toilet paper, I think (?). Maybe that finally explains to me why public restrooms encase the toilet paper in plastic dispensers that have a convenient serrated cutting edge—to assist those of us who are not strong enough to rip the perforated seam in the toilet paper! But do I choose softness over absorbency? That's a sticky dilemma! It's a good thing that Charmin makes a "Sensitive" toilet paper (now the bear is shown cuddling a bottle of lotion), because by the time I get to wiping, all these choices have made me cranky enough to desperately need that "Soothing Lotion with a touch of Aloe and E" (Vitamin E, I presume. I dunno).

Now that my anus will be happy, let's stroll to the "Oral Care" section to buy something for my mouth—an entire isle of products with an even more dizzying array of choices in toothbrushes, toothpastes, mouthwashes, flosses, denture products, teeth whiteners, and whatever "probiotics for oral care" are. This could take a while. So as not to beat a dead horse, let's just look at my choices in Colgate-brand toothpaste *alone*: "Max Fresh with Cooling Crystals," "Max White with Micro Cleaning Crystals," "Total Advanced Whitening," "Cavity Protection," "Maximum Cavity Protection," "Total," "Total Whitening," "Total Mint Stripe," "Optic White," "Sparkling White," "Sensitive Fresh Stripe," "Sensitive Pro Relief," and "Sensitive Whitening." What a mouthful! While the main purpose of brushing teeth is to prevent gum disease and tooth decay, in our study of how people manage odors, Phillip Vannini and I (2008) found that people brush their teeth as much to manage breath odor as for dental hygiene—clearly, toothpaste manufactures know this and have added "whitening" to the seduction.

Products for deodorizing and odorizing rituals (Largey and Watson 1972; Waskul and Vannini 2008) that occur in the bathroom are by far the most numerous. Even the most casual of observers must notice how soaps have become perfumes, perfumes have become body washes, and body washes have become skincare products for any one of at least a thousand ways that we can buy a product to get clean, smell fragrant, and tend to the urgent needs of our skin. Certainly cleanliness is important to health, but the sheer range of these products would surely compel an alien observer to believe that the human body is ridiculously rank, the largest of our human organs (our skin) has failed to adapt to our environment, and dangerously puts us at constant risk—and especially the bodies of our women. "Indeed the entire feminine hygiene industry is built on the dubious contention that women's bodies naturally stink and thus require potent remedies" (Waskul and Vannini 2008: 66; also see Classen, Howes, and Synnot, 1994), and likewise the vast number of skincare products marketed to women to fix their flawed bodies. I pause for a moment to look at a makeup mirror that magnifies *and* reflects; it occurs to me that if we look at something that closely, then it's small wonder we always find flaws.

Clearly, the number of products we purchase for use in the bathroom is not only enormous, but oftentimes reveals curious and sometimes concerning themes. In 1956 Horace Miner observed that the "fundamental belief underlying the whole system" of things people do in the bathroom "appears to be that the human body is ugly" (503). More than a half-century later, Miner's observation not only remains true but the apparent ugliness of the human body appears even more manifest than ever before, and especially if we are to take cues from advertising.

Wiping it Up

Since the bulk of this essay is emergent from casual reflections and observations of everyday life—rather than the usual academic labor of literature review, data collection, and analysis—this essay is essentially a series of observations that I've pulled out of my ass, fittingly enough. Nonetheless, I hope in these few pages I have made at least one point clear: bathrooms matter, and not only as a gracious relief for the people who have to use them, but socially and culturally as well. It's rather curious that the acquisition, preparation, and consumption of food and drink have been the subject of considerable social and cultural analysis, and especially throughout the history of anthropology. Yet, the opposite end of the digestive system is equally fundamental to the human condition, but wastefully ignored as irrelevant, wiped clean from the existing literatures, and flushed from our collective sociological imagination. Moreover, besides a place for eliminating waste, the bathroom is also the primary location in which we all must engage in "the disciplined management of personal appearance or 'personal front,' that is, the complex of clothing, makeup, hairdo, and other surface decorations" (Goffman 1963:25) which then comprises the people we are outside of the bathroom. Must we remind ourselves that individual acts are necessarily social and cultural—and that is no less true of what we do in bathrooms, be they public or private? Indeed, beginning with Durkheim's classic analysis of suicide, a century of sociological research has consistently shown that the most private things that people do are frequently among the *most* influenced by history, society, and culture—which is likewise true in the bathroom!

Dennis D. Waskul is Professor of Sociology and Distinguished Faculty Scholar at Minnesota State University, Mankato. He has authored or edited six books, and co-edits (with Phillip Vannini) Ashgate's *Interactionist Currents* book series. He has published many empirical studies, including various investigations of the sexual use of new media technologies, the sociology of the body, sensual sociology, and the intersections of fantasy and lived experience.

Notes

1. This, alone, is an extremely interesting quality of the bathroom. I can sleep in my bed, on the couch, and even in my office chair. I can eat in my kitchen, dining room, living room, and even in my car. Aided by my laptop computer, I wrote this essay in a total of six distinct locations between my home, campus, and even the waiting room of an auto repair shop. But if I need to bathe, shower, piss, or shit there is only one public or private place in which that can be done, and failure to abide by that rule is potentially a criminal offense, or casts serious doubts upon my sanity (i.e., to shit on my couch). To declare the bathroom "sacred" is no exaggeration.
2. I should add that I'm always extremely impressed by how quickly that graffiti are removed—and the most hateful of them are addressed the quickest.
3. Did you hear the one about the constipated mathematician? He worked it out with a pencil!
4. I'm guessing the bear is feminine from the pink bow in her hair, although I do not mean to be sexist. I wear pink clothing and accessories too.

References

Cahill, Spencer. 1985. "Meanwhile Backstage: Public Bathrooms and the Interaction Order." *Urban Life 41*(1): 33–58.

Classen, Constance, David Howes, and Anthony Synnot. 1994. *Aroma: The Cultural History of Smell*. London, UK and New York, NY: Routledge.

Cooper, Patricia and Ruth Oldenziel. 1999. "Cherished Classifications: Bathrooms and Construction of Gender/Race on the Pennsylvania Railroad During World War II." *Feminist Studies 25*(1): 7–41.

Durkheim, Émile. 1915 (1912). *The Elementary Forms of Religious Life*. (trans. Karen E. Fields.) London, UK: Allen & Unwin.

Farr, Jo-Ann and Carol Gordon. 1975. "A Partial Replication of Kinsey's Graffiti Study." *The Journal of Sex Research 11*(2): 158–162.

Goffman, Erving. 1963. *Behavior in Public Places: Notes on the Social Organization of Gatherings*. New York, NY: Free Press.

Goffman, Erving. 1971. *Relations in Public: Microstudies of the Public Order*. New York, NY: Basic Books.

Gomi, Tarō. 2001. *Everyone Poops*. (trans. Amanda Stinchecum). La Jolla, CA: Kane/Miller.

Grazian, David. 2010. *Mix it up: Popular Culture, Mass Media, and Society*. New York, NY: W.W. Norton.

Kinsey, Alfred, Wardell B. Pomeroy, Clyde E. Martin, and Paul H. Gebhard. 1953. *Sexual Behavior in the Human Female*. Philadelphia, PA: W.B. Saunders Co.

Largey, Gale and David Watson. 1972. "The Sociology of Odours." *American Journal of Sociology* 77: 1021–1034.

Miner, Horace. 1955. "Body Ritual Among the Nacirema." *American Anthropologist* 58(3): 503–507.

Vannini, Phillip and Aaron McCright. 2004. "To Die For: The Semiotic Seductive Power of the Tanned Body." *Symbolic Interaction* 27(3): 309–332.

Waskul, Dennis D. and Phillip Vannini. 2008. "Smell, Odor, and Somatic Work: Sense-Making and Sensory Management." *Social Psychology Quarterly* 71(1): 53–71.

Weinberg, Martin and Colin Williams. 2005. "Fecal Matters: Habitus, Embodiments, and Deviance." *Social Problems* 52(3): 315–336.

15

GETTING DRESSED

John C. Pruit

> One of the most evident means by which an individual shows himself to be situationally present is through the disciplined management of personal appearance or "personal front," that is, the complex of clothing, makeup, hairdo, and other surface decorations he carries about on his person.
>
> —Erving Goffman

Although getting dressed is part of our daily routine, it is a mundane activity laden with social and cultural implications. The time, effort, and thought we put into getting dressed convey its importance to social and cultural life. In fact, getting dressed is an inevitable part of our lives. From the beginning to the end of the life course, we wear clothing. It begins at birth when babies are wrapped in blankets and pink or blue hats are placed on their heads. When we depart someone will make us presentable to those attending our curtain call (your final impression management; see Goffman 1959; Turner and Edgley 1976). In the interim, we adorn our bodies with clothing and ornaments. Most of the time we are only briefly naked—taking a shower, having sex, or changing clothes. But even during sex an argument can be made that a condom is an article of clothing.

There is a dynamic social component to getting dressed in which we must anticipate and account for several future concerns in the present. One wrong fashion choice can leave us "feeling naked" (vulnerable). Ruth Barcan (2004) argues the act of getting dressed is a liminal condition in which we transition from being naked to being clothed. Nude/clothed represents a complex dialectic between natural and cultural states. The natural is equated with animals, while the cultural relates to sophistication and being human. Getting dressed is a universally shared aspect of what it means to be human (Williams 2002).

Getting dressed is marked with social and cultural significance. More often than not, we deliberately choose our clothes. Our closets, dresser drawers, hampers, and floors contain combinations of clothing to meet anticipated contexts. We have clothes for work, going out, exercising, weekends, Halloween parties, interviews, church, and court dates. We have clothes for traveling, swimming, watching football on the couch, and sleeping. And, when the season comes, we have our ugly Christmas sweater. There are clothes for every occasion. Hence, getting dressed is a collective activity (Grazian 2010), aiming at self-presentation.

In order to get our "personal front" ready to face the world, there is much we have to do, and not all of it is merely putting on clothing. We are not only putting on clothes, but we are also doing other necessities required by the social order to appear in public. This includes many of the tasks in Dennis D. Waskul's essay in this collection ("Going to the Bathroom"), such as cleaning the body, shaving, deodorizing, hair styling, and putting on makeup. Yes, getting dressed is something we "do" (Garfinkel 1967), a process undertaken to meet certain social and cultural standards of appearance and decorum. The amount of time and energy we put into getting dressed is substantial. It is not only the back-and-forth between the closet, the mirror, and your partner ("Does this look okay?"), but also the time it takes to go shopping.

Clothing is a ubiquitous representation of commercial culture and personal identity. Wearing clothes, at the very least, is a tacit endorsement of popular culture made individual—commonly referred to as "personal style." The products available for consumption, for example, largely determine judgments on what is appropriate and/or inappropriate to wear in public—what is "in style," so to speak—and relate to the resources in our cultural tool kit (Swidler 1986). Because most people do not make their own clothes or have a tailor craft them, popular cultural trends in mass-produced, middle-class fashion become the default for consuming and producing personal style. Middle-class lifestyles, then, drive consumption and identification with popular commercial culture (Gans 1974) and pervasive identification with the middle class (especially in America). While getting dressed expresses personal style, individuals are not so much producers of commercial and popular culture as they are its product.

Getting Dressed as Unremarkably Remarkable

From the point of view of sociological theory, the moral order consists of the rule governed activities of everyday life.

—Harold Garfinkel

Considering popular culture as everyday life provides an opportunity to peer into life's taken-for-granted corners. These include "seen-but-unnoticed" (Garfinkel 1967: 37) actions, products, and processes. Recognizing and studying the "seen-but-unnoticed" shifts our focus to the routines and rhythms most, if not all, of us experience but pay little attention to. Research analyzing social marking and unmarking (Brekhus 1998; Mullaney 2006; Pruit 2012) provides an analytic framework for understanding how people "do" popular culture in everyday life. Social marking originates in linguistics research. Linda R. Waugh (1982) traced it to the 1930s when Nikolai Trubetzkoy and Roman Jakobson used it to describe the inequality between phoneme pairs. One half of the pair is marked, emphasized, or highlighted, while the other side of the pair acquires its meaning through the absence of the quality. Markedness represents the "asymmetrical and hierarchical relationship between the two poles of any opposition" (Waugh 1982: 299).

Many articles of clothing keep the body a mystery but certainly draw attention to particular parts of the body synonymous with desire. Clothing is remarkable for what it reveals as much as what it conceals. Undergarments and outer garments are layers of clothing serving multiple purposes. The push-up bra lifts and separates breasts while concealing the nipples. Thong underwear is similarly provocative for what it reveals and conceals (compared to "granny panties"). The outer layer of clothing also conceals and reveals. A low-cut shirt partially conceals the breasts and accentuates cleavage. Tight-fitting t-shirts hug biceps, and tight-fitting jeans hold and accentuate curves.

If the clothes make the person, then the clothing can also make the setting. Getting dressed is a reflexive act in which our anticipations of future scenes influence our clothing choices in the present, and our clothing choices influence the scenes in which we will eventually find ourselves (Mead 1932). There are also many practical contingencies to account for prior to getting dressed, such as the activity, context, and our role in it.

When getting dressed we often consider what we will be doing (working, relaxing, exercising, eating, watching a movie). If we are going to watch a movie at a friend's house we are likely to make sure we have on clean socks without holes in the toes because it is customary in some places to partially undress (take shoes off) upon entering a home. We also consider the type of event we will attend (formal, informal, business casual, a backyard barbeque). If we are going to a wedding then we are likely to wear formal attire. Where an event takes place (indoors, outdoors, both, public, private) is also important to the act of getting dressed. If the event is outside we must consider the weather and time of day or night. Do I need gloves, sunscreen, or a sweater? If the event takes place inside, is there air conditioning? Movie theaters are always cold and somehow humid (better grab a cardigan!).

Aside from context, we take other actors into account and anticipate how they will interpret us (Cooley 1902; Mead 1934) and what they will expect from us. The leading question is, who will be there (employers, community leaders, friends, strangers) and what impression will I be giving off? In short, anticipated others influence our choices regarding clothing. For example, if we think someone we want to impress will be at an event, then we might put a little extra effort into our appearance to make a good impression. Will others think of us as put together, disheveled, or will we be unnoticed and overlooked? Getting dressed, then, is among the most influential forms of impression management because people tend to judge our appearance before speaking with us, potentially rendering a set of expectations into being.

A further consideration relates to our role in the event. Simply put, why will we be there? Our role in the event plays a part in getting dressed because roles have social expectations attached to them. Consider the differences between teachers and students. Students (and occasionally teachers) may not be motivated to come to class at 9:00 on a Friday morning. They may wear a baseball cap instead of fixing their hair. This is completely acceptable because the social expectations for the role of college student allows for a wide variety of clothing choices, or none at all. In 1992, a college student named Andrew Martinez achieved some fame by going to class naked at the University of California, Berkeley. College teachers, however, have differing social expectations attached to their role, and it is unlikely they will show up to teach class naked (depending on their tenure status, and if the class is taught online!).

The Consequences of Getting Dressed

My momma always said you can tell a lot about a person by their shoes. Where they go. Where they've been.

—Forrest Gump

Appearance is the product of getting dressed. A person becomes the object of others' gaze (Foucault 1977) and is evaluated based on appearance as well as regulatory and proscriptive forces relating to social and cultural power. Power differentials in class, gender, ethnicity, and race influence evaluations of appearance. Clothing is a form of social control with social, legal, and even fatal consequences. It symbolizes and is symbolic of the broader social order, and has varying meanings for its bearers and observers.

Having the "right" shoes, purse, or apparel can carry social prestige. Objects and the person as an object are woven together in a brief glimpse, telling the evaluator about the person. We make meaning of cultural objects, such as clothing and appearance, as if we were an audience (Kidd 2014). Our meaning-making activities, our interpretations, are a result of personal experience and the cultural context. This of course, involves stereotypes, generalizations, and the politics of labeling in which the clothing brand, for example, is used to categorize the person wearing it. The individual is socially marked in relation to the brand and its cost. Not only is having a designer label a marker of social class, in effect labeling its bearer, but it also indirectly signifies the social class of those making the clothing. We must not forget about the working conditions many endure while they produce our clothing.

Getting dressed reflects the gender order, its internalization, and is a way to police cultural boundaries. Candace West and Don Zimmerman (1987) argued people "do gender." Quite obviously doing gender is embedded in our clothing. For instance, there are more regulatory and proscriptive boundaries relating to clothing for women than men. Indeed, men get a "free pass" in most instances of clothing failures because they are men and are not expected to be fashion savvy.[1] Women, however, have no such free passes. Women are almost always expected to be dressed appropriately, with makeup on, hair fixed, and ready to meet the day's events. A woman failing to comply often receives looks, gestures, and whispers—negative sanctions ("Did you see what she was wearing?"). This is to say, women are on the evaluative end of getting dressed more so than men because the gender order does not allow women to claim ignorance and rarely gives them a day off. Appearance upholds the gender order and is yet another way in which men are socially unmarked and women are marked.

There is also formal social control for what, where, and how clothing is worn. Burqas and niqabs symbolize modesty and chastity, but in western societies they are marked as the garb of potential terrorists. News stories about French legislation banning burqas and niqabs (Willsher 2014) and Australian authorities wishing they did not exist (Griffiths 2014) are tangible evidence of prejudice and discrimination relating to clothing. Here, concealing and revealing represents a threat rather than desire. The burqa and niqab, then, are simultaneously symbols of modesty and Western fear. France's legislative maneuvers are a double move against minority ethnicity and gender, effectively banning Muslim women from carrying out day-to-day activities in public settings.

While the legislation in France aims at controlling what clothing is worn and where, in the United States there have been local movements to control how clothing is worn. Local politicians in several states are working as the fashion police to ban sagging pants (Huffington Post 2013), defined as pants worn two inches below the natural waistline (Figalora 2014). Most of the distress comes from the dominant culture being unable to impose its moral sensibilities on those wearing their clothes in a manner inconsistent with dominant norms. Banning sagging pants disproportionately affects younger black men, an already

disproportionately overrepresented group in the American criminal justice system. This becomes all the more apparent when we consider the
social construction of clothing: sagging pants may be "a phase" for white
male teenagers, but when black male teenagers sag it is a social problem.

The hoodie (hooded sweatshirt) is another example of how an article
of clothing can have diverse meanings. In general, hoodies are simply
an outer layer of clothing worn to keep warm. However, when a young
black man wears one, the meaning of the hoodie changes. It becomes
racialized—symbolizing threat. It is associated with "gang bangers" and
"thugs" (both euphemisms for racial slurs) and the potential for violence.
In the wake of the Trayvon Martin killing, hoodies became symbols of
racial and social justice. For some, the hooded sweatshirt was a way
to draw attention to the intersection of race, power, and violence in
America, and how black men are interpreted and acted upon as threats
(Hanna, Savidge, and Murgatroyd 2014). Quite significantly, there are
consequences for getting dressed beyond the occasional fashion faux
pas. The dominant culture's definition of where, what, and how clothing
is worn is a formal and informal expression of social control.

Conclusions

Getting dressed is a matter of routine, but it is also a transition chalked
full of meaning, symbolism, and reflexivity. It is an act of impression
management (Goffman 1959) often meticulously undertaken for specific
situations. Quite literally, our clothing influences other's impressions—
whether or not we like it, and has a range of consequences. The clothing
we wear has symbolic meaning for others and ourselves individually,
socially, and culturally. Getting dressed can place us in the "matrix of
domination" (Collins 1990: 18). The effects of race, ethnicity, class, gender, and other identity markers are brought to bear on clothing, which
then shapes experience and situates individuals within broader systems
of meaning. Some interpretations of clothing reduce the individual to a
single dimension, while others open up social worlds.

If clothing tells a story about a person, then that story is partial at best.
Clothing accentuates and problematizes social markers about race, class,
gender, sexuality, disability, and privilege. It also conceals and reveals bodies, behavior, attitudes, beliefs, and values. Getting dressed clarifies the

boundaries of personal identity through the lens of the broader cultural context for others and our selves. Using popular culture to interpret personal style simplifies the processes of "knowing" by providing us with shorthand understandings. More often than not, these interpretations are from a single perspective—white, male, middle class, heterosexual, and able-bodied—reducing "others" to objects. We always already know everything about members of some subcultures through their appearance. For instance, we know emo's, erotic dancers, gangsters, goths, hippies, hipsters, jocks, Muslim women, nuns, police officers, and preppies because of their clothing (or lack of clothing). Getting dressed, then, is a reflexively organized feature of social life made concrete through the interplay of personal identity and popular culture.

John C. Pruit is a Ph.D. candidate at the University of Missouri. His work has appeared in journals such as *Journal of Contemporary Ethnography*, *Symbolic Interaction*, and *Qualitative Inquiry*. His research interests include culture, identity, deviance, narrative, and qualitative methods. His current research is an ethnography, focusing on preschool teachers, gender, and identity work.

Note

1. Men's appearance is also subject to the gender order. Men who emphasize personal in a similar manner as women are sometimes labeled "gay" or "metrosexual." These become gendered markers for masculinity and femininity.

References

Barcan, Ruth. 2004. *Nudity: A Cultural Anatomy*. Oxford, UK and New York, NY: Berg Publishers.

Brekhus, Wayne. 1998. "A Sociology of the Unmarked: Redirecting Our Focus." *Sociological Theory* 16(1): 34–51.

Collins, Patricia Hill. 1990. *Black Feminist Thought*. New York, NY: Routledge.

Cooley, Charles Horton. 1902. *Human Nature and the Social Order*. New York, NY: Scribner's.

Figalora, Sarah. 2014, July 22. "Meet the Passionate 'Driving Force' Behind Fla. City's Saggy Pants Ban," *ABC News*. Accessed October 1, 2014. Retrieved from http://abcnews.go.com/US/meet-passionate-driving-force-saggy-pants-ban/story?id=24670963.

Foucault, Michel. 1977. *Discipline and Punish*. New York, NY: Vintage Books.

Gans, Herbert J. 1974. *Popular Culture and High Culture*. New York, NY: Basic Books.

Garfinkel, Harold. 1967. *Studies in Ethnomethodology*. Cambridge, UK: Polity Press.

Goffman, Erving. 1959. *The Presentation of Self in Everyday Life*. New York, NY: Anchor Books.

Goffman, Erving. 1963. *Behavior in Public Places: Notes on the Social Organization of Gatherings*. New York, NY: Free Press.

Grazian, David. 2010. *Mix It Up: Popular Culture, Mass Media, and Society*. New York, NY: W.W. Norton.

Griffiths, Emma. 2014, October 2. "Prime Minister Tony Abbott Reveals He Wishes the Burka 'Was Not Worn' in Australia." *ABC News Australia*. Retrived from http://www.abc.net.au/news/2014-10-01/abbott-says-he-wishes-the-burka-was-not-worn-in-australia/5782008.

Hanna, Jason, Martin Savidge, and John Murgatroyd. 2014, September 26. "Video Shows Trooper Shooting Unarmed Man, South Carolina Police Say." *CNN Justice*. Retrieved from http://www.cnn.com/2014/09/25/justice/south-carolina-trooper-shooting/.

Huffington Post. 2013, November 1. "Saggy Pants Ban," *Huffington Post*. Accessed October 1, 2014. Retrieved from: http://www.huffingtonpost.com/news/saggy-pants-ban/.

Kidd, Dustin. 2014. *Pop Culture Freaks: Identity, Mass Media and Society*. Boulder, CO: Westview Press.

Mead, George Herbert. 1932. *The Philosophy of the Present*. (Arthur E. Murphy, Ed.). Chicago, IL and London, UK: London Open Court Publishing Co.

Mead, George Herbert. 1934. *Mind, Self, & Society*. Chicago, IL: University of Chicago.

Mullaney, Jamie. 2006. *Everyone Is Not Doing It: Abstinence and Personal Identity*. Chicago, IL: University of Chicago Press.

Pruit, John C. 2012. "Peak Oil and the Narrative Construction of Unmarked Identities." *Symbolic Interaction 35*(4): 438–455.

Swidler, Ann. 1986. "Culture in Action: Symbols and Strategies." *American Sociological Review 51*(2): 273–286.

Turner, Ronny and Charles Edgley. 1976. "Death as Theater: A Dramaturgical Analysis of the American Funeral." *Sociology and Social Research 60*(4): 377–392.

Waugh, Linda R. 1982. "Marked and Unmarked: A Choice between Unequals in Semiotic Structure." *Semiotica 38*(3–4): 299–318.

West, Candace and Don H. Zimmerman. 1987. "Doing Gender." *Gender & Society 1*(2):125–151.

Williams, Raymond. 2002 [1958]. "Culture Is Ordinary." In B. Highmore (Ed.), *The Everyday Life Reader*. New York, NY: Routledge.

Willsher, Kim. 2014, July 1. "France's Burqa Ban Upheld by Human Rights Court." *The Guardian*. Accessed October 1, 2014. Retrieved from http://www.theguardian.com/world/2014/jul/01/france-burqa-ban-upheld-human-rights-court.

16
PUTTING ON MAKEUP
Rebecca F. Plante

Peering into the Mirror

I'm in the bathroom again. The light is better and all of my makeup (and there is a lot of it) is here, on the sink, in several drawers, and crowding into a cabinet. I am "making up" my face today, inventing a story for myself. Which face do I want to present to the public? Do I want a smoky eye, a crimson lip, or a "dewy" cheek? Do I want to seem sultry, beautiful, professional, or innocent? "Fresh-faced" is always a good look for someone like me; I think it's better than the opposite—haggard? tired? zombified? Do I want my made-up face to seem like a "better" version of myself, or just a "refreshed" one? Or like a version of myself that I don't normally present—a character, a fairy tale, an actor. Putting on makeup involves playing a part, and using cosmetics to create an illusion.

The mirror—a ubiquitous element of the process of putting on makeup—is both purposeful and symbolic. I peer into the mirror because, of course, I need to see what I'm doing as I apply my own makeup. And if a makeup artist applies makeup to me, when she is done, the first thing I do is to look in a mirror to see her work. Symbolically, we all peer into the mirror, or "looking glass," in the socially necessary process of assessing how we think others will see or regard us (Cooley 1964). Even on the rare days when I do not apply any makeup, I look in the mirror, attempting to imagine what others will make of me. How will they read the impression I am trying to make? Am I managing that impression effectively, actively creating a storyline or narrative for my self-presentation?

In this essay, I explore the idea that putting on makeup is a creative, indulgent, mostly gendered, possibly political, often engrossing act that is a ritual and a chore. Putting on makeup is one way to easily modify presentations of self, do literal "face work," and tell culturally-produced stories about beauty. Putting on makeup can simultaneously be experienced as conformity, as giving in to pressure to create beauty with cosmetics, *and* as an individualized creative act of transformation and self-expression. Note that I focus on women's everyday acts of "putting on a face," not, for instance, men wearing eye liner ("guyliner") and foundation, although I do briefly discuss drag makeup.

A (Very) Little History

The act of putting on makeup is at least 6,000 years old (Power 2010). The oldest cosmetic may be kohl, the smoky black powder Egyptians used to outline their eyes (think pharaohs and Nefertiti). The noun "cosmetics"—the products and objects otherwise called makeup—comes from the Greek *kosmetike*, the art of beautifying. The adjectival form, such as "it was a cosmetic adjustment," comes from the Greek *kosmein*, to arrange or adorn. Words associated with makeup and beauty—glamour, fetching, and captivate—have nefarious, dissembling origins, even if their current connotations are more neutral. Glamour was associated with magic, enchantments, and spells. To be fetching was to be crafty or scheming, and to be captivating was to be enticing, entrapping, or capturing (with beauty or charm). Even the word mascara means mask (from the Spanish *mascara*).

Around the world cosmetics are used to hide, disguise, enhance, change, and make over everything from freckles to acne scars and from wrinkles to baldness. Queen Elizabeth I, ruler of England (1558–1603), relied heavily on lead-based face powders and other concoctions to hide her poor, aging skin and poor health (Whitelock 2014). The paler the skin, the better for the aristocracy, as it showed that they did not need to labor outside like the proletariat. By the late 1800s, makeup had become associated with "loose women"—prostitutes (Peiss 1998). But changing culture, increasingly visible female Hollywood stars, and cosmetic industry marketing lead to women of all social classes in Europe and North America beginning to use at least some cosmetics by the 1920s

(Schweitzer 2005). Marketing efforts even suggested that middle class (white) women who did *not* use makeup were abandoning their responsibility to create beauty and to make their faces the center of that effort.

By the end of the 1940s, between 80 and 90% of adult women were using lipstick (Peiss 1998). But for decades after the Victorian morality of the turn of the century had ceased to be so prominent, the good girl/bad girl dichotomy persisted. Peiss described two new lipsticks, marketed in *Mademoiselle* magazine in 1938: "one was for "girls who lean toward pale lacquered nails, quiet smart clothes, and tiny strands of pearls," the other "for the girl who loves exciting clothes, [who] pins a [paste] pin as big as a saucer to her dress and likes to be just a leetle bit shocking" … The names of these lipsticks were "Lady" and "Hussy" (1998: 3). Lipstick names, in particular, take center stage in teaching women about "femininity and self-esteem" in hegemonic culture (Merskin, 2007).

Why Do People Use Makeup?

My grandmother's daily makeup consisted of eyebrow pencil and a particular coral lipstick by Coty. Her cosmetics were in a little cup in the bathroom cupboard. Without the pencil, she had no brows, having tweezed them to invisibility when she was young and it was *à la mode* to have thin, drawn-on eyebrows. Without the lipstick, she would not leave the house. She referred to it as "putting on my face"—inventing a look, an image. Grandmother created her face when she was a teenager in the 1930s, with a bold lip and her hair piled on top of her head. She maintained that face for decades, going through tube after tube and pencil after pencil. I spent a lot of time playing with her makeup (and my mom's) when I was nine or ten years old, imagining myself as an older girl, a woman. What face did I want to put on?

I began collecting my own makeup as a 13-year-old: eye shadows, under-eye concealer, foundation (to create a smooth, even face), finishing powder, mascara, eye liners, lipsticks, and lip glosses. My taste was a bit punkish, a little bit heavy metal, with a lot of dark, thick eyeliner and clumpy mascara. I wanted to look like a sexy, mysterious Joan Jett (google her, circa 1982). At some point in high school I began to think I'd call myself a feminist, and at my alternative, somewhat countercultural college, I got into heated debates about whether my makeup was a symbol of my and other women's oppression. I struggled to reconcile my feminism and my perceived individuality with cosmetics and the invented stories they helped me tell—that I was getting enough sleep (thanks to concealer covering my under-eye circles), that I was sexy (thanks to a lot of black eyeliner, carefully smudged), and that I was appealing (thanks to my glossy lips, made fuller by the illusion of a lipstick/gloss combo). I was a scared conformist, imprisoned by my belief that cosmetics made me look prettier and more attractive to men.

There is a culturally produced, socially and historically contextualized, story around makeup. I can't tell if it's a feminist story or its opposite (anti-feminist?), or an individualist story or its opposite (conformist?). Is putting on makeup a playful, transformative, creative act of individual expression? Or is it a "grit your teeth and bear it" chore—a frustrating reminder that you'll never make yourself look perfect. but that you'll spend a lot of money and time trying? Women tell their stories and these themes emerge:

> It makes me feel pretty. It gives me confidence to face the world.
> I feel like someone I'm not when I wear makeup, but it's someone I want to be ...
> It's fun to play with makeup / the colors / the effects created by different products.
> Makeup transforms me (Clarke and Bundon 2009; Darden and Worden 1994; Dellinger and Williams 1997).
> Makeup is a contradiction—I put it on so that it looks like I'm not wearing makeup (Holmes, 2013).
> Makeup is a chore. It's something I have to do; I don't really have a choice.

"Every morning, it's a chore," says Janet Pardo, senior vice president of global product development at Clinique, an Estee Lauder brand. The ritual of standing in front of a mirror to examine and camouflage imperfections is "a pain point for women," she says. "It's something they must do, like men have to shave" (Holmes 2013: D1).

Beausoleil (1994) interviewed a diverse group of about 40 women, asking about their daily use of makeup. They created faces to correspond to their expected activities, such as "going to work," "going out," "going to the store" (39). Respondents used makeup rituals to narrate their imagined lives, using their created faces to tell the story of their days and nights, their leisure activities, and their selves.

Men who wear makeup, by the way, seem to suggest that the products transform them from guys who may not care about their appearances into people who are well groomed. An analysis (Hall, Gough, and Seymour-Smith 2012) of YouTube videos of men putting on makeup includes one video commenter's reasoning: "same here, metro[sexual] since 14; I basically do make up every day to school, and not just 10 mins bud, I spend like 30 mins in front of the mirror, and 2 hours in the bathroom. some guys are just plain stupid. Men = smelly, ugly, hairy? fuck that shit." Yeah, fuck that shit.

Men who do drag and/or perform in drag shows talk about the experience of getting "vavoom … makeup, hair" (Lowder, Cracker, and Lesperance 2014). I asked my friends who do drag about why they wear makeup, and they told me about feeling pretty, creating a character, and becoming someone else for a night. This is similar to the motivations that some women have. Drag performers are so good at creating new faces that they are often asked about their makeup techniques (Wright 2006). Buzzfeed and the Citypages have step-by-step tutorials of the 13 or 14 stages of drag performers "making up."

Metaphorically and literally, "makeup" is a form of creative invention, whether performed by men or women. Among the many Merriam-Webster dictionary definitions of makeup, we find "forming by fitting together or assembling; combining to produce a sum or a whole; or preparing in physical appearance for a role." *(Merriam-Webster's online 2015)* To make up is *to assemble*, to produce *a new whole*, to prepare *for a role*. Each swipe of eye shadow, bronzer, luminizer, or lipstick creates a new, made-up self-story. The appeal of cosmetics is, in part, the possibility of self-invention. I can create illusion, contour, color, depth, sparkle, highlighting, "youth," allure. Drag performers can create the illusion of characters and drama, and metrosexual men can create the impression that they are not ugly and hairy.

Contemporary Cosmetics: Technologies

On YouTube there are hundreds of thousands of makeup haul videos, 15 to 20 minute exhibitionistic demonstrations of (mostly) women's latest shopping trips. They're blandly titled "huge high-end makeup haul (Dior, Chanel, Louboutin)" or "Clearance makeup haul from Walgreens." The hosts, all extensively made up—including a 14-year-old with lime green eyeshadow and magenta glossed lips—hold product after product to the camera. Some hosts sit in front of their closets. Most sit in their bedrooms, other aspects of consumer and material culture (shoes, clothing, attempts at decorating) scattered or carefully arranged around them. Some of the hosts also post videos of themselves putting on makeup, tutorials for making a smoky eye or a bronzed cheek. These women are participating in a 204 billion dollar global beauty industry that includes cosmetics and other grooming and beautifying products (WWD 2013). There's no way to know how much their consumption habits influence viewers' consumption habits, but there seems to be a persistent market for videos that show viewers what cosmetics to buy and how to use them.

The beauty industry also extends to nonsurgical cosmetic procedures, including permanent eyeliner, lip color, lip liner, and eyebrow pigmentation. One micropigmentation studio advertises its services in clichés and truisms: "If you're a busy mom, business woman, or have an active lifestyle, you'll save hours every week not having to stand in front of the mirror slaving over applying makeup. Not to mention you won't have to worry about sweating it off during a workout or melting by the end of an evening out" (Permanent Makeup n.d.). What permanent makeup companies neglect to acknowledge is that applying makeup isn't always seen as a chore, and part of the pleasure of "making up" is precisely that it's temporary. It's easy to play with, and mistakes are quickly erasable with makeup remover or water and a wash cloth.

The expansion of makeup extends to the products made specifically to enhance skin tone in selfies and smartphone photos, such as Radiant Cream Compact Foundation by NARS. And "selfie makeovers" abound, for those interested in making their smartphone self-portraits look more perfect. The Selfie Photo Editor and Photox apps allow users to add every possible makeup effect (Photox charges a fee): "Want your eyes to seriously shine? Make your eyes bigger and brighter. You can go as natural or dramatic as you like. Scroll through the eyeliner and eyelash overlays to create the look you're going for. You can even thicken your eyebrows" (Selfie Photo Editor). Children can practice selfie makeovers and beautification via hundreds of simple online computer games such as "Take a Selfie" and "Baby Mia Makeover," the games involve putting a full face of makeup on a computer figure, choosing an outfit and accessories, and then clicking "done." That's it—that's the whole game.

Makeup has become linked with perceptions of professional, white-collar occupational competency. In one study, women who wore makeup were judged to be healthier, more confident, better employed, and more promotable (Nash, Fieldman, Hussey, Lévêque, and Pineau 2006). Makeup artist Charlotte Tilbury has a 19-step tutorial for turning a red, aging face into a confident, professional face, using Tilbury's Magic Cream, Wonderglow Youth Elixir, Life Changing Eyelash Curlers, Filmstar Bronze and Glow, Lip Cheat Lip Liner (in Pillow Talk, no less), and First Love blush, among other products (Tilbury 2014).

(Brief) Conclusions

Putting on makeup can be a private or a very public act. At age 14 I began to wear makeup to junior high, and to my shame, one of my snottier classmates noticed. In history class she loudly told everyone that I was wearing makeup and that it "looked nice" (she was lying—she didn't think so). Wearing makeup was a way for me to take some control over my face and my appearance in the midst of puberty, perhaps the most compressed, out-of-control time in the life course. I felt like I had some agency every morning as I chose an eyeliner and eyeshadow to go with my outfit.

Putting on makeup seems as if it should be just one of many choices about the body that people may be or feel empowered to make it seems as if one's choice to wear makeup should be nonthreatening, but it clearly gets people worked up. As historian Kathy Peiss succinctly said, "Small objects sometimes possess great moral force" (1998: 4). For example lipstick, when worn by a lesbian, can lead to the application of potentially pejorative labels, like "lipstick lesbian," along with assumptions that "lesbian" + "cosmetic-wearing" = "problematic." There are Tumblr sites, as well as blogs and articles, about "lipstick lesbians"—fuckyeahlipsticklesbians.tumblr.com or belladonna.org's lipstick lesbian page, for example.

Then there is #feminist-makeupping, which is about the politics of combining the apparent oxymorons of feminist + makeup. An event in Wellington, New Zealand featured a long line of women, peering into the mirrors in a dance studio (think floor to ceiling down a long wall), all applying makeup (Morgan, 2014). The women talked about why they wear makeup, the way it makes them feel "powerfully visible" in male-dominated industries, or the way unusual lipsticks feel like "war paints." They talked about the constant questions: Do heterosexual women wear makeup to be more appealing to men? Are cosmetics an aspect of patriarchal culture determined to make boatloads of money from convincing women that they need tweaks and alterations to be considered attractive?

What's the problem with a tube of lipstick, named Lady or Hussy or Vamp, a bit of foundation or BB cream or CC cream, some sparkly eyeshadow, and a feathery pair of fake eyelashes? I've aged out of wanting to look like Joan Jett, but I do like to look a little more rested (under-eye concealer) and a little more alert (mascara) than I usually am. Small objects do indeed possess "great moral force," but they also possess great possibilities, pleasures, and creativity.

Rebecca F. Plante is Associate Professor of Sociology at Ithaca College, where she teaches courses on gender, sexualities, and sexual selves. She uses intersectionalities and qualitative methods to study hooking up and college campus sexual climate change; online dating, sexuality, and intimacy among U.S. adults; the concept of positive sexual reputations; and a sociology of sexual ethics. Her most recent books are *Sexualities in Context: A Social Perspective*, 2nd ed., (Routledge, forthcoming) and the *Handbook of the Sociology of Sexualities* (with J. DeLamater, Springer, forthcoming); and *Doing Gender Diversity: Readings in Theory and Real-World Experience* (with L.M. Maurer; Westview Press, 2010). "Latex & Vinyl," a radio call-in show at the University of New Hampshire, featured Plante (as "Dr. Victoria Monk") answering questions about everything from best sexual positions to having better orgasms.

References

Beausoleil, Natalie. 1994. "Make-up in Everyday Life: An Inquiry into the Practices of Urban American Women of Diverse Backgrounds." In Natalie Sault (Ed.) *Many Mirrors: Body Image and Social Relations,*. Rutgers, NJ: Rutgers University Press, 33–57.

Clarke, Laura Hurd and Andrea Bundon. 2009. "From 'The Thing to Do' to 'Defying the Ravages of Age': Older Women Reflect on the Use of Lipstick." *Journal of Women & Aging 21*(3): 198–212.

Cooley, Charles Horton. 1964 [1902]. *Human Nature and the Social Order*. New York, NY: Schocken Books.

Dellinger, Kirsten and Christine L. Williams. 1997. "Makeup at Work: Negotiating Appearance Rules in the Workplace." *Gender & Society 11*: 151–177.

Hall, Matthew, Brendan Gough, and Sarah Seymour-Smith. 2012. "I'm Metro, Not Gay!": A Discursive Analysis of Men's Accounts of Makeup Use on YouTube. *Journal of Men's Studies 20*(3): 209–226.

Holmes, Elizabeth. 2013, July 11. "Is It Me, or Is It Makeup? New Products Aim to be Invisible; P&G Finds a 'Natural' Look Signals Competence." *Wall Street Journal* (Eastern edition), D-1.

iTunes. https://itunes.apple.com/us/app/selfie-photo-editor-cosmetic/id781409730?mt=8. Accessed January 20, 2015.

Lowder, J. Bryan, Miz Cracker, and Christian Lesperance. 2014. "Ask a Homo: A Queen on Queens." (video) *Slateoutward*. Accessed January 6, 2015. Retrieved from http://www.slate.com/blogs/outward/2014/11/05/ask_a_homo_drag_queen_miz_cracker_takes_questions_about_her_art_video.html.

Makeup. n.d. In *Merriam-Webster.com*. Accessed January 12, 2015. Retrieved from http://www.merriamwebster.com/ dictionary/make%20up.

Merskin, Debra. 2007. "Truly Toffee and Raisin Hell: A Textual Analysis of Lipstick Names." *Sex Roles 56*(9/10): 591–600.

Morgan (no last name). 2014. "What is #Feminist-Makeupping? Going Beyond the Hashtag to Discuss the Politics of Makeup IRL." *xoVain* (website). Accessed January 30, 2015. Retrieved from http://www.xovain.com/makeup/what-is-feminist-makeupping.

Nash, Rebecca, George Fieldman, Trevor Hussey, Jean-Luc Lévêque, and Patricia Pineau. 2006. "Cosmetics: They Influence More Than Caucasian Female Facial Attractiveness." *Journal of Applied Social Psychology 36*(2): 493–504.

Peiss, Kathy. 1989. "Charity Girls" and City Pleasures: Historical Notes on Working Class Sexuality, 1880-1920. In Robert Padgug (ed.), Passion and Power: Sexuality in history, pp. 57-69. Philadelphia: Temple University Press.

Permanent Makeup. n.d. "FAQ." *Sheila Bella Permanent Makeup* (website). Accessed January 13, 2015. Retrieved from http://permanentmakeupsocal.com/permanentmakeupfaq/

Power, Camilla. 2010. "Cosmetics, Identity and Consciousness." *Journal of Consciousness Studies 17*(7–8): 73–94.

Schweitzer, Marlis. 2005. "The Mad Search for Beauty: Actresses' Testimonials, the Cosmetics Industry, and the Democratization of Beauty." *Journal of the Gilded Age & Progressive Era 4*(3): 255–292.

Tilbury, Charlotte. 2014, April 17. "Youth-boosting Makeup for 40+ Skin: How to Conceal Redness & Feel Great." *Charlotte Tilbury* (blog). Accessed January 14, 2015.

Retrieved from http://www.charlottetilbury.com/us/blog/2014/04/how-to-conceal-redness-and-feel-great/.

Whitelock, Anna. 2014. *The Queen's Bed: An Intimate History of Elizabeth's Court*. New York, NY: Sarah Crichton Books.

WWD. 2013. "The 2013 Beauty Inc. Top 100." *wwd.com*. Retrieved from http://wwd.com/beauty-industry-news/beauty-features/the-2013-beauty-inc-top-100-7824155/.

Wright, Megan. 2006, August. "Doing Drag: Masculinity Beneath the Makeup." Paper presented at the Annual Meeting of the American Sociological Association, Montreal, QC.

17

DRINKING COFFEE

Pernille S. Stroebaek

Coffee (and coffee consumption) has a long history. From its availability in European coffee houses and salons starting in the seventeenth century, coffee has grown to become a daily convenience drink in most parts of the world (Cowan 2005). Although coffee consumption in the past was limited to *Tischgesellschaften* (table societies) (Habermas 1991), coffee consumption today is an integral part of our daily life. We drink our coffee at work, at home, with friends, and on the go. Indeed, we drink so much coffee that coffee consumption is being linked to social concerns and problems (Troyer and Markle 1984), as well as being treated as a potential health risk to body and mind (Higdon and Frei 2006). Searching for the words "coffee" or "coffee consumption" on the Internet yields pages on medical and pharmacological studies and ongoing debates about coffee and its potential health risks and benefits. You have to look for a long time before finding results that will provide you with information about coffee itself and its history and ubiquity in the world—a focus that I think is much more interesting.

"Caffeine is the world's most popular drug and coffee is its most popular agent" (Topik 2009: 101). Caffeine is, as with other stimulants such as tobacco and chocolate, largely a "social drug." Admittedly, the phrase "let's have a cup of coffee" does not mean "let's get buzzed on caffeine!" Instead, it very often means, "let's have a conversation" and the sociality of drinking coffee is hereby marked (Topik 2009, page 99). Caffeine is a drug that has shaped the politics and economy of whole countries (Pendergrast 2010) and coffee consumption has been marked by a history of advertising conspiracy, colonialism, and capitalism (Wild 2004). Whereas coffee in North America came to signify industry— with its accompanying development, money, and privileges, elsewhere, for many coffee-producing countries, coffee came to mark exploitation (Pendergrast 2010).

The coffee industry is fast. Recently, we find examples such as Nestlé's successful 2010 launch of "Nespresso" and Starbucks' massive global growth in stores and locations. Within 10 years Starbucks has more than doubled its locations globally, from locations in 28 countries in 2004 (Ruzich 2008) to locations in 65 countries in 2014 (Starbucks 2015). As stated on its website, "it's clear that our passion for great coffee, genuine service and community connection transcends language and culture" (Starbucks 2015). According to Ruzich (2008), a major part of Starbucks' global success comes from its ability to associate coffee with love and social responsibility. In-store language associating coffee drinking with exotic and romantic experiences and promoting Fair Trade and small family businesses in the coffee-producing countries are important indicators of its global success. "Starbucks aims to seduce us with comfort, romance us with relationships, and assure us that we are all working together for the good of the underprivileged" (Ruzich 2008: 440). However, Starbucks, as well as other large coffee companies, such as Costa Coffee, could not have grown into the huge corperations they have become without the everyday popularity of coffee consumption that we see today.

In our culture, caffeine is the most significant, widely used, and virtually omnipresent "social drug" of all. Indeed, coffee consumption carries personal significance and demarcates our day differently in the privacy of our home than in public spaces and differently when consumed alone or with others. Coffee is significant in work environments (coffee is an employee benefit in many workplaces) and likewise in many retail locations (such as gas stations or hair salons). Coffee is significant to the travel industry as coffee is served on trains and planes. In sum, coffee drinking expresses personal and social rhythms of people engaged in living in our global and mobile society today. I use the next few pages to illustrate this in terms of how we generally practice coffee drinking in our everyday lives.

At Home

> I'm not human until I've had my morning coffe …
>   —Carrie Bradshaw in *Sex and the City*

In the seventeenth and eighteenth centuries, coffee was consumed inside the closed social space of a coffee house or coffee salon. Coffee houses were associated with intellectual and political discussion, and for this reason they provided a special social scene. "Inside a coffee house, if a gentleman had decided to sit down, he was subject to the free, unforbidden talk of his social inferior" (Sennett 1992: 82). Thus, coffee houses permitted people to interact on a common ground (Sennett 1992), and this common ground was largely one of the sociality of knowledge sharing (Berger and Luckmann 1966). Indeed, in large European cities like London and Paris, many coffee houses even published their own newspapers and acted as miniature universities (Cowen 2005).

As the industrial age approached, coffee grew more and more popular, and it moved out of the closed rooms of coffee houses and into the private sphere of people in their own homes. Thus, the indoor location of coffee consumption was retained, but its availability changed greatly. During the ninteenth and twentieth centuries coffee grew into a daily convenience drink (Topik 2009).

Today we find our bags of coffee beans in the supermarket alongside other daily groceries such as paper towels and milk. Coffee is part of our home. We equip our kitchens with coffee machines or espresso machines and we buy beautiful porcelain jars for coffee storage that we exhibit on open kitchen shelves or on the kitchen table. Many of us have become "home baristas," buying into the growing industry of home espresso machines and milk steamers, thus raising the quality and variety of coffee available to us in our own home. Coffee drinking creates a break from laundry, cleaning, and other domestic work routines. Whether we drink our coffee alone, with other family members, or with friends, it is a drink and activity that we use to feel good.

Though caffeine is enjoyed more as a social drug, it is hard to deny that it is a stimulant that many of us enjoy alone, especially in the morning! Many of us do not feel awake or "alive" before having our morning cup of coffee. We need our "caffeine fix" to get started, and having our first cup of coffee sets the psychological alarm clock for the social activities of the day ahead. Many of us feel that the world can wait until we have had our first sip of our morning coffee. When having our "after-dinner coffee" or "evening coffee," we start wrapping up the day and its activities as we get ready to sit back, relax, and go to bed. Since coffee contains caffeine, well known for its energizing effect, we may choose a decaffeinated coffee in the evening, or sometimes we exchange our evening coffee for a hot cup of tea.

Having friends over for coffee often means a quick visit outside dinner hours. The "coffee date" is more informal and low key than a visit for dinner. It is a "let's get each other up to speed" conversation about what is going on in our lives just now. Conversations held over coffee are often spontaneous and somewhat unpredicatable. Of course, if the purpose of the coffee date is to discuss some particular events in our lives, then the content may be quite predictable. But regardless, having some occurring events in our lives that are motivating the coffee visit, then the content of the conversation is often pre-programed to these specific happenings. But, regardless, having coffee with friends is as much about conversation as consumption.

At Work

> … you don't get stress from sitting here. Here you can also get a cup of coffee.
>
> —Employee in a public service industry

Drinking coffee is an integral part of our work and business behavior. Many of us drink coffee while we work, and we drink coffee when we take a break from work. Serving coffee to customers and clients is a gesture of hospitality that often serves as the "icebreaker" of an encounter. Very often a meeting starts with the question, "Do you want some coffee?" In conference programs, "coffee break" appears as an already scheduled part of the program.

What goes on in a meeting where coffee is served of course, much more than just drinking coffee. Coffee drinking is a social gateway. As Fineman and Sturdy (2001) have suggested, offering coffee to participants in meetings at work is important, since it aides the human creativity that needs to take place there. This is especially true as regards the informal social order at work. As workers meet informally over a cup a coffee in the corners and corridors of their workplace, they create a social scene that allows conversations to take place in "hidden transcripts" in the "offstage" or outside of the hearing of the management or of other power holders, such as clients and customers (Scott 1990).

As I explored the social rhythms of a newly merged and changed organizational scene I encountered the importance of drinking coffee at work (Stroebaek 2013). I found coffee drinking among coworkers to be an anonymous acknowledged social norm of sharing. For the employees, coffee drinking was a social coping strategy at work. When sharing a cup of coffee with coworkers, employees were able to vent feelings of frustration and stress. Coffee drinking also mediated the relationships between newly hired employees and longer-term employees as they met and got to know each other through the cups of coffee that they got from the office vending machine. For these reasons coffee was of the utmost importance to employees. Indeed, coffee was one of the most important factors in group life at the office.

Thus, drinking coffee at work is not only part of workplace routine and culture, but also associated with personal and social well-being. Opening our eyes to the social significance of coffee at work makes us aware of the social psychology behind work-break behavior. Elton Mayo (1945) described this in terms of organizations carrying social value for workers. The social value of work makes employees feel like human beings and not machines, but it can also hold monetary value for the organization. Indeed, researchers have found that employees who had an extra coffee break during the working day performed better than employees without the extra break (Waber, Olguin, Kim and Pentland 2010).

On the Go

Traffic can wait.

—Tweet by Starbucks on Twitter

Drinking coffee "on-the-go" offers perhaps the starkest contrast to the ways in which coffee was consumed in the past. Although coffee drinking once was going on in salons and coffee houses (and later in cafes and diners), coffee consumption nowadays is almost as often "on the go." Used, "to go" coffee cups fill up garbage cans and street trash. When Starbucks created the slogan "traffic can wait," it was actually a bit ironic, since much coffee, in fact, is consumed in traffic. Starbucks' own share of the "to go" coffee industry is itself an example thereof. Coffee on the go is matching the fast food industry of our time and culture (Leidner 1993). Moreover, coffee that can be drunk inside an establishment or outside "to go" is a significant portion of the coffee service industry. This flexibility simply appeals to our modern way of living, where individual choice and selection is pivotal (Habermas 1991).

People traveling any considerable distance often get coffee to go. This is as a matter of practical necessity; indeed, we spend a lot of our daily life in transition. Coffee is frequently available to us in places connected with our commute: subway stations, gas stations, train stations; even on ferries. Coffee available in the public space of our everyday lives has become a special branch of coffee industry. New businesses are making their appearances, entering very selectively into the market for coffee to go. On the streets and corners of Copenhagen, the city where I live, there are mobile coffee carts parked at strategically chosen locations at chosen hours. Figure 2 shows such a cart, which I walk by every morning on my way to my son's daycare. It is parked outside the Danish Broadcasting Corporation's (DR) headquarters in Copenhagen. Like CNN and BBC headquarters, DR's headquarters has many employees and visitors coming in and out of the building every day, making it a perfect location for a coffee business. "Street coffee" is a business that competes with in-house coffee establishments, such as the workplace canteen. Today, not only do coffee drinkers come to coffee shops— the coffee shops are also coming to us, wherever we are in our daily routines and activities.

Figure 2

Coffee Drinking—Mixed and Stirred

Much more could have been said about both the history and presence of coffee consumption. I have chosen, however, to spend my few pages on the everyday routine of drinking coffee. "Drinking coffee" is a routine activity that we only occasionally think about or take special notice of. It is part of our popular culture and social existence every single day. I hope to have made one central point clear: Coffee is so much more than its caffeine effects and health risks or benefits. Coffee and coffee consumption are about sociability.

Much of our coffee drinking is routinized and helps us feel more comfortable in social occasions. It is a "social lubricant:" we share moments and make conversation when we share a cup of coffee with someone, whether we know each other already or not. Coffee is a modern gesture of "the syntactical relations among the acts of different persons mutually present to one another" (Goffman 1967: 2).

Coffee bridges the gap between what is private and what is public in our lives. When having our morning coffee at home, we may plan our day at the office. When sharing a cup of coffee with friends or colleagues, we create a social space where we are able to share personal feelings and opinions.

Exploring the ways that we drink our daily coffee reveals much about the "social rhythms" of our modern society (Blumer 1937: 877) in which our individual activities and social relations are subjected to social media such as Twitter and Facebook. Images connected with coffee drinking frequently appear on social media. For example, one of my friends on Facebook just posted a picture of a cup of coffee on a table, with the skyline of Sydney, Australia in the background. This picture was posted with the text "rooftop coffee." There was no picture of her. The picture of her cup of coffee with this particular backdrop says it all: "She is having a fabulous time in Sydney, Australia just now." Drinking coffee is part of our social life, whether our presence to one another is mediated face-to-face, through virtual reality, or simply when symbolically decoding a social scene of drinking coffee.

The coffee industry helps us to mediate our social and cultural beings as it guides us toward what, where, and which coffee we prefer. It offers us numerous establishments where we can drink or buy coffee. It provides commercials that help us learn about our choices, which are many. Indeed, coffee comes in all different kinds and flavors. It is not just the hot, black beverage it once was. Ice coffee, coffee syrup, and mixed coffee drinks are on the menu today. In fact, not all coffee drinks taste like coffee. I have a friend who does not like coffee and normally prefers tea as her chosen hot beverage. However, the other day she ordered a café latté with licorice. "I thought you didn't like coffee!" I said. "Well, I don't, but this doesn't really taste like coffee," she replied. Just the other day I passed by a coffee shop promoting a new coffee drink: Café latte with salty caramel flavor! If you don't like café latte, well, then what about Cocio Natural Energy Chocolate Milk + Guarana?[1] This is a Danish invention of chocolate milk mixed with coffee and guarana. So non–coffee drinkers, please join us in the modern age of coffee drinking!

Pernille S. Stroebaek is an Assistant Professor at the Department of Psychology, University of Copenhagen, Denmark. She holds a master's degree in psychology and completed her doctoral studies in August, 2011, for which she specialized in the social psychology of occupational stress. She is currently studying the everyday social rhythms of workplace well-being. She is especially interested in employees' well-being in emotionally taxing occupations, such as in service industries, with emphasis on the implicit social order of collective coping.

Note

1. Guarana is a dried paste made from the seeds of a South American plant.

References

Berger, Peter and Thomas Luckmann. 1966. *The Social Construction of Reality. A Treatise in the Sociology of Knowledge*. Garden City, NY: Anchor Books.

Blumer, Herbert. 1937. "Social Disorganization and Individual Disorganization." *The American Journal of Sociology 42*(6): 871–877.

Cowan, Brian W. 2005. *The Social Life of Coffee: The Emergence of the British Coffeehouse*. New Haven, CT: Yale University Press.

Fineman, Stephen and Andrew Sturdy. 2001. "The Struggles for the Control of Affect—Resistance as Politics and Emotion." In Andrew Sturdy, Irena Grugulis, and Hugh Willmott (Eds.), *Customer Service: Empowerment and Entrapment*. Basingstoke, UK: Palgrave, 135–156.

Goffman, Erving. 1967. *Interaction Ritual: Essays on Face-to-Face Behavior*. Chicago, IL: Aldine Publishing Co.

Habermas, Jürgen. 1991 [1962]. *The Structural Transformation of the Public Sphere: Inquiry into a Category of Bourgeois Society* (Thomas Berger, Frederic Lawrence, trans.). Cambridge, MA: MIT Press.

Higdon, Jane V. and Balz Frei. 2006. "Coffee and Health: A Review of Recent Human Research." *Critical Reviews in Food Science and Nutrition 46*(2): 101–123.

Leidner, Robin. 1993. *Fast Food, Fast Talk: Service Work and Routinization of Everyday Life*. Berkeley, CA: University of California Press.

Mayo, Elton. 1945. *The Social Problems of an Industrial Civilization*. Abington, UK: Routledge.

Pendergrast, Mark. 2010. *Uncommon Grounds: The History of Coffee and How it Transformed Our World*. New York, NY: Basic Books.

Ruzich, Constance M. 2008. "For the Love of Joe: The Language of Starbucks." *The Journal of Popular Culture 41*(3): 428–442.

Scott, James C. 1990. *Domination and the Arts of Resistance: Hidden Transcripts*. New Haven, CT: Yale University Press.

Sennett, Richard. 1992. *The Fall of the Public Man*. London, UK: Penguin Books.

Starbucks. 2015. (website). "Company Information." *Starbucks.com*. Retrieved from http://www.starbucks.com/business/international-stores.

Stroebaek, Pernille S. 2013. "Let's Have a Cup of Coffee! Coffee and Coping Communities at Work." *Symbolic Interaction 36*(4): 381–397.

Topik, Steven. 2009. "Coffee as a Social Drug." *Cultural Critique 17*: 81–106.

Troyer, Ronald J. and Gerald E. Markle. 1984. "Coffee Drinking: An Emerging Social Problem?" *Social Problems 31*(4): 403–416.

Waber, Benjamin N., Daniel Olguin Olguin, Taemie Kim, and Alex Pentland. 2010. Productivity through Coffee Breaks: Changing Social Networks by Changing Break Structure. *Social Science Research Network*. Retrieved from http://papers.ssrn.com/sol3/papers.cfm?abstract_id=1586375.

Wild, Anthony. 2005. *Black Gold: The Dark History of Coffee*. New York, NY and London, UK: Harper Perennial.

18

EXERCISING
Michael Atkinson

My Other Significant Other

I have been a self-proclaimed exercise enthusiast for the better part of the last 20 years. Not a single day passes without an array of complex negotiations occurring with family, coworkers and bosses, friends and others so that I can squeeze about two hours of physical activity into my life. I am not a professional athlete, personal trainer, preparing for a sports contest or event, or even in dire need of weight loss (or at least, no one in my life is pressuring me to lose weight at this particular moment), so rationalizing great periods in the gym, on my bike, in the pool or running through the wooded trails is difficult. To be sure, exercising is neither leisure nor something one approaches with passive concern; to "work out" as "serious leisure" (Stebbins 2007, 2012) is to take on another vocation replete with commitments, activities, perspectives, identities and relationships often incongruous with the cacophony of everyday life.

Exercise in the so-called spare time arena is indeed a jealous lover. Unlike work, it seems, many people's exercise habits involve a level of commitment that blends meritocratic and neoliberal work ethics, commitment to popular cultural calls to at least look fit and invested in the ubiquitous healthism discourses, and passionate interpersonal involvement. In a sense, it is more work than one's paid career and can often foster more close-knit and meaningful social ties than other personal involvements (because, after all, one *chooses* one's exercise companions). Attending to exercising as a matter of daily habit involves at a minimum: buying workout clothing, eating for exercise (quantities and qualities of food, proper timing), organizing work and family schedules to accommodate one's exercise, being physically tired and sore on a regular basis, learning how to enjoy pain, actually engaging in the activity (and/or training for the activity) for hours on end, buying a gym pass or facility pass to engage in the activity, taking hundreds of "selfies" while doing the activity and promoting it online through social media, driving or walking to and from the activity at all hours and in all environmental conditions, finding and interacting with sympathetic co-dependents who engage in the activity with similar fervor, reading information (magazines, websites, blogs journals, etc.) about one's activity of choice to deepen one's expertise, dealing with others who are unsupportive or critical of the activity, and of course, wanting to quit on a regular basis. Because one has never completed enough exercise and because fitness is not something one possesses but constantly invests in corporeally and (pop) culturally, the veritable exercise treadmill never turns off and demands unwavering monogamy. Quite simply, when one becomes a consummate exerciser, the practice is woven into the fabric of one's existence without seams or separation.

Given the above, a highly planned, integrated, and expansive personal exercise regimen is the height of corporeal self-indulgence. To engage in physical activity is to constantly self-reflect, monitor, measure, consume, self-scan, and uphold an unyielding commitment to self-improvement. Running, weightlifting, Pilates, soccer, hiking, cycling, sailing, hockey, fencing, snowboarding, spinning, Crossfit, or aerobics are rarely about others—they are about me and how I look, how I wish others see me, how I feel, and bolstering the functional capacity of abject "things" of mine which I will likely never see first hand (i.e., my brain, lungs, heart, kidneys, muscles, ligaments, etc.). As with Narcissus, the significant other I am truly enamored with is precisely my own self, as it is projected into and reflected back to me from a pool of popular culture. Exercise involves gorging on sensual stimuli, and worshiping at the altar of self-gratification. When one becomes fully immersed in the world of here-and-now corporeal exercise, it offers a glimpse of personal control in a culturally schizophrenic and temporally obliterated cosmos. The swelling of memberships and queues in gym classes, fitness clubs, and sports facilities testifies to Bauman's (2000) liquidly modern world in which we are all disembedded, melancholic and in search of a point of re-insertion through shared cultural practice.

Within the broader context of Canadian society, disengagement from exercise is not an option, moral or otherwise. The social pressure to exercise (and to develop healthy, active living as a modality of existence) permeates through popular media, "educational" discourses in school settings, fashionscapes, in the physician's office, and through peer networks. Framed through overly simplistic accounts of health as being achieved through "just being active," "integrating exercise that suits your lifestyle" through the consumption of workout regimes, gym memberships and clothing brands, or boiled down to a techno-scientific equation of "calories in, calories out," exercise is the duty of the contemporary bio-citizen. And your exercise regimen is more than 60 minutes of daily health work; your choice of exercise, exercise clothing, exercise friends, extended exercise family, exercise food, exercise-based vacations, and integration of exercise into all aspects of your life defines you socially and morally.

Still, everyday exercise could also be considered from another perceptual tack entirely. Because exercise is so spectacularly sensual it also has the potential to be aesthetically moving in a range of ways described by Prosaics theorists (Battani 2011; Rautio 2009; Saito 2008; Yi-Fu Tan 1995). Prosaics focus on the aesthetic and sensorial qualities of seemingly simple practices and their associated symbolic meanings in everyday environments. The systematic disregard by academics of culturally "crass" forms of aesthetic representations (such as exercise) in everyday life was first pointed out by scholars including Mandoki (2007). Prosaics, in essence, turns classical aesthetic theories and visions on their heads by analyzing the social conventions of what is approached as beautiful, appropriate, normative, taken-for-granted, disruptive, or challenging within popular constructions and everyday interactions. Prosaics researchers analyze a vast array of 'common' sensory-stimulating aesthetics in everyday existence (such as the moving body in exercise settings) and what they mean to people in the here and now of social interchange. The uptake and social use (of may we say even incredibly banal) everyday aesthetic practices can be studied in a host of physical cultural contexts. Prosaics thus democratizes the analysis of aesthetics in (popular) culture as a core disciplinary project, further pointing to the active social constructions and meanings of common aesthetics in shaping social life and consciousness. Building on Prosaics, I attend to exercise as one of the understudied mainstream arts of corporeal existence and aesthetics of everyday physical cultural life.

Doing Ashtanga

My corporeal proclivities for physical cultural pastimes, including triathlon, Parkour, long-distance running, mountaineering and orien-teering, and (most recently) yoga, have been loosely justified (or perhaps thinly justifiable to loved ones) in the last two decades, because I have chosen to study physical culture as a vocation. Without such a thinly veiled excuse for constantly doing physical activity, I am not sure I could wedge it into a daily schedule in which a partner, three young children, a professional career, and other social responsibilities compete for my consciousness.

As a woefully inflexible recreational athlete, I started practicing Ashtanga Yoga (hereafter, simply referred to as "Ashtanga") as a com-plementary strength and recovery technique to my running, duathlon, and triathlon adventures. Ashtanga is an ancient brand of yoga derived from the *Yoga Sutras of Patanjali* and the *Yoga Korunta*. The practice of Ashtanga focuses on generating heat in the body through a set of prescribed bending, balancing, and strength-building postures (called *asanas*), deep and cleansing breathing, and meditation. Like other forms of yoga in Canada, Ashtanga's popularity has grown almost exponentially since the 1990s and has become quite a popular cultural trend. Where one might have been hard-pressed to locate an Ashtanga studio in most Canadian urban environments in the early 1990s, options now abound.

Almost immediately after commencing my Ashtanga practice at a small studio in Hamilton, Ontario in 2005, I delved deep into Ashtanga culture and physical practice. I took classes, I read books, I bought yoga clothes, I started listening to yoga music and meditating, and I hung around with "yoga people." I moved away from the practice briefly while working in the UK (owing only to the lack of qualified instructors in my small town), only to resume it after returning to Canada in the summer of 2009. In the autumn of 2009, I stumbled across a traditional Ashtanga studio in Toronto (traditional studios are called *shalas*) and became engrossed with the practice once more.

Being an Ashtangi is arduous, life changing, and replete with suffering and pleasure for many reasons. First, there are two essential paths (*sadhanas*) one follows in traditional Ashtanga culture: the total devotee who abandons all else to pursue the practice, and the householder—the common Bill or Sally who has a family, career, and friends outside of yoga, but who wishes to practice Ashtanga nevertheless. And yes, Ashtanga yoga is a *total practice* of/for living. I once believed that Ashtanga simply referred to a set of traditional exercises performed in discrete time blocks of 60 to 90 minutes per day. In the *Yoga Sutras* (the textual basis of present-day Ashatanga culture), however, Patanjali writes that the two core principles for practicing yoga are abhyasa (devotion, or single focus on practice) and vairagya (non-attachment). Abhyasa means having an attitude of persistent effort (a physical, mental, and emotional practice) to attain and maintain a state of stable tranquillity (equanimity). To become well established, this needs to be done for a long time, without a break—it means, in the first instance, practicing asana (poses) six days a week, every week, without fail. This is not easy. The body, let alone the mind, wants to reject such idiocy. Vairagya is the essential companion of non-attachment; learning to let go of the many attachments, aversions, fears, and false identities that Ashtangis believe are clouding the true, and eternal, self.

The term Ashtanga is a composite of the Sanskrit words "ashta," meaning eight, and "anga," meaning limb. The practice of Ashtanga is an eight-fold path—distilled differently, there are eight steps or limbs for doing abhyasa leading to vairagya. Respectively, the eight limbs are: Yama (five moral restraints—non-violence, truthfulness, control of the senses, non-stealing, and non-covetousness); Niyama (five observances—purity, contentment, austerity, study of scriptures, and surrender to God's will); Asana (postures); Pranayama (breath control); Pratyahara (withdrawal of the senses); Dharana (concentration); Dhyana (meditation); and, Samadhi (a super-conscious state). Although the asanas and breathwork exercises are straightforward, morally controlling your life (not having sex too much, washing at particular times of the day, eating specific vegan dishes only, not socializing with morally questionable friends, avoiding public places and large crowds, turning off the media and focusing on quiet around the house) became for me overwhelming. Only then, when I had this realization, did I know I was "exercising" as a zealot.

Ashtanga is traditionally taught at The Ashtanga House using "Mysore style." This method is named after the city in India where Ashtanga originates; Mysore means "self-practice." Mysore style involves students moving through the practice at their own pace and level. The Ashtanga House in Toronto opens daily at 5:45 a.m. and Mysore practice runs until 1:30 p.m., with the exception of Saturdays (the prescribed one day off during the week). Mysore style is the traditional method of learning the practice, in which an individual is progressively given poses from an Ashtanga series by a teacher when the student is ready to receive them. One may enter the main Mysore practice room in a shala (like the one at The Ashtanga House in Toronto) at any time during the morning session and commence the asanas one has received to date. My teacher oversees Mysore practice every morning (after doing his own asana practice at home at 3:30 a.m.) along with 2–4 of his assistants who aid students with physical alignment in particularly problematic postures. The Mysore room is stiflingly hot, humid, dimly lit, sweat soaked, packed with bodies, and deathly quiet. The only audible sounds are feet hitting the mats at points and heavy, deep nasal breathing from practitioners. An individual with an established Ashtanga practice might take between an hour and two hours to complete Mysore-style practice in the morning, depending on his or her own personal level and experience.

The sheer demand of a daily practice constantly reminds me of the absolute centrality of *living* and not merely *doing* exercise. Daily practice is strongly encouraged in Ashtanga culture as a means of taking the first steps toward pursuing abhyasa. I knew, from very early on, that my entire style of life would need reorganization for me to pursue this practice. Why? In order for me to practice, I needed to manage the following: fitting daily practice into a schedule packed with work commitments that serve as "distractions" to one's exercise preferences (teaching schedule, committee meetings, research activities, reading, traveling to work, writing, and daily exchanges with people), family responsibilities (escorting my sons to and from school, spending time with my wife, wanting to do other physical things with them even when I was aching and sore from yoga, etc.), friendship duties, long-standing eating and sleeping habits, and a million other things. Breaking, shifting, realigning, and struggling with these everyday practices causes a range of suffering experiences at first; from the physical, to the affective, to the social. For instance, I hated carrying around sweat-drenched yoga gear after practice, but loved that I sweat profusely each day. One is asked, or rather forced, to be personally involved in these new aesthetics of everyday life. New people, new feelings, new places, new movement, new smells and sounds, new modes of movement, disrupted senses of balance, new aches, new everything. I had to travel nearly 80 kilometers from my house to the shala to practice asanas at 6:00 a.m. before work (which meant getting up each morning around 4:00 a.m. and having three espressos before heading out the door), get to bed by 8:30 p.m. most evenings, never eating after 6:00 p.m. (Ashtangis believe in practicing on an empty stomach), convincing my wife to assume all morning child-care duties, relinquishing many of my research projects and university-related responsibilities, culling my circle of friends outside of the culture for some time, and neglecting my running practices—in which I had found great pleasure for nearly two decades. Ashtanga, like any other physical culture, is indifferent to your life "beyond the mat."

By late 2010, I learned to hate the sound of my alarm clock and felt perpetually hung-over for weeks at a time, but I watched and experienced my body changing considerably, developed close friendships with a core group of people at the shala, and did whatever I could to participate in different aspects of the culture emanating from the studio, such as workshops, a 100-hour immersion course, and shala-organized social events like potlucks and art exhibits. After my evening bedtime story rituals with my two sons, I spent most nights reading yogic texts and sutras. Suffering transforms into pleasure. I now love yoga. I love surrounding myself with yogic "things." I love the smell of the mat, the heat in the practice room, and I am actually able to stand properly upright now, the complicated thoughts and philosophies rattling around in my head, and the small corner of my house that has become my personal practice room. Nearly four dozen ancient yogic texts and several 100 magazine articles fill a cabinet in my office. Vedic art adorns walls of my office and bedroom. My modality of living has changed dramatically, and I increasingly find it difficult to squeeze the rest of my life into daily life. The physical culture has become real in my life, structuring my daily activities, thoughts, and relationships.

The Aesthetic Art of Yoga as Exercise

Although exercise is, to a certain degree, about the feeling of vascularity after one has pumped the muscles, a moment of exhilaration discovered through the cultivation of a new physical skill, or joy in seeing inches melt away from the waistline, exercise is complicated along many social and cultural lines. As I became more involved in yoga, I lost weight, transformed my muscular shape and abilities, experienced pain and agony, became flexible, and pushed myself in new directions. I also redrew friendship lines and an array of social habits. But in surrounding myself with and embracing the other trappings of the practice, I also adorned my life with yogic material(ism) and inserted myself into a new aesthetic physical network. The objects of my cultural concern shifted, as they often do in exercise circles, and I transformed from a runner to a yogic "om boy."

Curiously enough, at the same time I immersed myself in yoga, popular culture has immersed itself in the practice headfirst as well. I started seeing dozens, then scores, then multitudes of scantily clad yoginis and yogettes sauntering to the supermarket in their lululemon gear. Endless types and manifestations of yoga are showcased in hip urban exerciseries and New Age centers in the city. Om symbols, images of Ganesh, and renderings of mystical third eyes are represented on t-shirts, billboards, and bumper stickers. It seems that exercise aesthetics truly know no bounds. My everyday yogic aesthetics are not mine; they are potentially everyone's. Like the bodies performing downward dogs, the images of yoga are not divorced from popular cultural trends, aesthetics, material productions, and broader systems of representation. From my body, to my yoga shala, to the community of practitioners in Toronto, to the vacuuming up of yogic practices and symbols into the sea of commercial health and exercise signifiers, I am reminded that yoga in the broader social sense (as in all forms of exercise) is not really about me after all. It never was, really. Yoga taught me that I may know exercise starting with my glycogen-drained muscles and sickeningly sweat-soaked mat, but I have experienced exercise through a range of senses, cognitions, and my cultural location as a seer.

But notwithstanding the above, Ashtanga is a perfectly suited physical cultural practice in the new millennium, because in the end, yoga is really about me and me alone. Yoga is my practice about my self, and my self-liberation. It is self-work in the most self*ish* consumptive sense. While one ostensibly follows a tradition, a pre-determined set of asanas, aesthetics, and life-rules, the real "somatic work" of yoga (Vannini, Waskul and Gottschalk, 2012) focuses on me. As a total physical cultural practice, it feeds my insatiable desire to self-explore, self-customize, and self-demarcate from others. That's why we love it, in the end. The flexibility and the sweat and the strength may invigorate, but the focus on my favorite subject, me, absolutely fulfils.

Michael Atkinson is Professor of Kinesiology Physical Education at the University of Toronto, Ontario, where he teaches physical cultural studies and research methods. His main areas of teaching and his research interests pertain to the experiences of human suffering as physical culture, existentialism, and ethnographic research methods. Michael's ethnographies have included the study of ticket scalping, tattooing, fell running, cosmetic surgery, animal blood sports, yoga, critically ill athletes, and child abuse in ice hockey cultures. He is the author of 10 books, has published over 70 journal articles and book chapters on physical culture, and his research has appeared in diverse academic journals around the world. Michael is past Editor of the *Sociology of Sport Journal,* former Chair of the Social Sciences, Humanities, Health and Ethics Committee at the Canadian Institute of Health Research, and is Director of the Sport Legacies Research Collaborative at the University of Toronto.

References

Battani, Marshall. 2011. "Aura, Self, and Aesthetic Experience." *Contemporary Aesthetics 9*: 1–2.
Bauman, Zygmunt. 2000. *Liquid Modernity*. Cambridge, UK and Malden, MA: Polity Press (in association with Blackwell Publishers).

Mandoki, Katya. 2007. *Everyday Aesthetics: Prosaics, the Play of Culture and Social Identities.* Aldershot, UK: Ashgate Publishers Ltd.

Rautio, Paulina. 2010. "Beauty in the Context of Particular Lives." *The Journal of Aesthetic Education 44*: 38–59.

Saito, Yuriko. 2008. *Everyday Aesthetics.* New York, NY: Oxford University Press.

Stebbins, Robert. 2007. *Serious Leisure: A Perspective for Our Time.* New Brunswick, NJ: Transaction Publishers.

Stebbins, Robert. 2012. *The Idea of Leisure: First Principles.* New Brunswick, NJ: Transaction Publishers.

Tuan, Yi-Fu. 1993. *Passing Strange and Wonderful: Aesthetics, Nature and Culture.* Washington, DC: Island Press.

Vannini, Phillip, Dennis D. Waskul, and Simon Gottschalk. 2012. *The Senses in Self, Culture, and Society: A Sociology of the Senses.* New York, NY: Routledge.

19

KICKING ASS

Dale C. Spencer

In June 2014, *The Onion* cited a fake 80-page report by the Department of Health and Human Services entitled "Average Male 4,000% Less Effective in Fights Than They Imagine" (Onion 2014). While meant to be a spoof, the article points to a truism regarding (primarily) men's perceptions of how much they "kick ass" and how little actual "kicking-ass" occurs in everyday life. This essay engages with one source of that paradox: the divergence between depictions of kicking-ass in popular culture (primarily in the martial arts film genre) and the scarcity of kicking-ass in everyday life.

In this essay, I delve into "kicking-ass." What I mean by this phrase is a state of being that involves the ability to single-handedly defeat multiple opponents in armed and unarmed combat. It is a formal adherence to a dominant masculine ethos that prescribes martial arts practice as a path for men (primarily) to kick-ass (cf. Connell 2005). The claim here is that the vision of kicking-ass presented in popular culture *influences* North American young and adult males, who think of themselves as able to kick-ass and, to a lesser extent, *animates* their choice to make martial arts practice part of their everyday lives. In relation to the latter, I am not referring to the very small minority of men and women who participate in cage-fighting contests (see Spencer 2009, 2011), but instead to the overwhelming majority who fill the ranks of (traditional) martial arts clubs across North America.

This essay draws on two sources to explore the divergence between popular culture visions of kicking-ass and the scarcity of kicking-ass in everyday life. First, I engage with writing, film, and academic materials on martial arts. Second, I draw on insights gleaned from a four-year sensory ethnography that I conducted of mixed martial arts (also known as cage fighting, or the Ultimate Fighting Championship), continuous engagement with Brazilian Jiu Jitsu and everyday life experience of not-kicking-any-ass-at-all.

Kicking-Ass in Popular Culture

As a young boy, martial arts and martial arts films fascinated me. If I behaved and hadn't picked on my younger sister, my dad would rent me martial arts movies. I can recall being filled with adrenaline at even the prospect of watching *Fists of Fury* or *Double Impact* on a Friday night. During the movie I would throw punches and kicks in the air, trying to emulate Bruce Lee or Jean-Claude Van Damme, letting out "eeee-yyaaas." What amazed me was that no matter how outmatched and overpowered, one guy, with skill and technique could overcome all odds and beat the "bad guys." This was, in many ways, in variance with my everyday experience of being bullied, as I was always the smallest kid in my elementary school classes. While my childhood experience is not necessarily typical for all children, very few boys in Western countries that grew up during and after the 1960s can claim that they did not have a fondness for this film genre and other "action" genres at some point.

For John Fiske (2006: 4–5), popular culture is "the culture of the subordinated and disempowered and thus always bears within it signs of power relations, traces of the forces of domination and subordination that are central to our social system and therefore to our social experience." Gender distinctions serve as sites of struggle for control over the meanings of masculinity and femininity in forms of popular culture. In relation to martial arts films, the allure owes "to the fact that they are ritual performances which symbolically deal with fundamental questions of human existence—power, the question for control, the search for identity" (Donohue 2002: 74). Martial arts films, as much as any action genre, taps into manifold forms of masculine desire for power and control.

The forms of fighting in martial arts, and action movies more broadly, are a flashy form of violence (at odds with the bungled form of violence that characterizes street fights) and is predicated on unlikely situations (Wetzler 2014). For example, it does not matter if the hero is heavily outnumbered in a street fight, his or her enemy combatants will patiently wait to attack them, dancing around in a threatening manner until the hero has defeated their predecessors. This propagates a mythic understanding that street violence is honorable and one man can take on many opponents, overcome adversity, and reign victorious. In addition, popular cultural representations of martial arts rarely, if ever, are invaded by the concerns of everyday life. The hero fights non-stop without the need for sleep, food, or to use the bathroom. In the next section, I consider the relationship of this vision of kicking-ass to the experience of everyday life.

Everyday Life and Kicking-Ass

For Henri Lefebvre (1947, 1971, 2008), everyday life is a product of the modern world and is the realm of quotidian, taken-for-granted experiences, beliefs, manners, and practices, all of them dominated by reproduction and maintenance. The everyday is taken to be banal and seamless, undifferentiated by events, and centered on consumption (rather than production). Antipodal to everyday life is the heroic life (Simmel 1907). A figure primarily of a distant history, the heroic life places emphasis on resisting everyday routine activities and subjugating the everyday for a higher purpose. Featherstone (1992: 164–165) argues that heroic life is based on "the courage to struggle and achieve extraordinary goals, the quest for virtue, glory and fame, which contrasts with the lesser everyday pursuit of wealth, property and earthly love." The heroic life is the sphere of danger, violence, and the courting of risk to which the hero seeks to prove himself by displaying courage and sacrificing one's life (Featherstone 1992). The heroic life is analogous to the life of the hero in martial arts film. The heroic life, then, is that which is suppressed by a growing civility in Western societies (Elias 2000; Pinker 2012), where the mounting concerns of everyday life predominate.

For Norbert Elias (2000), the theorist of all things "civilized," Western society has gone through successive civilizing spurts. These spurts are reflected in our manners and in an overall reservation about violence. The civilization of Westerners demands a greater level of restraint, with far fewer moments for cathartic acts of violence. We come to act more civilly towards cantankerous neighbors and colleagues. For example, we are less apt to ask our continuously obnoxious colleague, who seems to be consistently naval gazing and oriented toward making everyone else's lives more difficult, to step outside and have a good old fashion scrap. This was, as the histories of street fighting and gun and sword-based dueling demonstrate, a past reality for all classes (Kennedy 1999; Muir 1998).[1] I am not lamenting a somehow better, more violent past. I only emphasize, as Elias does in his own way, there is much less kicking-ass going on in contemporary Western society.

In a different vein, Randall Collins (2009) also illustrates why there is a lack of kicking-ass in contemporary society. In his study of the micro-sociology of violence, he asserts that "violent interactions are difficult" (Collins 2009: 20) and states that in every violent interaction there is what he refers to as confrontational tension. He utilizes this concept to discuss those moments of higher intensity before violence that shade over into fear. It is this emotional component, according to Collins, that inhibits individuals from engaging in violence. He explains that disfunctioning bowels and other unsavory reactions are found in situations of high tension and fear. Only those who learn to overcome confrontational tension—the violent few—are able to effectively engage in kicking-ass.

What is, for the most part, eschewed in Collins' account is the impact of civility *and* the demands of everyday life that mitigate even a "trained" fighter's propensity to refrain from violence. Consider the following vignette, written after a turbulent afternoon:

> It is 3:00 p.m. on a Saturday and I am taking my six-month-old daughter to Costco to pick up groceries, which after looking at the list, looks like enough food and toiletries for the next year or so. We arrive at the parking lot and it seems like everyone in Ottawa is shopping at Costco. I drive around the one side of parking lot, going up and down the aisles, occasionally looking into other people's cars that are trying to find a spot, seeing the sort of grimace humans only get when they are behind the wheel. Eventually I make my way over to the other side of the parking lot and spy a car pulling out of a spot. I throw my left hand turn signal and

prepare to drive my car into the spot. The medium-sized sedan pulls out and I make my way into the opening. Pulling forward I get half way into the spot and in my peripheral vision see what looks to be a monstrosity qua over-sized truck also pulling in. We are both half way into the spot and I throw up my hands and look over at them in astonishment. Emptying their jumbo pick-up truck like a hillbilly clown car, mother-daughter-father-son come lumbering up to my vehicle, shouting as they get closer, throwing their hands up in the air. Here I am thinking, should I get out of the car? Heat wells in my head and my eyes are wide open looking out the driver side window as the son has his face pressed up into the window, pointing his finger at me and saying in a really loud voice, "I am going to kick your ass if you don't move!" I am now incensed. Right before I begin to roll down the window, I look up in my rear-view window and see my daughter unaware of what is going on, her mouth pumping away on her soother. I shake my head at the clowns to my right and pull my car out of the spot and drive past them shaking my head. I swallow the saliva in my mouth which now feels like a piece of sandpaper going down my throat …

This seemingly preposterous, potentially violent, situation may not be commonplace, but it points to a number of elements of everyday life that stand in the way of kicking-ass. First, driving is a mundane element of everyday life (Thrift 2004, 2007), which produces a cyborg body that impacts on ways in which people experience, sense, and encounter driving and other drivers. It is also a site of high levels of tension and "road rage" (Lupton 1999). A highly trafficked parking lot transforms into a site of high levels of tension as people try to find a parking spot. Due to the fact that drivers transform into cyborgs, my attempt to take what the other driver thought was his spot is seen as an affront to the other driver. Second, everyday life is filled with concerns over one's loved ones. My affection for my daughter mitigated my decision to even attempt to get out of the car and kick-ass as such concerns are antithetical to a heroic life. The third, and perhaps the most salient blockade to getting out of the car and kicking-ass, is my interpretation of such a ridiculous situation as barbaric and at odds with my sensibilities as a professor and a feminist.

While my clown-like opponents are seemingly not beholden to the civilities of the law and the generalized other that is society, the restraints of a more civilized approach to interpersonal relations overrides a more visceral reaction to such road rage. Lastly, there is the matter that this situation clearly does not meet the situations customary of kicking-ass in martial arts films. In the next section I consider the aspirations to kick-ass and the actual practice of martial arts as part of everyday life.

Sport, Friendship, and Kicking-Ass

One modality by which, primarily men, engage in violent cathartic activities is through sport. Through pacification and parliamentization, much of the violent aspects have been cleansed from sport (Dunning 1999). While participation in martial arts is cathartic, there is an added presumption of being able to kick-ass. Across North America, adults join martial arts clubs in the hope of being able to defend themselves. In 2003, the Simmons Market Research firm reported 18.1 million Americans participated in some martial arts during that year (American Demographics 2003). While this indicates some of the prevalence of martial arts schools, over the last decade there has been an additional explosion due to the ever-increasing popularity of the Ultimate Fighting Championship and mixed martial arts (a.k.a. cage fighting) more broadly (Downey 2014; García and Malcolm 2010). The practice of martial arts, then, makes up a part of the everyday life of a significant proportion of North American population.

With so many people making martial arts practice part of their everyday life, one would expect a whole lot more kicking-ass. But kicking-ass is, as will be demonstrated, contravened by the realities of life in martial arts clubs and how bodies speak back against efforts to kick-ass. In relation to the former, martial arts take on a neotribal character for those that get hooked on martial arts practice. Michel Maffesoli (Maffesoli 1993, 1995) asserts that our friendship relations are increasingly characterized by "fluidity, periodic assemblies and dispersals" (Maffesoli 1993: xv). The rituals associated with martial arts, founded on cooperation between neotribal members, intensify and reinforce the affective bonds between practitioners. Friendship serves as one of the key reasons that individuals remain committed to martial arts practice, and concomitantly stands in the way of fully kicking-ass. As a general rule in respect to one's training partners qua friends, the mantra remains: "What happens in the gym stays in the gym." That is, even in the event of something that looks like kicking-ass, it stays within the confines of the club out of respect for the tribe.

With friendship and cooperation serving as the bedrock of everyday life in the martial arts gym, there is also the fact that flesh and blood bodies participate in martial arts practice (cf.Wacquant 2006). As shown in the following field note created after a Brazilian Jiu Jitsu (a ground fighting style of martial arts) training session, the act of training contravenes kicking-ass, even in the gym.

It is a half hour before the end of class and Henry is in front of the class and the rest of the class is lined up along the wall waiting for his instructions. "Alright, time for rolling;[2] pick your partner and we are going to have 6 minute rolls. Remember, you are not fully warmed up, so go easy for the first round". Ryan picks me and I am hesitant to roll with him because of his tendency to go hard. We pick a spot on the mat and when the bell rings for the timer, we slap hands and get ready to roll. I immediately pull guard[3] and the match goes to the mat. Ryan immediately breaks the guard by pushing down on my leg and stepping over, putting me in half guard.[4] Immediately he spins around and goes for a knee bar (on my already injured knee). As he applies the technique my knee pops and I yelp in pain. I stumble off the mat and sit down on the side for the rest of the session. I am pissed and in pain at the same time. Ryan comes over and says, "I am sorry; I did not mean to hurt you." I keep my head down and acknowledge his apology by bobbing my head up and down. The bell rings and the rolling session ends and Henry comes over immediately and asks me if I am ok and I inform him I am out for the rest of the class. He walks back in front of the class that is now lined up for the next roll. He pauses and then addresses the class, "You know guys, when you are rolling with your teammates, you are placing a lot of trust in them. Your safety and health is in each other's hands. It is so important that you are careful with your partners or you will not have anyone to train with."

The reality of kicking-ass in martial arts is exposed in this excerpt: flesh and blood bodies break down and continuously stand in the way of kicking-ass. Pain and injury are a normal part of everyday life in martial arts clubs, especially those whose practice is based on real time physical techniques. While I was injured in this case, Ryan has been hurt numerous times (perhaps more than anyone else), because of his propensity to go hard and try to kick-ass. This reaffirms Thrift's (2007: 10) assertion that the everyday experience of embodiment is characterized far more by failures and suffering than focused intensity. Concomitantly, for those that are careful with their training partners, this joint action is far more cooperative and playful than they are "violent" situations.

(Not) Kicking (Much) Ass

As I sit and watch *Shrek* for what seems like the fiftieth time with my son and daughter, a film filled with ogres and princesses kicking-ass, it reaffirms just how absurdly otherworldly kicking-ass is. It is, in the end, a product of media culture. While it is to a degree encouraging to find unlikely heroes and female heroines in children's action and adventure films like *Shrek*, it also points to the continuous infusion of kicking-ass in popular culture. At the same time, the everyday practice of watching TV sitting slouched on a sofa with my two kids involves not-much-kicking-ass, and for this author's broken down old body that is just fine.

Dale C. Spencer is a criminologist and socio-legal studies scholar and is an Assistant Professor in the Department of Law and Legal Studies at Carleton University in Ottawa, Ontario, Canada. His main interests are violence, gender, victimization, and the criminalization of marginalized populations. He has published two books, *Reimaging Intervention in Young Lives* (with Karen Foster, University of British Columbia Press) and *Ultimate Fighting and Embodiment* (Routledge), and two edited volumes, *Emotions Matter* (with Kevin Walby and Alan Hunt, University of Toronto Press) and *Fighting Scholars* (Raul Sanchez Garcia, Anthem Press) and his work can be found in a number of journals, including *Body and Society*, *Punishment and Society*, and *Ethnography*.

Notes

1. In the American context, the most famous duel was between then Vice President Aaron Burr and former Secretary of the Treasury Alexander Hamilton, which ended with Hamilton's death and Burr's exit from politics (Rorabaugh, 1995).
2. Rolling is the practice of grappling with an opponent on the ground in real time (at a high level of intensity), where participants use ground techniques, including guard positions, sweeps, holds, and submissions. Opponents try to submit their opponents using chokes, arm-bars, and leg-locks. When a participant gets caught in a submission technique, he taps on his opponent three times or says "tap" to his opponent to signal that she or he can no longer withstand the submission. The opponents then start over and resume grappling.
3. In this guard, legs are wrapped around an opponent's waist to control their posture and apply submission techniques.
4. In this guard, legs are wrapped around one of an opponent's legs tries to control the opponent's balance and base and sweep the opponent on to their back.

References

Collins, Randall. 2009. *Violence: A Micro-sociological Theory*. Princeton, NJ: Princeton University Press.

Connell, Raewyn. 2005. *Masculinities (2nd ed.)*. Berkeley, CA: University of California Press.

Donohue, John J. 2002. "Wave People: The Martial Arts and the American Imagination." In D. E. Jones (Ed.), *Combat, Ritual, and Performance: Anthropology of the Martial Arts*. Westport, CT: Praeger.

Downey, Greg. 2014. "'As Real As It Gets!': Producing Hyperviolence in Mixed Martial Arts." *Journalism, Media and Cultural Studies Journal [JOMEC Journal]* 5: 1–28.

Dunning, Eric. 1999. *Sport Matters: Sociological Studies of Sport, Violence, and Civilization*. New York, NY: Psychology Press.

Elias, Norbert. 2000 (1994). *The Civilizing Process: Sociogenetic and Psychogenetic Investigations*. (trans. Edmund Jephcott; Eric Dunning, Johan Goudsblom, and Stephen Mennell, Eds.). Oxford, UK and Malden, MA: Blackwell Publishers.

Fetto, John. 2003, May 1. "Your Questions Answered." *Advertising Age* (website). Accessed October 10, 2014. Retrieved from http://adage.com/article/american-demographics/questions-answered/44147/.

Fiske, John. 2006. *Understanding Popular Culture* (6th ed.). New York, NY and London, UK: Routledge.

Kennedy, Roger. 1999. *Burr, Hamilton, and Jefferson: A Study in Character*. Oxford, UK: Oxford University Press.

Lefebvre, Henri. 1971. *Everyday Life in the Modern World* (S. Rabinovich, trans.). London, UK: Allen Lane.

Lefebvre, Henri. 1991 [1947]. *Critique of Everyday Life, Volume 1*. (trans. John Moore,). London, UK and New York, NY: Verso.

Lefebvre, Henri. 2008 [1961]. *Critique of Everyday Life, Volume 2: Foundations of a Sociology of the Everyday*. (John Moore, trans.). London, UK: Verso.

Lupton, Deborah. 1999. "Monsters in Metal Cocoons: 'Road Rage' and Cyborg Bodies". *Body & Society* 5(1): 57–72.

Maffesoli, Michel. 1993. *The Shadow of Dionysus: A Contribution to the Sociology of the Orgy.* (trans. C. Linse and M. K. Palmquist). Albany, NY: State University of New York Press.

Maffesoli, Michel. 1995. *The Time of the Tribes: The Decline of Individualism in Mass Society.* Thousand Oaks, CA: Sage Publications.

Muir, Edward. 1998. *Mad Blood Stirring: Vendetta and Factions in Friuli During the Renaissance.* Baltimore, MD: Johns Hopkins University Press.

Onion. 2014. "Report: "Average Male 4,000% Less Effective in Fights Than They Imagine." *The Onion 50*(24): 1. Retrieved from http://www.theonion.com/video/report-average-male-4000-less-effective-in-fights-36321.

Pinker, Stephen. 2012. *The Better Angels of Our Nature: Why Violence Has Declined.* New York, NY: Penguin Books.

Rorabaugh, William. 1995. "The Political Duel in the Early Republic: Burr v. Hamilton." *Journal of the Early Republic 15*(1): 1–23.

Sánchez-Gárcía, Raúl and Dominic Malcolm. 2010. "Decivilizing, Civilizing or Informalizing? The International Development of Mixed Martial Arts." *International Review for the Sociology of Sport 45*(1): 39–58.

Simmel, Georg. 1907. *Simmel on Culture: Selected Writings* (David Frisby and Mike Featherstone, Eds.). London, UK and Thousand Oaks, CA: Sage Publications.

Spencer, Dale C. 2009. "Habit(us), Body Techniques and Body Callusing: An Ethnography of Mixed Martial Arts." *Body & Society 15*(4): 119–143.

Thrift, Nigel. 2004. "Driving in the City." *Theory, Culture & Society 21*(4–5): 41–59.

Thrift, Nigel. 2007. *Non-Representational Theory: Space, Politics, Affect.* New York, NY and London, UK: Routledge.

Wacquant, Loïc. 2006. *Body and Soul: Notebooks of an Apprentice Boxer.* Oxford, UK: Oxford University Press.

Wetzler, Sixt. 2014. "Myths of the Martial Arts." *JOMEC Journal 5*: 1–12.

20

WATCHING THE SUPER BOWL

Bernard D. Glowinski and Joseph A. Kotarba

A recent Pew Research Center's social trend study titled "Who's a Sport Fan?" concluded that 46% of all Americans, just under half the total population, are sports fans (2010). There is something special, however, about the Super Bowl and its fans: the Super Bowl is not simply another football game or even another championship football game. The Super Bowl has a way of magically transforming all the experiences and activities of an entire day into a special *day*. Metaphorically, Super Bowl Sunday is much like Christmas, which is a day much more complex than the singular celebration of the birth of Jesus Christ or the culmination of a month-long shopping orgy.

One of the most interesting aspects of the power of Super Bowl Sunday is the way simple and common places like sports bars (and bars in general) are transformed into Super Bowl scenes. *Scenes* are rich and complex cultural settings that produce much more than just music, art, or other cultural events (Irwin 1977; Kotarba, et al. 2009). In this project, we will describe the rituals, anticipations, social rhythms, and emotional webs that together turn the bar into much more than a place to meet and drink. The Super Bowl scene is a place and space that include a range of players who include football fans, non-football fans, waitresses, bartenders … and sociologists!

We watched Super Bowl XLIX at two sports bars and one regular bar in San Marcos, Texas over the course of game day, February 1, 2015. Sports bars generally have a number of flat screen televisions to show sports programming, may have billiard tables and electronic dart boards, and also serve liquor and food (Eastman and Riggs 1994). We compared notes in terms of our contrasting viewpoints as a NY Giants fan (Bernard) and a Houston Texans fan (Joe) navigating through what would ordinarily be Dallas Cowboys country on a typical Sunday. The core phenomenon in question is the way Super Bowl Sunday draws disparate fans and non-fans into an arena to reflexively construct and share Super Bowl Sunday (Mehan and Wood 1975).

Pre-Game Rituals

Bernard awoke on Super Bowl Sunday realizing that his favorite team was not playing for the Vince Lombardi trophy, but he still determined to watch the game because he is a Super Bowl fan. Bernard's major pre-game ritual today was choosing what jersey to wear. The wearing of a sports jersey by any fan is an indication that the individual shares an identity with others who wear the same jersey (Cottingham 2012). The sports jersey symbolically creates a sense of moral superiority among those who wear the same jersey. It also functions as a *sacred* object (Durkheim 1975) because it symbolizes the essence of a team's fandom more than simply serving as a piece of clothing. One shortcoming of the sports jersey is that no one really knows what kind of fan he or she "really" is (Borer 2009). Some jersey wearers are hard-core fans and will wear their jerseys no matter how the team is doing, while other jersey wearers are fair-weather fans and only put on the jersey when the team is winning, or as a fashion statement (Borer 2009). Bernard quickly decided to wear his Giants jersey.

The Beginning: a Journey to the Sports Bar
(Suiting Up for the Super Bowl)

As Bernard walked down the path to downtown San Marcos on this warm and sunny morning, he entered a convenience store to purchase a drink. The checkout clerk was wearing her Cowboys jersey, so Bernard asked her, "Who is going to win today?" She responded, "It won't be the Cowboys, so I don't care, plus I have to work on Super Bowl Sunday." Bernard told her supportively, "Super Bowl Sunday should be a legal holiday and she should be paid double time for working on Super Bowl Sunday," and she readily agreed. In the parking lot, a carload of college kids noticed Bernard's jersey and yelled out the window of their car, "Go Cowboys!" so Bernard yelled back, "Go Giants!"

The relationship between one's favorite team and the Super Bowl teams can be complex. One can cheer for a team as a secondary favorite. For example, Bernard noticed two teenage boys sitting on a park bench and asked the boys who they thought would win the Super Bowl. Both said that they were Cowboy fans but hoped the Seahawks would win because they represent the NFC, the conference in which the Cowboys compete.

Bernard arrived downtown about half an hour before Super Bowl XLIX's five and a half hour pre-game show began, so he decided to stop at the local downtown supermarket to purchase a cannoli. The shoppers, many of whom wore Cowboys jerseys, had carts filled with chicken wings, beer, chips, and house party accessories. These shoppers were fans preparing for a very different type of Super Bowl Sunday experience: the house party. They had the luxury of sporting their Cowboys jersey because they did not have to choose between Super Bowl teams as fans in the sports bars later did.

The Pre-Game Show

Bernard arrived in front of two sports bars, The Purge and Picture Perfect, which are located next to each other. The Purge has sliding glass doors that open so patrons can be seated up to the sidewalk, where they can enjoy the sunshine, eat and drink, but can still view and hear the TVs. Picture Perfect is similar in design, but is larger and offers dozens of beers on tap. Patrons are able to gather on the sidewalk in front of both bars to smoke, socialize, and play with their dogs.

Approximately four hours before the game, employees and customers began to enter both bars. The bartenders—all very attractive, cheerleader types of women—wore sports jerseys. They were of similar build, height, and hairstyle, and dressed in black tank tops and mini-skirts. As the pre-game show began, most patrons paid little attention to any of the TVs, only to the menus and each other. A number of these customers were there only for Sunday lunch and left in time to watch the Super Bowl at home or at private parties.

The sports bars had opened their doors and set out their food and drink specials, which included chicken wings, brick-oven pizza, and drinks. The specials began at four-thirty, but a number of fans remained out front sipping cocktails, watching people, and enjoying the weather. The Purge has a round bar for fans to sit and drink at, and the sports viewers can experience viewing round television screens that are circular with the bar. Some of the TVs had the pre-game show on, but other TVs showed women's college basketball, the World Series of Poker, professional soccer, and other regular Sunday afternoon fare.

The pre-game show on NBC started off with coverage on the investigation of "inflate gate," the term coined by the media for the scandal following the 2015 AFC Championship Game, when the New England Patriots were accused of cheating by under-inflating the footballs that were used for the championship football game. In a sanctimonious tone, the announcers boldly claimed that the Super Bowl today would not commit that sin. After an hour into the pre-game show, Bernard noticed how all of the ex-NFL players, who were now expert announcers for the game of football, were all showing off their Super Bowl Championship Rings: a symbol of masculine achievement of using the body as a weapon (Messner, et al. 2000), and signifies the pain and suffering the wearer had to endure to deserve the privilege of wearing it (Jones 2015).

The sports bars maintained other pre-game Super Bowl rituals, generally involving drinks and food. The bars had free food giveaways, ranging from a raffle for pizza to actual trays of finger food available at the bar. For example, drink specials included "three dollar calls," for drinks including "top shelf" liquor. This special hospitality served not only to entice customers into the bar, but also encouraged them to stay for the duration of the upcoming game.

As we approached game time, and Joe joined Bernard, patrons' appearance and demeanor changed. Several Cowboys fans were talking to a male bartender who was wearing a Detroit Lions jersey, but they all appeared to be buddies. A significant feature of Super Bowl Sunday is the way sports bar regulars feel free to project their typical and authentic team identifications (Vannini and Williams 2009). Joe recalls, when he was considerably younger and the American Football League was new, how wearing a Cincinnati Bengals or Denver Broncos jersey in Chicago marked one as adventurous, creative, and not parochially limited to being a Bears fan just because one lived in Chicago. The manager of Picture Perfect maintained the celebrity atmosphere surrounding the Super Bowl, taking pictures of her all-female bar staff. A few of those pictures would soon appear in the college town's free and promotional weekly newspapers. Picture time was over; it was 10 minutes after five o'clock and time for Joe and Bernard to find a seat for the Super Bowl.

The Game, First Quarter: Gender at the Bar

Bernard and Joe settled in at Picture Perfect for the Super Bowl. As the last of the pre-game activities proceeded, the importance of gender distinctions came to the fore. A female fan reverentially reminded the bartender all TVs must be tuned in to the game (Eastman and Land 1997), as opposed to other sports events on which the men would be betting. Men and women fans were enjoying spicy chicken wings, the preferred food of the Super Bowl (Messenger 2010). The Seahawks won the coin flip, and the game began.

Over the last thirty years or so, women have become major consumers of professional sports memorabilia, but the memorabilia has different gendered meanings (Borer 2009). Professional sports are still male-dominated. However, women are choosing identities "within the hegemonic masculine symbolic code that defines the boundaries of authentic sports fandom" (Borer 2009: 2). Males are expected to have sports knowledge, and the more sports knowledge the male has acquired, the more masculine and devoted fan he is perceived to be. Women who have greater sports knowledge than most men are considered deviant because they are attempting to present themselves as an equal to the dominant male sports fan (Wenner 2013). Some females wear football jerseys to accessorize themselves and are more interested in the material and social aspects of the game (Borer 2009). According to Eastman and Land (1997), some women go to sports bars just for the social interaction because there are single men in sports bars, but their increasing knowledge of sports can blur gender distinctions.

On this Super Bowl Sunday, the women held their own. Even as the game began, the sports bars were humming with fans who were drinking, eating, and playing with their cell phones, but not really paying attention to the TVs. Surprisingly, most men were playing with their cell phones while most women were paying attention to the football game. The men were in fact involved with the game, but through the framework of gambling information (e.g., "Vegas boards") or game analysis shared with friends at other locations.

As Bernard and Joe enjoyed their buffalo wings, Number 12 threw an interception in the end zone. The crowd cheered and everyone at the bar had a shot of liquor, but no shots specifically designated as Super Bowl favorites. As the game progressed, patrons were talking so loud that it was hard to hear the TVs. The essential sociality aspect of Super Bowl Sunday was clear. At the end of the bar, there was a group of men and women who were not costumed in jerseys, but they all seemed to have an interest in the Super Bowl. They were playing "squares," a game of chance in which the winner has the correct two last numbers for the game score at the end of each quarter. A bartender held the money collected—ranging from 5-dollar to 50-dollar squares—and then distributed it to the winners. The involvement of the bar keeps the squares honest, and the game attracts football fans to the bar. Interestingly, playing the squares was open across the bar, without fear of police surveillance. As Aziz (2015) notes, betting on the Super Bowl is yet one more way seasonal fans can fit in to an entertainment activity that creates excitement, self-esteem, chance, self-delusion, and potential addiction.

The Second Quarter: Families at the Bar

When we stepped next door to The Purge, the front of the bar and the porch were filled with smokers and drinkers, so we quickly exited to the rear where there was better seating and healthier breathing. We ordered a couple of beers with our chips and noticed that this sports bar housed a wider array of patrons. The Purge seemed to be the place where older non-fans would go just to be able to say, the next day at work, that they went to a sports bar to watch the Super Bowl.

There were several tables occupied by families. Some of the adults wore Cowboys jerseys, while some of the children wore Cowboys t-shirts. In one corner, a father sat with his two young children, feeding them chicken tenders and soda pop while explaining what was happening in the game. The kids seemed much more interested in the chicken tenders. The waitress walked up with beers and chips, and Joe asked if she was excited about halftime and Katy Perry and her mostly snotty response was, "Why? Should I be?"

Through the second quarter, the announcers spoke through the affirmative ideology of the NFL, how "inflate-gate" is being controlled, and how the NFL builds communities and wholesome family values. The elephant not in the room was talk about the players who had domestic violence issues throughout the season. The commercials were wholesome and family oriented—we did not recall seeing so many fathers in previous Super Bowl commercials. The fans we talked with almost all agreed that there were not any cutting edge commercials this year, only family-orientated perceptions that everything will be alright as long as you buy this product—very religious, very capitalistic, or very Marxist depending on your political persuasion. The second quarter ended in a 14–14 tie, so whoever was doing fandom by gambling and had double fours on the squares made a nice hit.

Half Time: Katy Perry, Lenny Kravitz and Missy Elliot

Half time had started, and there was a lot of movement in The Purge—to the bathrooms, to the porch for a smoke, etc. We were glued to the TV to watch the halftime show. Katy Perry started the show by riding a huge mechanical lion into the stadium as she sang "Roar." She was dressed very conservatively, but her wardrobe was colorful—typical of Katy Perry. After a quick costume change, she was singing "I Kissed a Girl" with rocker Lenny Kravitz. Katy Perry started "twerking" with Lenny, but only for a short but suggestive moment. Then, Lenny left the stage and Missy Elliot and Katy Perry sang "Get Your Freak On," but even this version of the song seemed pretty clean and conservative. After another quick costume change, Katy Perry was dressed to make her look like a wholesome pinup girl from the 1950s. Dancing sharks on either side reminded us of Katy's ill-fated experience with Sesame Street. Katy Perry ended the half time show by singing "Firework," and it was a great production where she was raised over the crowd on a shooting star. Joe paid the tab and left for home. As we walked out the front of The Purge, we both noticed that the front portion had emptied out. The patrons who conversed, played with their dogs, and smoked out front lost their interest in the game and left.

Third Quarter: A True Tavern is Discovered

Bernard gravitated to a third bar on the square for the third quarter. La Peppiest was nothing spectacular, and it is not considered a sports bar. It contained a traditional horseshoe-shaped bar with a big screen TV in the front of the bar and a few smaller TVs over the back of the bar. In the back, off to one side, there was a table with food provided by La Peppiest as occurs every Sunday. Everyone was playing squares, and all drinks were three dollars. Bernard placed himself right in the middle of the establishment so he could see both big screens and to be right in the middle of the contrasting team fans. The NFC fans—likely Cowboys fans during the regular season—up front were rooting for the Seahawks, and the New England fans were standing behind Bernard. The kickoff began the third quarter.

The Seahawk fans were all grouped at one end of the bar as a show of solidarity. They appeared to be locked in conversation with their dates and also seemed bored with the game. We will refer to these fans as *cocktail-party fans*, very formal in a sense. In contrast, the New England fans—seven women and five men—were partying. All of them but one were wearing some kind of sports jersey that represented the New England Patriots. The women in this New England crowd were more into the game than their male counter parts; they were hooting and hollering while the men pretended to be cool and collected. One female Patriots fan rubbed a Tom Brady doll, praying that her dedication to the Patriots would bring them good luck. Bernard asked a group of women, "Why Tom Brady?" Their response was, after looking at each other and snickering, "Just because." The third quarter came to an end, and the numbers for the squares is double fours again, just like the end of the second quarter … lucky bastards who drew double fours.

The Fourth Quarter: The Game of Chance

The fourth quarter started, and the fans who were rooting for the NFC began to do shots of top-shelf booze while toasting the NFC team for having a 10-point lead. However, the New England fans did not give up. They were encouraging each other to keep the faith so that good things would happen. All eyes were glued to the TVs as New England scored, but were still down three points. The Seahawks fans had noticed the score and began to minimize the sanctity of the Seahawks by stating that "the defense was getting tired, and you cannot always stop Brady." After the ball changed possession a few times, New England scored a touchdown to take the lead, and all of the NFC fans shivered as the momentum shifted to the New England fans. The NFC fans had gone completely silent while the New England fans were going wild and thanking God while *basking in reflected glory* (End et al. 2002). Seattle had possession of the football and completed a play for which the receiver caught the ball in a gracefully acrobatic way, putting the Seahawks on the three-yard line with three time-outs and the best running back in the game.

Now those cocktail party fans were acting like they were at a Super Bowl sports bar. The vibe of the room had shifted again after the catch, and the NFC fans were *basking in reflected glory* while the New England fans appeared to be praying and cutting off *reflective failure* (End et al. 2002) because all fans needed to protect their social sports identity. Then it happened: instead of running the ball into the end zone, the Seahawks chose to throw the ball, and it was intercepted by New England. The New England fans went crazy while basking in reflected glory, the miracle they were praying for came through, and Bernard heard a female Patriots fan say snottily to him, "How about that, New York?" Both Seattle and New England fans could not believe how the game ended on a miracle. The cocktail party fans seemed to be handling the loss in a very sophisticated manner by pointing out the errors made by the Seahawks, and how they could have prevented the loss. The New England fans only knew that they were witnesses to a miracle—party time!

It seemed like everyone who stuck it out at the bars for the entire day were exhausted. What a great Super Bowl … but, aren't they all great?

Bernard D. Glowinski is a graduate student in the master's degree program in the Department of Sociology at Texas State University. He is also a Student Associate with the Center for Social Inquiry at Texas State. Bernard's thesis focuses on the impact of mindfulness meditation on the experience and interpretation of violent popular music. This interdisciplinary study involves the collection of cardiovascular psychophysiological data from respondents. The sociological portion of this study is the "norming of a violent song." Bernard received his Bachelor of Science degree from Texas State University, San Marcos in December, 2012. He is also a veteran who served in the United States Navy from 1982–1986. Bernard is still very proud of the New York Giants, whose jersey he wore on Super Bowl XLIX Sunday and which was given to him by his Uncle Eddy in 1980.

Joseph A. Kotarba, Ph.D., is Professor of Sociology at Texas State University, where he serves as Director of the Center for Social Inquiry. He is also a faculty member at the Institute for Translational Sciences at the University of Texas Medical Branch, Galveston. Dr. Kotarba received his doctorate from the University of California, San Diego. His major areas of scholarly interest are culture, science, health and illness, everyday life social theory, and qualitative methods. Dr. Kotarba's most recent book is *Baby Boomer Rock 'n' Roll Fans* (Rowman and Littlefield, 2013), for which he received the 2014 Charles Horton Cooley Award for Best Book from the Society for the Study of Symbolic Interaction. He also received the Society's George Herbert Mead Award for Lifetime Achievement (2009), and the Mentor's Excellence Award (2010). Dr. Kotarba's other recent books include *The Present and Future of Symbolic Interactionism*, co-edited with Andrea Salvini and Bryce Merrill (FrancoAngeli, 2012), and *Understanding Society through Popular Music*, 2nd ed., co-authored with Bryce Merrill, Patrick Williams, and Phillip Vannini (Routledge, 2013).

References

Aziz, John. 2014, February 5. "How did Americans Manage to Lose $119 *Billion* Gambling Last Year?" *The Week*. (online journal). Retrieved from http://theweek.com/articles/451623/how-did-americans-manage-lose-119-billion-gambling-last-year.

Borer, Michael Ian. 2009. "Negotiating the Symbols of Gendered Sports Fandom." *Social Psychology Quarterly* 72(1): 1–4.

Cottinghan, Marci D. 2012. "Interaction Ritual Theory and Sports Fans: Emotions, Symbols, and Solidarity." *Sociology of Sports Journal* 29: 168–185.

Durkheim, Émile. 1915 (1912). *The Elementary Forms of Religious Life*. (trans. Karen E. Fields.) London, UK: Allen & Unwin.

Eastman, Susan Tyler and Arthur M. Land. 1997. "The Best of Both Worlds: Sports Fans Find Good Seats at the Bar." *Journal of Sport and Social Issues* 21(2): 156–178.

Eastman, Susan Tyler and Karen E. Riggs. 1994. "Televised Sports and Rituals: Fan Experiences." *Sociology of Sport Journal* 11: 249–274.

End, Christian M., Beth Dietz-Uhler, Elizabeth A. Harrick, and Lindy Jacquemotte. 2002. "Identifying With Winners: A Reexamination of Sports Fans' Tendency to BIRG." *Journal of Applied Social Psychology 32*(5): 1017–1030.

Irwin, John. 1977. *Scenes*. Beverly Hills, CA: Sage Publications.

Jones, Jack. 2015, January 21. "Cost of Super Bowl Rings." *Bet Firm*. Retrieved from http://www.betfirm.com/cost-of-super-bowl-rings/.

Kotarba, Joseph A., Jennifer L. Fackler, and Kathryn M. Nowotny. 2009. "An Ethnography of Emerging Latino Music Scenes." *Symbolic Interaction 32*(4): 310–333.

Mehan, Huge and Houston Wood. 1975. *The Reality of Ethnomethodology*. New York, NY: Wiley.

Messner, M.A., M. Dunbar, and D. Hunt. 2000. "The Televised Sports Manhood Formula." *Journal of Sport and Social Issues 24*: 380–394.

Messenger, Stephen. 2010. "By the Numbers: Super Bowl Facts and Figures." *Treehugger*. Retrieved from http://www.treehugger.com/culture/by-the-numbers-super-bowl-facts-and-figures.html.

Pew Research Center. 2010, November 4. "Who's a Sports Fan?" *pewsocialtrends.org*. Retrieved from http://www.pewsocialtrends.org/2006/06/14/americans-to-rest-of-world-soccer-not-really-our-thing/135-3/.

Vannini, Phillip and J. Patrick Williams (Eds.). 2009. *Authenticity in Culture, Self, and Society*. Farnham, UK and Burlington, VT: Ashgate Publishing Ltd.

Wenner, Lawrence A. 2013. "The Mediasport Interpellation: Gender, Fanship, and Consumer Culture." *Sociology of Sports Journal 30*: 83–103.

21
HOME-MAKING
Karen McCormack

Ten years ago, my family and I bought a 25-year-old house at the end of a cul-de-sac, a house that had been owned by only one family before us. Prior to that purchase, we had lived in several apartments, as well as in a house owned by the college where I was teaching. These were spaces which left some room for personalization (e.g., photographs on the wall, furniture), but in which many elements remained impersonal, chosen by landlords, and the same for all tenants. Choices such as whether we would have wallpaper or paint, hardwood floors or carpet, single sink or double, were decisions (often happily) out of our hands. Exterior spaces were similarly maintained and controlled by others, who would mow the lawn, plant flowers, trim trees, and maintain driveways or garages.

And so the day we signed the papers and picked up the keys to our house, life shifted a bit. Suddenly we were walking into the highly personalized space of a family who had lived there for 25 years. The walls were covered with paisley and striped wallpaper, the kitchen and living room were painted a deep brown, two overgrown blue spruce trees shaded the front of the house. While structurally the house needed very little care, we immediately began to make changes in an attempt to make it into not just our house, but also our home. We wanted the space to express our own style and to feel more modern.

The sense that we were creating a home for our children and ourselves permeated the choices that we made. The word "home" signifies many things and conjures for many people warm and fuzzy feelings of comfort and family. The notion of home implies stability and continuity, along with control over the space and the boundaries separating it from the outside. Home appears to offer its occupants a sense of predictability and control in an often chaotic world, a sense of ontological security (Dupuis and Thorns 1998; Giddens 1991). Yet "home" is not quite synonymous with dwelling, be it apartment, condominium, or house. Rather, home represents only a subset of these places. How, then, does a house or other dwelling become a home?

Ontological security must be constructed not only through residence, but also daily routine (Dupuis and Thorns 1998). The daily routines of home—from making breakfast to using the bathroom to building Lego towers—over time create home from the dwelling. These routines have always included activities that maintain the physical space both inside and out, including such things as chopping wood for the fire, repairing leaky roofs, or displaying beloved objects and photographs. Personalization of space is one particular aspect of home maintenance, and one that is created and maintained on an ongoing basis. Each repair is often an opportunity to choose a new style, a new product, a new look, a new you.

The objects in the home are all a part of material culture, which refers to the way that objects are invested with meaning and come to represent more than their utilitarian function might suggest. One obvious example of this can be found in objects that are handed down from one generation to the next, which are associated with history, family, and continuity. But even consumer objects that we purchase are often meaningful to us and may symbolize our understanding of ourselves and our place in the world. A particular sofa, for example, can represent class status (a Mission-style settle or a couch from Bob's Discount Furniture?), or the importance of comfort, leisure time, and family.

Defining the Style

Home renovation and do-it-yourself (DIY) projects are one central locus through which the house becomes home. DIY is often a practical solution to repairs, and it can be less expensive than hiring professionals for repair and remodeling. Along with cost savings, an ethic of independence and self-sufficiency often shapes the choice of DIY, which can symbolize competence, craftsmanship, and independence in a world dominated by mass-produced consumer products. Sweat equity, connoting the investment of labor in a project, is often used to describe an investment in a home that rivals or even trumps the monetary expense of the house.

One of our first projects, removing the wallpaper, is a long and tedious process that highlights several of the ways that DIY invests the occupant/do-it-yourselfer in the physical space. Removing wallpaper involves steaming and then carefully removing the paper one small strip at a time. The paper peels away, revealing the wall underneath—sometimes covered in additional paper, sometimes just drywall. Every scratch, marking, and irregularity becomes visible. Every cobweb or dusty corner must be addressed. And, when the drywall begins to peel off along with the wallpaper, the do-it-yourselfer must in fact figure out a way to repair the damage. Painting similarly leads to a familiarity with every inch of the interior, and then an often painful awareness of any imperfection in the application of the paint itself.

This familiarity with the dwelling and the responsibility for maintenance and improvement confer a sense of ownership, of control. We were peeling off the paper of a house that belonged to someone whose tastes shaped the structure—from their built-in drawers for sewing materials to the chair rail in the dining room. The house was theirs, and we had to make it ours.

Popular Culture and Personal Style

Clearly this process of personalization happens in particular contexts and is shaped by cultural discourse, one important part of which is "lifestyle television," reality programs designed to provide expert advice on everything from diet and exercise to home repair and decoration. While the domestic sphere had been relegated to the private and female realm in the Victorian period, matters of taste and lifestyle have spread from women's magazines into the mainstream and now flood our homes through television and the Web.

As one piece of the phenomenon known as reality television, lifestyle television has become a dominant genre, with networks devoted to these programs, like Home and Garden Television and the DIY Network in the United States. The rise in lifestyle television promotes a belief in an identity constructed through individual choices made about daily tasks, from choosing foods for dinner to choosing the "right" color scheme for your living room. Lewis (2011: 21) describes lifestyle television as providing "etiquette manuals for the twenty-first century;" manuals designed to provide advice and direction along with information. Often this advice seems to filter from professionals to the working class. Palmer (2007: 168) describes *Extreme Makeover: Home Edition* as a site where "… the working class learn taste, [and] the petit[e] bourgeoisie learn about 'real people' (i.e., the sort of people they would not normally ever encounter in their lives as designers for the rich and famous)." Through changing the home, *Extreme Makeover* promises a transformation of family life, a transition to a better and easier way of living.

While advice may be the clearest offering of the lifestyle series, these shows also act as advertisements for vested industries (such as Lowes and Home Depot)—yet also for a *self* that can be transformed through new products. These shows produce a world in which "you, too, can have a new identity, a new persona, in a manner of days, weeks, or months, just as long as you have the necessary capital to finance such a drastic reconstruction of the self" (Dixon 2007: 52).

Lifestyle television brings the gaze of the public into the home, rendering it open to the judgments of experts as well as the neighbors. While the home is often imagined as a backstage space where personal choice and style might be exercised away from the public eye (Goffman 1959), decisions around style and taste in the home become disciplinary choices. Rosenberg (2011) points to the unique structure of DIY culture in nations obsessed with home ownership, countries like the United States, Canada, England, and Australia. Lifestyle television provides not only an etiquette manual, but also "guidelines for living."

DIY and lifestyle television bring the outside gaze into the home, and brings "expert" advice and judgment to the personal taste and choice of the individual dweller. Along with the growth of lifestyle television, the increase in residential mobility may also have brought the public gaze in. Rosenberg (2011) argues about Australia that the increase in residential mobility has brought the property market to the fore in individual decision making about home decor. He uses the term "residential ethics" to describe the way that homeowners often must consider future owners, or house hunters when choosing styles for the house. The HGTV show *House Hunters* illustrates this process from the point of view of the hunters, who compare houses during each episode to choose the right property. This focus on the future owner depersonalizes the home improvement choices of current owners and leads toward a homogenization of style and choice, dependent as much on expert advice and popular imagery as on personal style or choice (as if the two could be separated). "The aesthetic demands of the contemporary property market," Rosenberg (2011: 17) writes, "have governmental implications, as they require individuals to engage in forms of self-monitoring and self-disciplining in relation to DIY decoration and renovation."

Even the most personal of decisions around creating a home are suffused with the effects of mass-produced popular culture, and dwellers actively work to produce cultural artifacts that satisfy public judgment. While people actively construct their identity in the home, both through stylistic choice and through the objects that fill their homes and invest them with personal meaning (Csikszentmihalyi and Rochberg-Halton 1981; Cuba and Hummon 1993), these choices are constructed and sustained through popular culture and are increasingly subject to the discipline of the market. While many conform to the mass-produced norm, others defy it through different choices—by furnishing with antiques or restoring a historic home. While these choices do not conform to the modern styles promoted on reality television, few remodelers are unaware of the property market and expectations of potential future buyers.

The retail market, especially the impact of large box stores like Home Depot, Lowe's, and Sears, disproportionately influence the styles and products that are advised in these popular programs. *Extreme Makeover: Home Edition*, for example, is sponsored by Sears, which is a major partner in the show and a sponsor of its host, Ty Pennington. Along with promoting particular products, Sears reaps the reward of positive public relations, since the show is identified with charitable work and renovation (Palmer 2007). Other large box stores promote DIY both through advertising and through in-store workshops and the sale of magazines and DIY books.

The Home and Technologies of the Self

After peeling the wallpaper and mending the wall beneath, the choice of paint colors looms large. Retailers from small hardware stores to large box stores offer hundreds of small paint samples, and we buy many of these, painting 2x2 squares of color on the walls to determine "our style." Are we considering future owners in the process? While at the time I would have dismissed this out of hand, when I look at our walls 10 years later, our choices certainly conform to the style—soft, off-white shades, absence of patterns or bright colors—that fit in any house. In other words, while we chose these colors, they are likely the same as those chosen by neighbors, although our own identity and lifestyle are quite different.

The popular culture of home repair and home decor, exemplified through television programming and DIY websites and magazines, creates a set of expectations around the appearance of the home as a reflection of the self. Foucault (1988) describes these models of the self located in the culture as one basis for what he calls "technologies of the self," techniques and practices for enacting the self in recognizable and culturally appropriate ways. He writes that technologies of the self "permit individuals to effect by their own means or with the help of others a certain number of operations on their own bodies and souls, thoughts, conduct, and a way of being, so as to transform themselves in order to attain a certain state of happiness, purity, wisdom, perfection, or immortality" (1988:17). While home repair does not promise immortality, the ecstatic reactions of families whose homes are renovated in shows like *Extreme Makeover: Home Edition* suggest that happiness and a more efficient, better life are possible through implementing the correct techniques of the home. In fact, a radically new and improved self is promised through these technologies, a self that is better, happier, more beautiful, and more successful.

Expert advice, and the images of rooms, furniture, color, decor, and the like that are the stuff of "real estate porn"[1] govern a particular set of tastes and subjectivities that move the home from the backstage of social life, as a place where you can let down your guard, to the forefront of the display of appropriate forms of taste. This narrative of transformation is best understood as one response to the shift of responsibility for collective concerns, such as poverty and homelessness, from governments onto individuals. Lewis (2011: 24) writes that "in neoliberal settings, the personal health, and relationship advice increasingly offered on Anglo-American lifestyle makeover shows […] can be seen to be attempting to fill the gap left by the state as it passes on responsibility for once-public concerns like obesity onto the self-regulating consumer-citizen." Along with the particular choices—food, home decor, what to wear—more importantly reality TV has promoted "… grammars of choice, personal responsibility, and self-empowerment …" (Oullette and Hay 2008: 73) that place responsibility singularly on the individual and the nuclear family. This advice is class-specific, promoting values and styles consistent with, and affordable to, the upper middle class. These choices are deeply imbued with moral value; good taste becomes a way of enacting responsible contemporary citizenship (Miller 2012).

David Grazian (2010: 6) writes of pop culture that it is "produced, consumed, and experienced within a context of overlapping sets of social relationships," and lifestyle television and contemporary style highlight the breadth and depth of these relationships. Within a larger shift of responsibility from the collective and the state to the individual, choices around lifestyle—including choices about the home—take on more importance and have greater consequence. Lifestyle television promises to discipline these choices, offering advice on a wide range of matters from home decor to food preparation to weight loss. These reality programs are inexpensive to produce and have established a popular fan base, so they minimize risk to production companies and provide a source of advertising for home-related products. These programs create and perpetuate a set of stylistic choices to be emulated by those at home, and so DIY, which suggests perhaps a growing set of skills or craftsmanship, is shaped to fit a standardized model, one that fits into a property market where people buy and sell homes more frequently than in the past. Shows like *Flip This House*, a television show that aired in the United States from 2005 to 2009 and told stories about purchasing and renovating housing units in an attempt to increase the value of the property to be sold for profit, highlight this trend. These elements are all overlapping social relationships, often outside of any individual home renovators consciousness when choosing the color of their dining room or the pattern on their sofa. And yet the context demonstrates that these choices are far more complex than we might imagine.

Karen McCormack is an Associate Professor of Sociology at Wheaton College (MA). Her work is animated by a desire to understand how individuals and groups respond to social dilemmas related to poverty, debt, and inequality. Her recent research has been on the foreclosure crisis, which led to consider home-making and to contribute this essay to this volume. Her work has appeared in *The Sociological Quarterly*, *Symbolic Interaction*, and *Critical Sociology*. Her most recent work explores the role of digital communication in the formation and sustenance of community.

Note

1. Baudrillard (1983) first suggested that the gaze of reality television is somewhat like pornography, based on the 1970s American show, *An American Family*, which brought cameras into the home of an American family and watched it fall apart. Deery (2004) explores this further, noting how the intrusion and overly close-up lens of the reality style used elements more familiar in pornographic voyeurism.

References

Baudrillard, Jean. 1983. *Simulations*. New York, NY: Semiotext(e).

Csikszentmihalyi, Mihalyi and Eugene Rochberg-Halton. 1981. *The Meaning of Things: Domestic Symbols and the Self*. Cambridge, UK: Cambridge University Press.

Cuba, Lee and David Hummon. 1993. "Constructing a Sense of Home: Place Affiliation and Migration Across the Life Cycle." *Sociological Forum* 8(4): 547–572.

Deery, June. 2004. "Reality TV as Advertainment." *Popular Communication: The International Journal of Media and Culture* 2(1): 1–20.

Dixon, Wheeler Winston. 2007. "Hyperconsumption in Reality Television: The Transformation of the Self Through Televisual Consumerism." *Quarterly Review of Film and Video* 25(1): 52–63.

Dupuis, Ann and David C. Thorns. 1998. "Home, Home Ownership and the Search for Ontological Security." *Sociological Review* 46(1): 24–47.

Foucault, Michel. 1988. *Technologies of the Self: A Seminar with Michel Foucault* (Luther H. Martin, Huck Gutman, and Patrick H. Hutton Eds.). Amhherst, MA: University of Massachusetts Press.

Giddens, Anthony. 1991. *Modernity and Self-Identity*. Stanford, CA: Stanford University Press.

Goffman, Erving. 1959. *The Presentation of Self in Everyday Life*. New York, NY: Anchor Books.

Grazian, David. 2010. *Mix It Up: Popular Culture, Mass Media, and Society*. New York, NY: W.W. Norton.

Lewis, Tania. 2011. "Making Over Culture: Lifestyle Television and Contemporary Pedago-gies of Selfhood in Singapore." *Communication, Politics & Culture* 44(1): 21–32.

Miller, Daniel. 2012. *Consumption and its consequences*. New York: Polity.

Oullette, Laurie and James Hay. 2008. *Better Living through Reality TV: Television and Post-Welfare Citizenship*. Oxford, UK: Blackwell Publishing.

Palmer, Gareth. 2007. "*Extreme Makeover: Home Edition:* An American Fairy Tale." In Dana Heller (Ed.), *Makeover Television: Realities Remodelled*. London, UK: I.B. Tauris, 165–176.

Rosenberg, Buck Clifford. 2011. "Home Improvement: Domestic Taste, DIY, and the Prop-erty Market." *Home Cultures: The Jounral of Architure, Design and Domestic Space* 8(1): 5–23.

22

HAVING PETS

Leslie Irvine

Years ago, whenever I mentioned that I lived with three cats and had even moved them with me across the country, people's eyes would widen. Why go to that trouble? After all, one can easily obtain a new cat. And why have *three* cats, all of the very ordinary, domestic short-haired variety? Today, bringing pets on a cross-country move would take few people by surprise. Now, websites such as BringFido.com offer worldwide resources for those planning to travel with their pets. A majority of the households in the United States (69%) and Canada (57%) currently include pets (American Veterinary Medical Association 2012; Gibb 2013). Cats outnumber dogs, with most feline-owning households having more than one cat; to borrow the old advertising slogan used by Lay's potato chips, when it comes to cats, "You can't have just one."

The figures increase when one also counts the creatures with feathers, fins, hooves, and scales. Depending on how one defines "pet," any species can count. If we think of a pet simply as a favored animal, then the category can include those considered "production animals," or those raised for meat, milk, wool, or other products. But scholars of pet-keeping limit the designation to those animals we (a) give individual, personal names; (b) allow in the house; and most importantly, (c) would never eat (Thomas 1983). Because pets live with us, we grant them honorary status as members of the family, and long-standing taboos prohibit the eating of kin (Sahlins 1976).[1] To be sure, farmers do consider some of their animals as pets; they sometimes name them, and then later eat them. However, the status of "petted livestock" (Wilkie 2010) is temporary. When the time comes to send that animal to market—in other words, to be slaughtered for food—he or she regains the status of commodity.

To this point, most pets—in the sense that I use the word here—have no economic or instrumental value. Dogs and cats once had jobs, but today, we seldom rely on them to hunt, guard or herd livestock, or keep vermin away. Beginning early in the twentieth century and accelerating since World War II, the roles of dogs and cats changed (see Fogle 1999; Serpell 1996). Currently, many people prefer the term "companion animals" to "pets" and consider themselves "guardians" rather than "owners." San Francisco was the first city to implement this language in ordinances. Boulder, Colorado, and Amherst, Massachusetts, soon followed. Before long, municipalities far removed from these liberal boroughs also adopted the language of "guardian" and "companion animal."

These days, it seems that every other person drives a Subaru Outback—the vehicle advertised as "Dog Tested, Dog Approved"—embellished with a bumper sticker proclaiming, "Dog is My Co-Pilot." The ubiquity of that sticker, as well as others identifying the driver as a "Crazy Cat Lady" or announcing that "My Dog is Smarter than Your Honors Student," illustrates how having a pet draws on, reflects, and shapes popular culture. In this brief essay, I highlight how media, consumer goods, and celebrities—both human and animal—have shaped what it means to have a pet.

Screening the Pet

The 1905 British film *Rescued by Rover* was the first to feature a dog in the starring role.[2] The film opens as a beggar woman kidnaps a baby. When the child's nurse tells the waiting mother, Rover listens intently. He leaps out a window, runs through the streets, and swims across a river to the poor side of town. After finding the apartment where the woman has taken the baby, he again crosses the river and runs home to alert the distraught father. Rover leads the father to his child, and they return home to a joyful reunion with mother. *Rescued by Rover* wore out through repeated screenings. "Rover" became the most popular dog name in Britain. The movie started the trend of putting dogs in heroic starring roles.

For heroism and devotion, few dogs could compete with Rin Tin Tin. The original dog starred in nearly 30 movies throughout the 1920s and 1930s (Orlean 2011). On television, dogs from his bloodline played the faithful companion of a boy orphaned during an Indian raid and adopted by a U.S. Cavalry troop. Their far-fetched adventures conveyed weekly lessons about adventure, bravery, and loyalty. And, with a cast devoid of female characters—human or canine—the show also broadcast the "no sissy stuff" message of post–World War II masculinity (Kimmel 2012).

Another boy-and-his-dog pair embodied different messages on the media landscape. Lassie first appeared in a 1938 story, and then in a series of books. Lassie's adventures evolved as the medium changed from print to film, then radio, and finally, to television. Each week, through her intelligence and communicative abilities, fearless Lassie saved Timmy (Lassie's longest-appearing television companion) from various mishaps and crises. As in *The Adventures of Rin Tin Tin*, each episode concluded with a moral lesson. In contrast, however, the nurturing, female heroine of *Lassie* (albeit played by a male dog), extolled the importance of home and family (see Jenkins 2007). Likewise, in the animated feature *Lady and the Tramp*—a 1950s canine romantic comedy—home and family offered a refuge from life on the street, where not only adventure but danger also awaits. And similarly, the lovable dog in the *Benji* series used Lassie-like skills to first win a home with a family and then to find his way out of the trouble that would keep him away.

The heroic *Lassie* and *Rin Tin Tin* formula continues in new variations. On HBO's *Game of Thrones*, and in the books on which it is based, legendary dire wolves have a supernatural connection to the six Stark children who raised them. Other shows subvert the formula to depict the humorous side of canine devotion. In the series *Frasier*, Eddie the dog listened only to Martin Crane, ignoring Frasier and even fixing him a defiant stare on him. The scripts played up the idea that Eddie understood the effect this had on Frasier.

Media not only shape our expectations of pets, they influence the kinds of pets we have. For example, in the 1920s, Rin Tin Tin and his predecessor, Strongheart, popularized German Shepherds, then a new breed. And records of the American Kennel Club indicate that the 14 years following the release of *The Shaggy Dog* brought a 100-fold increase in registrations of Old English sheepdogs. After the 1985 re-release of *101 Dalmatians*, the number of annual registrations of Dalmatian puppies spiked, peaking in 1993 at 42,816 dogs before dropping below 1,000 in 2008 (Herzog 2006).

Uploading the Pet

People have long photographed their dogs and cats (see Arluke and Bogdan 2010; Arluke and Rolfe 2013; Grier 2006; Hall 2000, 2002). The Internet makes it possible to circulate images at an unprecedented rate. Amateur videos of dogs and cats behaving in funny, heartwarming, and bizarre ways have appeared on YouTube since 2005, when one of its founders posted a clip of his cat at play. The following year, the first cat video went viral. Although it features six puppies, the single cat has the starring role in the 1 minute and 9 seconds of action. Between 2007 and 2009, videos of Nora, the piano-playing cat, were almost unavoidable. A search will quickly reveal videos of cats appearing to talk, playing patty-cake or tetherball with other cats, playing with an iPad, ingeniously opening doors, annoying birds, dogs, or children—or being annoyed by them. In recognition of the genre, the Walker Art Center in Minneapolis started an Internet Cat Video Festival in 2012. The Festival gives the "Golden Kitty Award" to the Internet's best cat video. In 2013, the Award went to "Grumpy Cat."[3] Her rapid ascent to fame brought her appearances on *Good Morning America, Today*, and at *South by Southwest*. She starred in a made-for-TV-movie, *Grumpy Cat's Worst Christmas Ever*, broadcast on the Life-time network in November, 2014.

Cats have also had starring roles in the viral images known as "lolcats," with "lol" standing for "laughing out loud." Lolcats involve a photo of a cat, often caught in a bizarre or humorous pose, and a caption conveying the cat's putative words. For instance, in one, a particularly wide-eyed cat says, "Thermometer goes where?" The captions often employ Internet slang or strangely-spelled words. For example, a popular lolcat features the caption, "I can has cheezburger?" Another pairs a picture of a tiny, fuzzy kitten rolling on his back with the message, "I iz furrocious. Not to be messin wif me."

Despite the popularity of cats online, dogs have led the trend since 2012.[4] Well over a 100 million viewers have watched "Mutant Giant Spider Dog," featuring a dog wearing tarantula costume.[5] The current trend makes dogs themselves into filmmakers. GoPro, maker of small, durable, waterproof cameras, offers the "Fetch" harness, which secures a camera to a dog's back or chest. As the GoPro website proclaims, pet owners can now "capture the world from a dog's point of view" (GoPro 2014). My quick search turned up over eight million videos taken by dogs as they run, play, swim, and just do whatever dogs do.

Doing Things with Pets

Having a pet involves doing things with and for the animal. These practices reveal themselves in artifacts, or consumer goods, themselves examples of popular culture. For example, consider the ritual of walking the dog. One could simply tie a rope around the dog's neck, step outside, and go. But the iPhone app called MapMyDOGWALK can locate and store routes, measure distance and calories burned, upload photos taken on the walk, and share the information on social media.

A walk typically involves not a rope, but a leash and collar, perhaps a matching set, since both come in colors and patterns ranging from geometric to camouflage, skull-and-crossbones designs, and logos for sports teams and Harley-Davidson motorcycles. Reflective collars provide visibility at night, and some even have built-in blinking lights. Retractable "Flexi-leashes," wound on a spring-loaded mechanism inside a plastic handle, allow dogs to explore at distances ranging to 26 feet.

Along with the leash, a dog walker needs a plastic bag or two to clean up after the dog. Reusing bags will suffice, but one can also purchase bags made for this use, in colors to match leashes and collars. Some are scented. Some are biodegradable or compostable. Martha Stewart even manufactures her own brand of poop bags. Pouches and dispensers to hold a supply of bags come in every design imaginable. And depending on the dog's size and breed, he or she might need protection from the weather. Pet supply stores stock a variety of clothing for dogs, ranging from utilitarian coats to princess dresses.

Apart from the artifacts involved in walking the dog, the activity of dog walking is, in itself, a popular cultural phenomenon. Until around the turn of the twentieth century, when most dogs were *working* dogs, they lived outdoors. Walks were unnecessary. People allowed their dogs to roam, and when they moved to cities, they continued to do so. As cities grew, however, roaming dogs became a nuisance (see Irvine, forthcoming). The threat of rabies eventually prompted city governments to initiate laws about muzzling, licensing, and finally, leashing dogs (Brady 2012; Grier 2006). Thus, the daily walk became a requirement and ritual for dogs and their people.

Some owners, unable to walk their dogs, hire others to do it for them. Of course, the neighbor's kid could do it, but walking a particular dog may require some skill in dog handling. Insured, professional dog walkers can often handle six or more dogs at once. Another option, especially for owners who work long hours or travel, is doggie day care. These facilities offer supervised play with other dogs; a fee is charge for the day or half day. Some provide "report cards" that note how nicely the dog played or how affectionate she or he was with the staff. Some report cards include pictures of the dogs at play or rest, and a few doggie day care facilities provide closed-circuit video observation, so an owner can go online and watch the dog throughout the day.

Another option for active dogs comes in the form of the dog park. Having removed free-roaming dogs from the streets, many municipalities now fence in plots of land for their use. Offering dogs room to run, play, and socialize, dog parks also foster interaction among owners. By acting as "social facilitators" (Irvine 2004, 2013; Messent 1983; Robins, Sanders, and Cahill 1991; Sanders 1999), dogs allow for violations of the rule that Goffman (1963) called "civil inattention." This refers to how we ordinarily avert our gaze in public, avoiding interaction with others. Dogs, however, transform their human companions into "open persons" (Goffman 1963), amenable to friendly interactions. Capitalizing on this, some bars offer "yappy hours," with play groups for dogs and discounted drinks for their people. *Food and Wine* magazine has even rated the top yappy hours in the United States (Wippman 2014).

Conclusions

The astonishment I once encountered when describing my bond with my cats has given way to nods of recognition. As dogs and cats became members of the family, popular culture responded with products, media, services, and professions dedicated to having a pet. Even the basic act of feeding a pet highlights how popular culture shapes the practice. The selection in the grocery store's pet food aisle requires deciding not only whether to feed beef, chicken, or fish, but whether the dog or cat should have grains and vegetables, too. Dry food or wet? Does the cat prefer clumping litter? Scented or unscented? What about odor control? Would this brand live up to the promises of the ads? The options make it hard to know what is best.

And if these members of the family fail to uphold their end of the bargain, popular culture comes to the rescue. Programs such as *Dog Whisperer*, with Cesar Millan; *It's Me or the Dog*, featuring Victoria Stillwell; and *My Cat from Hell*, with Jackson Galaxy counsel pet owners on a range of behavioral problems. They visit clients in their homes to observe the situation. Their advice emphasizes understanding the needs of the animal and how owners influence their pets' behavior. Fans can purchase all manner of dog and cat products online, along with t-shirts for themselves featuring Millan's, Stillwell's, or Galaxy's logos.

The artifacts associated with having a pet reveal how even taken-for-granted practices rely on and contribute to popular culture. The examples I have offered are illustrative rather than exhaustive. A full list would include pet photographers, portrait painters, communicators, groomers, pet sitters, pet cemeteries, cremation services, and more. It would also include the ways people include pets as *bona fide* participants in family rituals, celebrating their birthdays, for instance, or filling a Christmas stocking with dog or cat treats. These examples could be taken as evidence that having a pet is frivolous, or a consequence of misplaced priorities stemming from affluence or isolation. I would argue instead that they reveal the creativity, playfulness, and care that people bring to this particular human-animal relationship. In doing so, they reveal the importance of animals in shaping human lives and identities.

Leslie Irvine received her Ph.D. in sociology from Stony Brook University (SUNY). She is Professor of Sociology at the University of Colorado, Boulder. She studies the roles of animals in society through a symbolic interactionist perspective. Her research topics have included animal selfhood, human-animal play, and gender in veterinary medicine. Her most recent book, *My Dog Always Eats First*, examines homeless people's relationships with companion animals.

Notes

1. Even cultures that consume dogs and cats do not eat pets; see Podberscek 2009.
2. See *Rescued by Rover* on YouTube: https://www.youtube.com/watch?v=LlhNxHfyWTU.
3. https://www.youtube.com/watch?v=INscMGmhmX4. Accessed October 12, 2014.
4. http://www.google.com/trends/explore#q=dogs%2C%20cats&gprop= youtube&cmpt=q. Accessed October 12, 2014.
5. https://www.youtube.com/watch?v=YoB8t0B4jx4. Accessed October 12, 2014.

References

American Veterinary Medical Association. 2012. "U.S. Pet Ownership & Demographics Sourcebook; Did You Know?" *avma.org*. Retrieved from h.ttps://www.avma.org/KB/Resources/Statistics/Pages/Market-research-statistics-US-Pet-Ownership-Demographics-Sourcebook.aspx.

Arluke, Arnold, and Robert Bogdan. 2010. *Beauty and the Beast: Human–Animal Relations as Revealed in Real Photo Postcards, 1905–1935*. Syracuse, NY: Syracuse University Press.

Arluke, Arnold, and Lauren Rolfe. 2013. *The Photographed Cat: Picturing Human-Feline Ties, 1890–1940*. Syracuse, NY: Syracuse University Press.

Brady, Benjamin. 2012. "The Politics of the Pound: Controlling Loose Dogs in Nineteenth-Century New York City." *Jefferson Journal of Science and Culture 2*: 9–25.

Fogle, Bruce. 1999. "The Changing Roles of Animals in Western Society: Influences upon and from the Veterinary Profession." *Anthrozoös 12*: 234–239.

Gibb, Rhys. May, 2013. "Pet Ownership is the 'Cat's Meow' in Canada." Vancouver BC: Ipsos Reid. Accessed August 17, 2015. Retrieved from http://www.ipsos-na.com/knowledge-ideas/public-affairs/thought-starter/.

Goffman, Erving. 1963. *Stigma: Notes on the Management of Spoiled Identity*. Englewood Cliffs, NJ: Prentice-Hall.

GoPro. 2014. "GoPro Unveils First Mount For Pets." GoPro.com Accessed August 16, 2015. Retrieved from https://gopro.com/news/capture-the-world-from-a-dogs-point-of-view-with-gopros-fetch.

Grier, Katherine C. 2006. *Pets in America: A History*. Chapel Hill, NC: University of North Carolina Press.

Hall, Libby. 2000. *Prince and Other Dogs, 1850–1940*. New York, NY: Bloomsbury, USA.

Hall, Libby. 2002. *Prince and Other Dogs II*. New York, NY: Bloomsbury, USA.

Herzog, Harold. 2006. "Forty-two Thousand and One Dalmatians: Fads, Social Contagion, and Dog Breed Popularity." *Society and Animals 14*: 383–397.

Irvine, Leslie. 2004. *If You Tame Me: Understanding our Connection With Animals*. Philadelphia, PA: Temple University Press.

Irvine, Leslie. 2013. *My Dog Always Eats First: Homeless People and their Animals*. Boulder, CO: Lynne Rienner Publishers.

Irvine, Leslie. Forthcoming. "Animal Sheltering." In by L. Kalof (Ed.), *The Oxford Handbook of Animal Studies*. New York, NY: Oxford University Press.

Jenkins, Henry. 2007. *The Wow Climax: Tracing the Emotional Impact of Popular Culture*. New York, NY: New York University Press.

Kimmel, Michael S. 2012 [1996]. *Manhood in America: A Cultural History* (3rd ed.). New York, NY: Oxford University Press.

Messent, Peter. 1983. "Social Facilitation of Contact with Other People by Pet Dogs." In A. Katcher and A. Beck (Eds.), *New Perspectives on Our Lives with Companion Animals*. Philadelphia, PA: University of Pennsylvania Press, 37–46.

Orlean, Susan. 2011. *Rin Tin Tin: The Life and Legend*. New York, NY: Simon & Schuster.

Podberscek, Anthony L. 2009. "Good to Pet and Eat: The Keeping and Consuming of Dogs and Cats in South Korea." *Journal of Social Issues* 65: 615–663.

Robins, Douglas M., Clinton R. Sanders, and Spencer E. Cahill. 1991. "Dogs and Their People: Pet-Facilitated Interaction in a Public Setting." *Journal of Contemporary Ethnography* 20: 3–25.

Sahlins, Marshall. 1976. *Culture and Practical Reason*. Chicago, IL: University of Chicago Press.

Sanders, Clinton R. 1999. *Understanding Dogs: Living and Working with Canine Companions*. Philadelphia, PA: Temple University Press.

Serpell, James. 1996. *In the Company of Animals: A Study of Human-Animal Relationships*. Cambridge UK: Cambridge University Press.

Thomas, Keith. 1983. *Man and the Natural World: Changing Attitudes in England 1500–1800*. London, UK: Allen Lane.

Wilkie, Rhoda. 2010. *Livestock/Deadstock: Working with Farm Animals From Birth to Slaughter*. Philadelphia, PA: Temple University Press.

Wippman, Brianna. 2014. "7 Best Yappy Hours, A.K.A. Happy Hours for Dogs." *Food and Wine.com [FWx]*. Retrieved from http://www.foodandwine.com/fwx/drink/7-best-yappy-hours-aka-happy-hours-dogs.

23

ON NOT DRIVING

Sherryl Kleinman

"I don't drive," I confess to someone who might become a friend.
"So, you know how to drive, but you don't drive?"
I'd like to claim modern competence. Or say I'm an environmentalist extraordinaire, living in a U.S. town of 60,000 with a limited bus system and without driving.
I always tell the truth.
"I never learned," I say.

*

My parents moved from an urban neighborhood in Montreal, Canada, to a suburb when I was 14 years old. I missed the old buildings, thick trees, and bakeries. Ville Saint-Laurent was so much farther by bus to downtown Montreal than Notre-Dame-de-Grâce.

My mother delighted in moving to a newly built house that no one had dirtied. She migrated from Poland to Quebec City at age 6, growing up poor, adding French and English to Polish and Yiddish, dealing with anti-Semitism, and helping her parents navigate new languages at the bank and grocery store. She moved to Montreal after she married my father, at age 25.

Newness meant upward mobility. Keeping the house spotless meant sustaining middle class status, though my father had a one-person printing shop and permanent ink under his fingernails. He received a Bachelor of Commerce in 1935 from McGill University—"when there were quotas on Jews," my mother added—but after apprenticing as an accountant for a firm, his father died and he took over the printing shop.

He worked there until a year before he died, in 1984. My mother said, "He could have sold the shop and been an accountant. But he couldn't work for anyone, someone telling him what to do. And he didn't care about money—like you."

I don't know when he first bought a car, something that went along with moving far from the shop and up a class level. I think he had one when I came along in 1952.

As a girl I was supposed to stay away from the shop, in what my mother considered a dirtier part of town. I visited once, a fire hazard filled with paper, hulking machines, and a tiny bathroom with a rust-stained toilet and chipped seat. Later I resented that they'd kept me from knowing this enclave of immigrant Jews.

My mother didn't drive, but whose mother did? My father drove, but it was clear he hated it. I asked him to take me to a friend's place in the evening to study. "Don't bother me. Take a taxi." We never took taxis; his answer was a no. He was tired from work, but the rejection stung.

A male friend who put off driving until 28, said, "Hating driving is a euphemism for fear." In my father's case, he was right.

*

I'm 7, living with my sister and mother in a small country house at Trout Lake, north of Montreal, for June and July. My father drives up for weekends. My parents are foreigners in the country: they can't swim; my father's skin burns in the shade. Kids my age have started going to camp, not the country, by that point, so I have few friends. I teach myself to swim short distances. The best part? Walking around the lake.

My mother fears summer storms, especially in the country. The lightning feels closer, the winds harsher, the walls thinner. She insists that my sister and I hide under our beds at the first sign. We obey; we've heard "with our luck …" since forever.

My sister, 5 years older, has friends in Trout Lake, and a boyfriend per season. The teens go to the dance hall in the evening, doing the jitterbug to music in the jukebox, hanging out at the two places that sell ice cream and sweets during the day. There are lots of country places to hide in, though mothers don't seem worried about where the teens disappear to, by foot, or what they might be doing.

The city feels safer—alive, peopled, and solid.

It's Friday afternoon. I'm outside, waiting for my father to drive up.

I see a figure walking up the dirt road. He gets larger, and I see—but it can't be—it's Daddy. My head tilts with the shift in my world. There should be a car; he should be in it. Driving.

I remember only what the adults repeated later. He fell asleep at the wheel, crashed into the median, rolled three times. The officers gave him up for dead, but he crawled out the window, the car upside down. "Thank God it was a Buick," everyone said. A Tank. Only a military vehicle might protect you.

He had already been to the hospital, somewhere. They took X-rays of his ribs, front and back, and everything looked fine. But my stoic father weakened with pain by the day. In Montreal (I have no memory of how we returned) he had X-rays taken of the sides of his ribs, each of them broken.

*

The subway is built in time for Expo '67, the World's Fair. The finished basement in the suburb has a bedroom, with its own bathroom and separate entrance. My mother, the one with entrepreneurial ideas, decides to rent the room to tourists.

I play tour guide for bus money, meals, and tips, taking Americans on the bus, transferring to the new subway, with its speed, beauty—art work at every station—peopled with strangers who don't attend Winston Churchill High. I hear French once I leave (we live in the Jewish English-speaking section of Ville Saint-Laurent) and other languages I don't know. Ah, the transfer station at Berri; people crisscrossing to catch their next train. Don't worry if you miss one; the next will arrive in a few minutes. Even in our suburb there's no need for a bus schedule; you'll wait only 10 minutes.

All summer I escape the white bricks of suburbia that offer me only opportunities for babysitting. Young mothers who don't work outside the home, their husbands disappearing in big cars they drive to work they don't like doing, taking their wives out once a week. I babysit children who try talking me into watching TV until their parents come home—in the parents' bedroom.

The parents haven't taught the kids to go to their own rooms and entertain themselves. The women bore me with talk about clothes and hair after they return, so I say I must leave to finish homework. The men ignore me. It's the women who take care of everything in the house, including the babysitter.

I want to get on the bus, move with the subway, get out.

*

In grade 9, I make three best friends. Leora is our ringleader in music, knowing the best coffee houses downtown, where local and visiting folksingers play. We hear people who write their own songs; that's the standard of the coffee houses, and so it's ours.

In high school we're neither in nor out, just off the radar. We write poetry, listen to music, occasionally write a song, wear big brown sweaters, jeans, and comfortable shoes. We disdain wall-to-wall carpeting, flocking on wallpaper, and anything we call plastic.

Twice a week we take the bus and subway downtown, and emerge into the Middle Of It All. Winter doesn't keep Montrealers inside: We're people watchers and you're interesting just for being in public, unlike the suburb that zips up at dinnertime.

We use our babysitting money to eat out at ethnic restaurants. Then we squeeze into the Yellow Door, so small you're never far from the performer. It could be locals we have crushes on, or Bruce Cockburn, not yet known. Or Jesse Winchester, a soft-spoken draft dodger from Tennessee.

They sing about the kind of love and heartbreak we hope to have, and politics. Our main political act is girls-escaping-the-suburbs-at-night, sitting close to strangers in speedy trains, then squashed by older-than-teens in coffee houses.

Leora discovers Joni Mitchell. We buy her first album, *Song to a Seagull*, but "Night in the City" is our favorite cut.

*

So how about escaping the 'burbs by car?

You'd have to drive your father's car! As unthinkable as having him drive you to the Yellow Door, picking you up afterward (our fathers would have refused anyway—they'd returned via traffic to suburbia, retiring to the television den with our mothers).

You didn't drive to an adventure. That consumerist tank was private. You took public transportation; rubbing shoulders with strangers, drinking coffee at cafes, looking through albums at Phantasmagoria, finding bookstores. That short walk from the bus stop to the suburban house at midnight, no one around, that's when I worried about a man lurking behind the hedges.

The worst danger: becoming a bored housewife and mother. Some women could drive their kids around, but not escape.

*

I grew up on U.S. television, but failed to equate driving with freedom. Initially, cars were for the rich, leaving cities to drive to their estates in the country. But why not expand the market? Why not persuade politicians to use tax dollars to build highways everywhere? Cars and tire companies still had to sell the *idea* to the people, and freedom—the key word in American exceptionalism—became equated with driving. Go wherever you want whenever you want. For teens, this meant time away from parents, a bed in the back seat, speed for young men. Does this sound like a commercial? It more or less was. And still is. A 2010 commercial for Goodyear tires has the slogan "Serious Freedom," though we're told it's not only the open road that beckons ("Go where you want to go"), but "Freedom from Worry." Should anyone, especially women, fear the freedom of traveling with children or by themselves, the "Serious Technology" of the tires will protect us.

The image of driving to the country wouldn't have worked for me anyway. How did the Quebec people live in Trout Lake all year? Wintry isolation, then the monotonous green of summer. Suburbia was another version of the same cycle, but you could leave: the bus and subway a moving public square.

*

I don't remember rejecting Driver's Ed. My friends didn't learn to drive. Were we the exception?

Montreal is known for bad driving and assertive walking. I used to cross a four-lane boulevard downtown one lane at a time. On cross streets, as the light turned red, we'd keep walking en masse. You'd move faster downtown by subway and walking, drivers are stuck in cages.

*

McGill University was a commuter school. You lived with your parents and took the bus and subway downtown. The one-hour trip out didn't bother me. I resented the return trip, wanting to stay downtown, study in the library, grab a burger at the greasy spoon in the "McGill Ghetto," hang out.

I longed to live near the university. Buildings that meshed with the city. Not only students, but also professors and staff on the streets. An urban campus; a part of the whole that is the city.

I knew two students who lived downtown. One close friend moved out of her parents' home in order to stay sane. The other friend was from the U.S.

Jane taught me the phrase "going away to college." She rented an efficiency in a high rise close to McGill. She hadn't mentioned working, so I asked how she paid for it.

"My parents," she said, nonchalantly.

I explained the concept to my parents.

"You have a perfectly good home," my mother said. "Only a brazen hussy would live downtown under those circumstances."

That wasn't the worst part.

"You would have to pay for it yourself. Your grades would suffer."

I'd fallen in love with sociology, and my professors encouraged me to get a Ph.D. I'd learned to equate my worth with grades from the time I could understand words. My mother sounded like the Hebrew God, sending me a warning. I believed in God only on occasions like this.

All right. I'll live in a city near the university once I become a professor.

*

I moved to Ontario for the one-year M.A. at McMaster, living in a high-rise 20 minutes away by foot from the sociology department. Hamilton was barely a city, but I'd soon move on. Graduate students from small towns in Ontario had cars. Many of us did not, and no one asked why. I thought it strange that one friend insisted on picking us up to go out. A bus stop next to my building meant a straight shot to downtown. Would she feel hurt if I said no?

Four of us hung out a lot. We didn't distinguish between driver and passenger, depending on each other for shop talk, humor, and kvetching.

I visited the campus and neighborhoods in Minneapolis the spring before I started the Ph.D. program at the University of Minnesota and immediately felt comfortable. A large university, with East Bank and West Bank—and their neighborhoods—connected by a walking bridge. I picked the high-rise complex on Cedar Avenue. The street had a food co-op, local bookstore, Annie's Parlor for hamburgers and shakes, a hippie restaurant when you wanted healthy, a pharmacy, clothing stores, and a community theater around the corner. I walked to the sociology department in five minutes.

I took the bus downtown. No match for Montreal. But I had my neighborhood, the university, and Dinkytown on the other side of the river.

A friend had a car. She discovered a fancy grocery store farther away, and I'd accompany her to help bring the groceries to the car and into the building, up the elevator (she lived in the same complex). She loved to cook, and going with her and paying for half of her groceries (and doing the dishes) seemed fair. I rarely cooked; I preferred to be out and ate at cheap places, alone or with friends. My apartment was for writing, reading, and sleeping. The department was for classes and socializing. I'd finish writing at home in the morning, walk over, and have lunch with friends.

*

Then I got a job in 1980 at the University of North Carolina in Chapel Hill. Everyone said it was a good job and I had few options. I remember calling up Howie Becker, my sponsor while I'd been a visiting graduate student at Northwestern University, near Chicago. He understood: "Too bad the job's not in a more urban area. But you'll find people who are like you." Off to exile.

*

Avoiding the move, I called to ask a UNC colleague to find me an apartment. I wanted to live near the center (the university is there) and fairly close to a grocery store. I'm not sure if I said I didn't drive; if I did, it was for practical reasons.

I lived in the only high-rise (six floors). I walked to an A&P and to what was called downtown, but clearly one built for undergraduates: stores with school paraphernalia, mediocre restaurants, and no decent cafe. So, "college town" meant sports and school colors.

Suburbia in search of a city.

*

Then the refrain started:
"You can't live in Chapel Hill and not drive."
But, nothing is far away, and there's nowhere to go!
"You'll like Chapel Hill better when you find someone."
I'd rather be in love in a city!
Urban transplants liked it here, especially if they had kids. Quick trips by car.

*

I learned to feel embarrassed about not driving, failing to fashion an acceptable account. I admit that the idea of driving gave me a chill. Would I feel comfortable? If I learned, would I drive instead of walk to campus, forgo buses? Would I become the car-dependent suburbanite?

I moved to a roomier apartment, still walking distance to UNC and shopping. I became friends with another tenant, who asked me to go food shopping at a large grocery store 10 minutes by car. Janet liked my company and we became friends, giving me plenty of opportunities to do things for her. But I knew that others would have labeled me dependent.

Auto-mobility connotes autonomous movement—independence—no matter how many traffic jams one sits through. In this town, moving one's body without the extension of a car, such as walking, means exercise, not an autonomous source of mobility (I have ability privilege so far). Undergraduates consider bus riding low-status, though the lack of campus parking has led many to take buses to class. Most have cars and use them otherwise.

It feels natural, apparently, to live in a space arranged for driving. Even intellectuals who argue that humans are interdependent—and that driving is bad for the environment—accept this arrangement. If five friends meet for dinner, five cars show up. If I am one of the friends, and it's late, I'll be in one of those cars, passengering. Why? You'll find few people walking; streets are dimly lit, and lots of trees and bushes obscure vision. I'm a woman.

Yet I have car guilt. I look through the window to see when a friend pulls up so I can leave immediately and pop into the car.

Michael and I met in 1988 and we moved in together in 1990. He teaches at a university 30 miles from here and commutes a few days a week. I gave up my cherished walk to campus so he could easily get on the highway. I take a bus to work. Otherwise, I walk to stores, restaurants, and doctor appointments in about half an hour. Michael does the grocery shopping and other errands in our car (so I paid for half of it). I'm in the car when we go out.

We rarely plan our days around my not driving, and I'm careful about asking him for rides.

*

The difficult comments: "I can't see being a feminist and not driving. I'd want to be independent."

As a practicing feminist, it hurts and angers to hear this. Must I give a lecture on the limits of the kind of feminism that ignores interdependence? Or do they think I secretly judge *them* for driving, increasing the carbon footprint? Enriching the car corporations who work with highway politicians to keep us all car dependent?

*

Back to the opening scene:

Because I live where I do, I tell the potential friend that I don't drive. And see where we go from there.

*

My story about not driving shows the conditions under which people come not to use—or even to resist—technologies. Even in the case of cars, a ubiquitous feature of the North American landscape, it is possible to understand how someone could become a non-user, taking the idea that pulled so many to adopt the technology (freedom) and applying it to an older technology that still exists. That old form is public transportation. The subway, introduced in 1967 in Montreal, became a new form of speed and escape, yet still a part of the teeming public in mass transportation. The suburbs represented sameness, superficiality, and conventionality. The city drew us in, with its mix of people, places, sounds, and the attraction of moving with others on the sidewalks and across the car-dense streets. As teens who resisted consumerism and felt drawn to the beginnings of the counterculture, we resisted cars; they symbolized unnecessary expense and the kind of individualism that kept people of different classes, ethnic groups, and languages away from each other. Instead, we dropped a few coins into a metal box and off we went, the adventure beginning with strangers who, in close proximity, let us be free.

Sherryl Kleinman is a Professor of Sociology at the University of North Carolina, Chapel Hill. She is the author of *Equals before God: Seminarians as Humanistic Professionals* (University of Chicago, 1984), *Opposing Ambitions: Gender and Inequality in an Alternative Organization* (University of Chicago, 1996), *Feminist Fieldwork Analysis* (Sage Publications, 2007), and co-author with Martha Copp of *Emotions and Fieldwork* (Sage Publications, 1993). She writes poetry and sociological memoirs and is currently writing a book on teaching about inequality.

24
SNOW-GAZING
David Redmon

As a born-and-raised Texan living in Montreal, I find snow especially difficult to endure—marvelous, but immobilizing. Although outwardly I love to complain about snow, inwardly I can't wait for its arrival. I love the simplicity of watching snow continuously fall, day and night, in different rhythms, accumulating inch-by-inch as it settles in the alleys, collects atop mounds of trash, and forms unusual shapes and unexpected colors in white drifts on a brick-enclosed expanse of a narrow passage. As a pristine, vital element, snow beckons to be seen, touched, and contacted through immersion. I love to hear the crisp crinkling sounds of snow settling on the ground, to see its refractions of light in the early morning, to observe its multifaceted patterns drifting across the sky, to feel its cold grip on my face. At the same time, snow can be an indicator of danger; something to avoid—especially for vulnerable people susceptible to its frigid temperatures. Within hours, its beauty can turn to slush and ice. Aesthetically and acoustically, the rituals of snow-play transform: from laughter to loud industrial snow-removal machines. These material aspects of snow are contradictorily romantic and enlivening, grating and tormenting. Such contradictions speak to the affective power of our sensory dwellings, but also of mediated weather.

The first snowfall marks the impending arrival of winter in Montreal. I gaze out my apartment window and feel the snow's hypnotic transfixion during brief bouts of wonder as my body yields to contemplative moments. Two television reporters in the background are debating whether the extreme increase in snowfall is attributed to global warming or the impending polar vortex. The television screen is impressionistic; red, white, and blue colors swirl as an ominous voiceover and scrolling text warn of blizzard-like conditions for the weekend. I flippantly ignore their dire warnings and shut off the media. "I'm done with the hyperbolic threats," I tell myself. "I want un-televised communication, physical interaction with snow, not third-party forecasts dictating my experience." I step outside for a moment to consider how I will weather the weather. I feel my body encounter the flesh of snow as embodied experience; I take in its presence in corporeal ways.

Magnolia in Snow

I leave my apartment to stroll with Magnolia, my four-month-old daughter, as snow begins to fall delicately around us. Children wrestle with puppies; teenagers flirt with each other; cars spin their tires trying to gain traction—the standard signposts of a winter's day in Montreal. Fluctuations of delight, excitement, and energy course through my body as Magnolia also interacts with snow for the first time in her life. I talk to Magnolia about the snow and describe its sound as "crackling." I point out how snow is forever melting into wetness as it lands on hundreds of orange, yellow, and red leaves dangling from trees. Each crackling sound contributes to the patterned rhythms of the suddenly wintry cityscape. To my surprise, Magnolia is sticking out her tongue. I do the same. Sharing this moment with my daughter is a profound experience, a personal moment of corporeal wildness that generates warmth inside my chest. The fragility of this material experience is burned into my physical memory like the clash of an outdoor fire on a cold winter day. As Vannini and McCright (2011: 370) illustrate, these familiar and unfamiliar sensations "build personal memories and intersect with collective memories and common skills." For this visitor from warmer climes, however, those common skills haven't yet developed.

Snow is a skillful natural and social process. It starts wild, becomes acculturated, gets commodified, and is eventually integrated into the political economy. In this sense, snow is sentient and sensible; it is part of nature, the economy, culture, and the everyday. Economically, snow amasses millions of dollars for companies hired to remove it;

private conferences are organized around snow themes; lawsuits are filed yearly based on snow accidents; and factory workers manufacture snow equipment. An entire culture and educational industry is built around snow: media technology consisting of phone apps (On the Snow); television shows and movies that equate snow with holidays (*Frosty the Snowman*; *Rudolph the Red-Nosed Reindeer*); theatrical plays (*Snow Play*); songs (*Let it Snow!*); books (*The Snow Leopard*); desserts (snow cones); drugs (cocaine, aka "snow"); video-game characters (*Snow Villiers*); movie and book characters (President Snow in *The Hunger Games*); sexual acts (snowballing); research approaches (snowball samples), and beers (Snowdrift)—all embrace snow within their nomenclature. Scientists measure the amount of toxic pollution using snow; there are labs exclusively for the study of snow; melting glaciers and snow avalanches contribute crucially to the monitoring of global warming and rising ocean temperatures; and "extreme weather" shows, "polar vortexes," and the notion of "threatening weather" in general have all emerged in everyday language. Authorities seize on these weather threats to shut down entire cities and transportation systems in the name of risk. Snow is infused in the everyday life of ritual and risk in taken-for-granted ways.

Physically, snow is alive—it transforms with material and sensory force. Snow enlivens bodies' awareness beyond cognitive understanding. At the same time, it is difficult to disengage our sensory experience from mediated symbolic impressions of snow. Significations and culture influence how people experience, interpret, and think about snow. Snow is a chain of mediated signifiers that communicate to people through the transmission of mental sensory impressions. However, snow is also a physically transformative object that influences where people go, how people walk, and what people wear. Thirty minutes into my walk with Magnolia, I am forced to reflect on this point as the pace and intensity of the snowfall increases. It becomes unavoidable; my boots are constantly crushing flakes, transforming their delicate fineness into temporary slush. I cannot separate the wetness from the firmness; the tactile from the visible. Blowing wind further intensifies these encounters, piercing my ears, freezing my face, silencing my voice. Snow confronts me at every turn. Navigating this terrain is what Vannini and colleagues (2011: 365) call "to weather, skillfully." At this moment, however, I don't feel too confident in my ability to navigate the dwelling of which I am a part. As a child in Texas, I never learned how to move through snow, and my haptic skills have not yet been activated.

Wild Being and Somatic Work

Corporeal contact with snow is connected to what Merleau-Ponty (1969) calls wild being: a pre-reflective "becoming" prior to a set of manageable significations. Immersion with wild being occurs through various bodily contacts with snow. Body–snow contact is somatic work: "the range of linguistic and alinguistic reflexive experiences and activities by which individuals create, extinguish, maintain, interrupt, and/or communicate sensations that are congruent with personal, interpersonal, and/or cultural notions of moral, aesthetic, or and/or logical desirability" (Vannini et al. 2011: 368). Somatic work continually redraws the line between work and leisure. Navigating, or "weathering," snow can be a challenge, a method of adapting to a dwelling through understanding, controlling, or remaking it familiar and sensible;—"to weather also means to struggle, to endure, to suffer, to brave, and to strive to cope with climatic elements, at times even failing, experiencing pain and discomfort" (Vannini et al. 2011: 369).

Embodiment, culture, media, and somatic work all enmesh to create continuities, rather than separations, among subjectivities, dwellings, and somatic work. Snow enacts personal, social, economic, and cultural occasions—it immerses us in sumptuous, brute contact with its multiplicity of textures encountered during winter activities. We expect, for example, that kids will play in snow; machines and people will remove it; weather stations will produce spectacle by reporting it. People work skillfully to interpret this mediated spectacle in expected ways: some turn off the report, others take precaution by stocking up on food, and still others prepare their video cameras to chase the storm, turning its dangerous elements and beauty into news, documentaries, entertainment, or even "disaster-tainment." Snow and its practices, therefore, are both experiential and mediated, a challenge and a threat; we engage with snow reflexively as we shape and are shaped by it, perceptively and materially. Snow, in this capacity, is self-willed—*wild*—self-governing as well as shaped by people, predicted by technologies, and commodified into media and economic resources.

Magnolia is inside her sling, falling asleep against my chest. I look upward and notice a floating white forest swirling in the air; it falls on and around me. The thickness of snow renders the depth of the sky almost invisible. I connect intimately and naïvely with snow's fleeting wilderness prior to its transformation into mush—and with it, I connect to Magnolia's presence as part of the snow. It is my contact with brute being and the dwelling's inability to separate sky from ground, clouds from snow, Magnolia from me, or the air from my frigid breath. I exhale and see my breath clashing with the atmosphere's breath in the form of condensation. There is no barrier separating us: my body is of the earth, and of the snow, through each element's raw enveloping contact with the others.

Snow Business

An entire industry of skis, snowmobiles, snow blowers, snow chains, Canadian goose jackets, fur coats, and snowplows all transform snow into a resource. Entrepreneurs of snow rely on its seasonal arrival to sell leisure and snow experiences. A consumer economy is built around the manufacturing of material and cultural experiences, including winter food and snow games. In other words, "snow assumes meaning and value in relation to the function it plays for our capitalistic system and consumer culture" (Vannini and McCright 2007: 57). Quebec City's snow festival, for instance, generates a tourist economy organized around the design of snow castles and numerous snow jobs. Snow, like fire, contains *natural* and *cultural* elements that bring people together. Culturally, snow offers people opportunities for experiential encounters. Snowboarding, winter concerts, Papa Noël (or Santa Claus), and Quebec City's Winter Carnival all bring people together. Snow is the central theme and major facilitator of these social and cultural rituals. According to Gary Fine (2003:12), as groups deal with miniature occasions, "they reproduce the larger cultures in which they are embedded, they demonstrate processes of contention and control, and they negotiate meanings through similar processes that occur in larger units."

I continue my walk around the back of Montréal's eponymous landmark, Mount Royal. Fresh-fallen snow covers the trees on the mountainside. As I round a curve in the path, I encounter a surprising cacophony generated by people engaging in various monetized snow activities. Men and women pay money to slide down the mountain on tubes; adults pull children in sleds; cross-country skiers glide overland; barking dogs chase each other; a woman sells hot chocolate. The dwelling has transformed the space from one of solace to one of excitement and commercial transactions; the energy is absolutely electrifying. Within minutes, I move from sharing solitary intimacy with Magnolia and the snow, to sudden immersion in a collective celebration, an effervescent gathering of restorative vitality. These interactions are the collective fleshness of snow, facilitating active engagement between people and the natural world. It is the embodiment of collective, lived experience; wild and domesticated gatherings oriented by rituals and culture.

Snow is central to organizing these collective occasions. In this sense, snow is transformed from a passive thing falling inertly to a vital material that enacts the social. Snow facilitates rituals that generate laughter, winter activities, social transactions, and skillful play—all of which are elements of dwelling and weathering. Snow isn't simply an occurrence of nature, but is foundational to the fabric of Quebec's social life and cultural identity; its presence is essential to a unique array of physical interactions between human and non-human objects. Snow is sensual and symbolic, residing along a continuum between natural and cultural, pristine and soiled.

Snow Fright

The intensity of the snow is rapidly increasing in pace and thickness, and the wind begins flinging snow directly into my face. I feel stinging sensations of bitterness on my cheeks; they start to numb. My legs move faster, and I walk briskly while covering Magnolia's infant skin, otherwise protected only by a small jacket and thin baby clothes. My steps are smaller, more careful, and paced with caution; patches of ice form on the sidewalk; I hear myself from the inside out breathing faster and faster with shorter and shorter breaths; I feel my heart thumping harder in my chest; my teeth chatter. Perhaps this is my body's way of developing weathering skills, a technique of generating warmth as a skill to navigate the potential threat and fear of bitter cold. Magnolia's four-month-old flesh cannot withstand the infinite age of winter. I feel guilt for not taking more precautions prior to leaving our apartment on this simple snow escapade. I temporarily question whether I'm a responsible parent; I imagine Magnolia with pneumonia; I get depressed and feel the touch of despair swirling in my chest like the snow around us. I clearly have not acquired the necessary skills to traverse this dwelling.

My mood has shifted as fast as the indifferent weather. I am now contemplating what I would have done to avoid this current situation, had I had the foresight to listen to the weather report or check the weather app on my phone. I should have left Magnolia home with Ashley, my spouse, and gone shopping to prepare for the snowstorm. The typical stops usually include the grocery store, liquor store, hardware store to buy salt, and the European food store to stock up on goat cheese, olive bread, and Belgian chocolate. This fashioning of my subjectivity is an aspect of what Vannini and McCright (2007) refer to as "weather discourse." Weather discourse arises from the everyday popularity of radio, television, reality TV, and Internet narratives that shape the received patterns of behavior through which we experience and understand the weather. Weather discourse "contributes to the constitution of the subjectivity of the weather as a socio-cultural, historical, geo-political, and ideological phenomenon, as well as the subjectivity of 'weather citizens'" (Vannini and McCright 2007: 54).

We're close to home now and the neighborhood has changed drastically. The light snowfall and solace of our early walk, the heavy snow and exuberance of our time on the mountain, have been replaced by the industrial sounds of heavy machinery removing snow in the late evening. Red lights repeatedly flicker on the snow as numerous men in orange safety uniforms control traffic. Engines roar, loud beeping sounds proliferate to warn people and animals of impending danger, and diesel trucks slowly roll through the streets, pushing thousands of pounds of snow as they grate their steel on concrete. This new dwelling is anonymous and alien. The abrasive sounds are raw on my ears, yet they are central to governing the ongoing movement of everyday life. In Montreal, and elsewhere across North America, these machines have accidentally killed homeless people seeking protection while sleeping inside wooden crates or boxes surrounded by snow. The elderly have died while shoveling snow (heart rate and blood pressure increases) and people living in poverty without access to heat or social networks freeze to death. Snow is fatal.

There's nothing intimate about these mechanical sounds or the death of vulnerable people or animals; the machines are here to create safety in public places, to ensure that people can buy groceries, that businesses stay open and vehicles can travel to meet basic needs, that a market economy goes on. The dwelling shifts, transforms, and slips into new moments. Snow is a key ingredient of dwelling, but also a taken-for-granted commodity in the everyday smooth functioning of the capital, rituals, and mobilities that enable everyday life to go on.

David Redmon is a Lecturer in the School of Social Policy, Sociology and Social Research at the University of Kent at Canterbury (UK). Together with Ashley Sabin, he has directed the following films: *Mardi Gras: Made in China* (2005), *Kamp Katrina* (2007), *Intimidad* (2008), *Invisible Girlfriend* (2009), *Girl Model* (2011), *Downeast* (2012), *Kingdom of Animal* (2012), *Night Labor* (2013), *Choreography* (2014), and *Snow* (2015). Some of these documentaries have premiered at Sundance, Toronto, and Viennale Film Festivals, and some have aired on PBS, POV, BBC, CBC, DR, ARTE, or NHK. David Redmon received his Ph.D. in sociology from the University at Albany, SUNY, and is an alumnus of the Radcliffe Institute for Advanced Studies at Harvard University and Harvard University's Film Studies Center. Routledge's Innovative Ethnography Series has released his first book, *Beads, Bodies, and Trash* (2015).

References

Fine, Gary Alan and Tim Hallett. 2003. "Dust: A Study in Sociological Miniaturism." *The Sociological Quarterly 44*: 1–15.

Merleau-Ponty, Maurice. 1964. *The Visible and the Invisible*. 1969. Chicago, IL: Northwestern Press. Vannini, Phillip and Aaron McCright. 2007. "Technologies of the Sky: A Socio-Semiotic and Critical Analysis of Televised Weather Discourse." *Critical Discourse Studies 4*(1): 49–73.

Vannini, Phillip, Dennis D. Waskul, Simon Gottschalk, and Toby Ellis-Newstead. 2011. "Making Sense of the Weather: Dwelling and Weathering on Canada's Rain Coast." *Space and Culture 30*: 1–20.

25

SHOPPING

Keith Berry

Most people loathe everyday shopping. This is what I tell myself to feel better, since I enjoy going to the dentist more than shopping. There are nearly 38,000 supermarkets in the United States (Progressive Grocer 2013), and shoppers take at least one trip to the store per week (Food Marketing Institute 2013). Although online options exist, most people still shop at brick-and-mortar stores (Pisani, 2014). Shoppers consumed, and consumed often, contributing to more than 620 billion dollars in sales in 2013 (Food Marketing Institute 2013). Grocery shopping is a pervasive and unescapable ritual in people's lives.

This essay explores practices related to shopping for the "stuff" that makes everyday living possible, like food. Shopping has commonly been discussed in terms of the choices available and desirable to consumers (Hitt 1996). As a communication scholar my research and teaching focuses on the ways interaction informs, and is informed by, culture and identity. I assume communication to be the "symbolic process whereby reality is produced, maintained, repaired, and transformed" (Carey 1989: 17). This orientation leads me to be interested in the practices and realities that are inherent to making food choices. Each "aisle" below engages a particular theme that is inherent to my shopping. I investigate how the "mundane" process of shopping is a complex and highly symbolic ritual in which people "do" shopping and become shoppers.

256

KEITH BERRY

Aisle 1: Approaching Shopping

Most people split their shopping between two or more stores (Storrs 2012). I shop in just one, and only after I have stalled for as long as possible. Stalling techniques include sitting in the car for a few minutes, talking with friends on my cell phone, and "people watching." I notice shopping carts everywhere, indicative of shoppers who did not bring their carts to the designated collection area. Apparently life is too busy for some people to care about cars being nicked by flyaway carts. There are fellow shoppers scurrying from cars to the store doors, rarely with a smile, and moving with a brisk, let-us-get-this-done walk. There are people who seem happy to be shopping, an appearance that puzzles me. Perhaps they are superhuman and possess the art and skill of mindful shopping. They may also be faking it.

As I walk from car to store many voices are in my head. I think of the tips for "healthiest" and "cheapest" foods that I routinely learn of when watching *The Today Show* and *The View,* and how those tips only sometimes match the groceries I plan to buy. As I and other incoming shoppers approach the doors, shoppers exit the store. Many outgoing shoppers look livelier than the people entering. They have completed the deed and survived. Indeed, they are in a much better place. I will hopefully soon be like them.

Often Boy Scouts and Girl Scouts, who are fund raising are positioned just outside the store. They entice shoppers to buy unhealthy foods with their adorable and needy faces. I typically respond, "Awww, good morning, no thank you, not this time." This seems to let me off the hook. "Catch ya' on the way out!" they respond. Their leaders have trained these mini-capitalists well. Even before entering the store, shoppers have to negotiate consumption and identity.

Once inside the store it is time to secure a shopping cart, a practice fraught with germ issues. Stores increasingly are providing sanitizing wipes, which creates a series of identity-related questions. For instance, if shoppers do not wipe handles, do fellow shoppers mark them as being dirty people? On the other hand, if shoppers use the wipes, exactly how thorough do we need to clean? This issue points to an inevitable reality: shopping means contacting germs. It means touching produce touched by other people, ducking wide-open-mouthed coughs, and being skeptical about whether employees take it seriously when they are told: "Employees must wash their hands before returning to work."

Aisle 2: Shopping Space

On average grocery stores measure 46,000 square feet (Tuttle 2011). They are large physical places that take the form of richly symbolic social spaces (De Certeau 2011; Humphery 1998). These spaces are often designed to resemble parts of houses, or to feel like home, so shoppers might stay longer and consume more. The store where I shop has façades that look like portions of house roofs, employees who are dressed as if they are in the kitchen, and pharmacists who look out for customers, who are "one of the family." Pumpkins, Easter baskets, and wreaths and food for upcoming holidays beckon shoppers when we first enter the store. These stress the importance, or supposed importance, of national holidays.

Shopping also provides a highly sensorial space. As I move more fully into the store, I smell freshly baked pastries and seasonal flowers. Overhead lights are dim enough to lessen the blow of fluorescent harshness, yet bright enough to see what shoppers are doing and notice the warm and lively pastel-colored walls. The worn wheels of the shopping cart rattle with every movement across the tiled floor. Beeps and other sounds flow from the checkout stations. Refrigerator units hum and motion-detector lights of refrigerator and freezer units flick on and off. Water mists over fresh produce and seafood, and occasionally thunder noises sound. Light music plays from overhead speakers, and the volume is not too soft or loud. In these ways, the space captures and enlivens senses, sensually (Hitt 1996) immersing shoppers within the buying experience.

Experiences in this space are conditioned by the intensity of its social activity, which varies based on a number of cultural factors. For instance, shopping just before a televised sports game, or at the last hour or two before stores close on holidays, is risky. Even worse is shopping around forecasted major storms, such as hurricanes and blizzards. At this time all hell could break loose. The charging rattles of shopping cart wheels signal the presence of people who are gaming for the last bread, eggs, milk, and water. For both occasions these shopping practices embody the competiveness of the game and the fear provoked by alarmist television meteorologists. Shoppers often fend for themselves. Second place is unacceptable, and injuries are not personal.

Aisle 3: Shopping Products

Shopping is about consuming goods and entails navigating through options that often speak to priorities in shoppers' lives. As I move through aisles I notice products that point to convenience (e.g., frozen dinners), health (e.g., gluten free), budget (e.g., "buy one get one free," or "BOGO"), the environmentally conscious (e.g., free-range chickens), and local interest (e.g., Florida Gators gelatin molds). Also, stores offer shoppers a plethora of options from which to choose. Will it be honey-roasted or peppercorn turkey luncheon meat? Thick or thin slices? Which is better, store brand or brand name? Offering an average of 43,844 items (Food Marketing Institute 2013), stores bombard shoppers with too many possibilities from which to choose, and more than enough to eat or use sufficiently.

My practice of choosing products is multilayered and speaks to consumption being relational and emotional. For instance, I notice the line of Coke Zero that shows personalized names on every can, and buy one with "Buddy." This is the term of endearment that a best friend and I use to address each other. I am also a "moody" shopper. It is not coincidental that comfort food items are in my cart when writing deadlines approach, or stress hits at home. Stores understand well the cultural phenomenon of "emotional eating" (Roth 1993). This should give shoppers pause, as 70% of the food people eat is highly processed (Warner 2013).

I often glance into the carts of passersby, and for fun reflect on aspects of their possible identities, given the products they have selected. For example, carts filled with plenty of cases of beer, chips, and solo cups might suggest partiers, and those carts with overflowing products, often giant packages of paper towels, point to shoppers who are there for large families, or maybe once-a-month shoppers. This observation and inference work involves ascribing identities that, to be sure, are speculative and stereotypical. Yet often these inferences are too hard to resist.

Aisle 4: Shopping People

Shopping is a significantly "peopled" ritual that surrounds people with what I take to be prototypical "types" of shoppers and workers. Page constraints lead me to just focus on shoppers. The list of shopping people includes: romantic couples who bicker about whether or not one partner "needs more fattening cookies;" shoppers who are on the phone with their spouses, the persons who wrote the lists and presumably know the store better; and parents who involve their child in shopping ("Sweetie, all we have left is the edamame and milk"). Shopping brings shoppers into contact with diverse beings, people with whom we share the need to be in the store, but who often perform shopping in unique ways.

Shoppers are people with stories, and who, like most people when they are communicating, understand shopping narratively (Fisher, 1984). We come to stores with stories about each other (alcohol-filled carts signify partiers), culture (Super Bowl is a time for celebrating), products (remember the time I puked after eating a bag of Doritos?) and shopping itself (do you recall our last marathon shopping session when we hosted your retirement party?). These stories speak to cultural realities of shopping, yet, the space rarely encourages a closeness that would allow shoppers to engage, let alone understand, each other's stories and realities well. As a result, the significance of stories and storytellers are backgrounded, and some more than others. Lost are stories about LGBTQ shoppers, like me, who try to locate our identities and needs and interests in shopping, a cultural ritual that is steeped in heteronormative assumptions and expectations. For instance, save for a few businesses that cater specifically to LGBTQ culture, I have yet to see greeting cards that are dedicated to same-sex relationships, or displays of families that show families with same-sex partners. Also lost are stories that convey how shoppers must grapple with racism (Boylorn 2011) and other social justice issues (e.g., sexism, classism, ableism). Indeed, while shopping stories might emphasize the need to consume goods in expeditious and individualized ways, they minimize the chance for personal and empathetic understanding. In this sense, shopping creates the conditions for relating as "its," or objects, and rarely as "thous," or people whose stories and beings are confirmed and valued (Buber 1970).

Aisle 5: Shopping Interactions

Similarly, shopping does not require sustained communication with others. Often interactions occur in passing, and are brief and tactical. These exchanges take the form of "seen but unnoticed" (Garfinkel 1967) relational dances, which shoppers are prone to perform but not explore.

For instance, as I move down the toiletries aisle, I approach someone who is coming directly at me. Another shopper is located to my side, filling the other half of the aisle. We are immersed in a shopping traffic jam. Noticing the break in smooth shopping, both shoppers stop in our tracks. One or both shoppers acknowledge the breach via smiles and eye contact, and say something like, "Sorry!" or "Ooops, sorry." Then one dance partner moves, often quickly, through an open space to get out of the other shopper's way. Sometimes this person draws attention to the quickness by adding nervous laughter, and maybe a joke ("Shall we dance?"). At least two levels of meaning inform what otherwise would seem like an innocuous dance. On the one hand, this response works as basic small talk. The apologies and movement serve as fillers for what is a physical impasse, and a brief pause in the normally steady flow of shopping. On the other hand, it also shows politeness (Brown & Levinson 1987) in the shopping ritual, wherein shoppers work to save the other person's face and convey ownership of the issue. The response is to say, "Ooops, this jam is my fault, not yours. Let me fix it." This response is often mutually performed by both shoppers. Here both show each other politeness, and each manages her or his own impression (Goffman 1959) as courteous and orderly shoppers.

There are additional dances, some more innocuous than others. Take, for example, a woman who says, "Hang in there, Dad, it gets easier," to a man whose child is doing nothing but screaming in the store. The statement serves to support the dad, whom she assumes is struggling. I have witnessed plenty of people saying this same line to women who are enduring children who have lost their minds, but not their voices. However, on another level, although kind and supportive, the utterance also points to essentializing cultural notions concerning sex/gender and parenting, namely that men need extra support in such situations. Or take the coordination of eye contact that occurs between men who are strangers. While this embodied relational practice might be a way to acknowledge the other, if it lasts for more than a second (or less!), it is not uncommon for the man on the receiving end to quickly evade contact. Suddenly a "hello" means something else, such as same-sex attraction, implicating the recipient as a shopper who works with a finely honed "gaydar." That it should even matter, and the dance should even exist, speaks to some of the ways in which shopping is informed by cultural assumptions and expectations rooted in homophobia. Still, today some shoppers must carefully manage how we dance.

Aisle 6: Checkout/Release

Arriving to the checkout area means anticipating imminent release from the throws of shopping. Yet it also means more choices, temptations, and people watching.

Shoppers often need to choose between ringing up our own groceries or dealing with cashiers. I choose living bodies and not machines as much as possible. I fear self-pay lines are another way to eliminate jobs, and I actually enjoy relating with cashiers. Stores also use this area to continue bombarding shoppers with things to consume. Tabloid magazines and other "pocket-sized" items (e.g., chewing gum, candies) are impossible to miss and sometimes too tempting to decline. Additionally, checking out means being a "good shopper"; thus shoppers must unload items from carts to conveyor belts in a timely and efficient manner. This process is affected by shoppers who are ahead of us in line, just as our process affects those behind us. As cashiers begin their ringing, they pose another choice to shoppers—selecting between paper and plastic bags. I often choose plastic bags, because they make it easier to carry groceries from my car to my home. I make plenty of environmentally conscious choices in my life. Yet, choosing plastic bags sometimes makes me feel guilty. I suspect bringing one's own bag to the store is most ideal, yet I know no one who builds this into their shopping ritual.

Once I have checked out I begin to feel a sense of relief. I have completed the deed. Granted, I emerge from shopping regularly feeling as though I have spent more time in the store than desired, spent far more money than expected, and spoken meaningfully to far fewer shoppers than I would normally speak to outside of this space. Nevertheless, shopping feels better on this end than the other. Few choices remain and I will soon check back into my everyday non-shopping rituals, practices, and identities.

Newly released from the throws of this ritual, I make my way to the exit, seeing some new shoppers enter and begin to sanitize their carts. Seeing shoppers skip this step makes me think of how the pen I just used to sign my credit card receipt is undoubtedly filled with germs. I work to let go of this concern. After all, I have survived shopping and am done with it all, until next time. As I move through the store's exit, I see an older woman enthusiastically say to the children pushing their goods, "Oh, so what do we have here?!" Her kindness is impressive. It also enables me to scoot to the parking lot unnoticed. Good exits like this prevent even more consumption.

As I walk to my car, I notice many incoming shoppers who appear listless look my way. They see me smiling widely and I wonder if they want to be me.

Once I am inside my car I let out a long sigh of relief. It is over. Paying attention to the moving and consuming within the store's aisles helps me to be more mindful of everyday shopping. While "mundane" in one sense, the practices of "doing" shopping and becoming shoppers are also personally and culturally symbolic and meaningful. I am thrilled to be checked out and able to move onto the next part of my day. But I then realize I have forgotten to buy some things and head back into the store.

Keith Berry is Associate Professor of Communication at the University of South Florida and past chair of the National Communication Association's Ethnography Division. His teaching and research primarily use cultural approaches to investigate identity negotiation as it occurs and is made influential within contexts of relational communication, especially those pertaining to marginalized populations. He also explores reflexivity in ethnographic and autoethnographic research, LGBTQ culture, and queer theory. His research has appeared in journals such as *Journal of Applied Communication Research, Text and Performance Quarterly, Cultural Studies ⇔ Critical Methodologies, Qualitative Inquiry,* and *Review* *of Communication*, and in books such as *Handbook of Autoethnography* (Left Coast Press, 2013) and *Identity Research and Communication: Intercultural Reflections and Future Directions* (Lexington Books, 2012). His book, *BULLIED: Stories of Bullying, Youth, and Identity* is forthcoming from Left Coast Press. Keith can be seen taking field notes at a grocery store near you.

References

Boylorn, Robin M. 2011. "Gray or For Colored Girls Who Are Tired of Chasing Rainbows: Race and Reflexivity." *Cultural Studies↔Critical Methodologies 11*: 178–186.

Brown, Penelope and, Steven C. Levinson. 1987. *Politeness: Some Universals in Language Usage* Cambridge, UK: Cambridge University Press.

Buber, Martin. 1970. *I and Thou*. (Walter Kaufman, trans.) New York, NY: Touchstone Books.

Carey, James. 1989. *Communication as Culture: Essays on Media and Society*. Boston, MA: Unwin Hyman Inc.

De Certeau, Michel. 2011. *The Practice of Everyday Life*. Berkeley, CA: University of California Press.

Fisher, Walter. 1984. "Narration as a Human Communication Paradigm: The Case of Public Moral Argument." *Communication Monographs 51*: 1–22.

Food Marketing Institute. 2013. Supermarket Facts. Accessed October 1, 2014. Retrieved from http://www.fmi.org/.

Garfinkel, Harold. 1967. *Studies in Ethnomethodology*. Englewood Cliffs, NJ: Prentice-Hall.

Goffman, E. 1959. *The Presentation of Self in Everyday Life*. New York, NY: Anchor Books.

Hitt, Jack. 1996. "The Theory of Supermarkets." *New York Times*. Retrieved from http://www.nytimes.com/1996/03/10/magazine/the-theory-of-supermarkets.html.

Humphery, Kim. 1998. *Shelf Life: Supermarkets and the Changing Cultures of Consumption*. Cambridge, UK and New York, NY: Cambridge University Press.

Pisani, Joseph. 2014. "Ditch the Supermarket: These 3 Companies Deliver." *USA TODAY*. Retrieved from http://www.usatoday.com/story/money/business/2014/06/21/ditch-the-supermarket/10966573.

Progressive Grocer. 2013. Research and Data. Accessed October 1, 2014. Retrieved from http://www.progressivegrocer.com.

Roth, Geneen. 1993. *When Food is Love: Exploring the Relationship Between Eating and Intimacy*. New York, NY: Penguin Books.

Storrs, Francis. 2012. "How Grocery Shopping got Personal." *Boston Globe*. Accessed October 1, 2014. Retrieved from http://www.bostonglobe.com/magazine/2012/10/13/how-grocery-shopping-got-personal/P3Fgfalj8jB4bNQ8fGnU7K/story.html/.

Tuttle, Brad. 2011. "Fewer Choices, More Savings: The New Way to Buy Groceries." *Time*. Accessed October 1, 2014. Retrieved from http://business.time.com/2011/01/25/fewer-choices-more-savings-the-new-way-to-buy-groceries/.

Warner, Melanie. 2013. *Pandora's Lunchbox: How Processed Food Took Over the American Meal*. New York, NY: Scribner.

26

TRICK-OR-TREATING

William Ryan Force

Trick-or-treating is a social practice in North American culture in which children wear costumes to solicit treats (candy, snacks, small toys, and other inexpensive items) from homes and businesses in celebration of Halloween. Although its origins can be traced to various pagan and folk practices in other cultures, by the 1940s it was widely established in the United States and Canada (Best 1985; Kawash 2001; Stone 1959). In this essay, I explore what appears to be a trivial activities to many people—handing out treats on Halloween evening—as representative of larger social patterns. This essay explores the micropolitical dimensions of this ritual, from the perspective of the individual distributing the treats (the "treater"). I reflect upon how moral, ideological, and cultural values informed my decision-making practices when treating those individuals who visited my home on Halloween 2013 and 2014. I argue the criteria and logic by which we evaluate individuals' "treat-worthiness" becomes a way of expressing our social identity and worldview.

The Meaning of Treating

In the summer of 2014 I was teaching abroad in London with a few students from my university in the United States. While leaving the Camden Market, our little group passed a middle-aged man—dressed in the typical trappings of a person who has lived without conventional housing or employment for some time—playing an accordion (and doing so quite well). As we walked past him, I fished out a pound coin from my pocket and tossed it into his hat, nodding to the musician in appreciation of his song. A few minutes later as I was reading on the "tube," one student turned to me and asked, "Dr. Force, why did you give that guy back there money?"

I was startled by the question, having assumed this was unremarkable behavior on my part. "Well, I can't play the accordion. He was pretty good. I like hearing music in public like that." She pressed, "But what if he spends it on drugs or something?" Many of the other students giggled and seemed to nod their heads in agreement with the inquiry. I responded impulsively and without filter, commenting sharply, "Does your boss tell you how to spend your paycheck?" The student shrugged her shoulders and said, "I guess," and the group returned after a moment to their prior interactions.

Georg Simmel observed that there is always a "return" on the gifts we give, although they are sometimes symbolic and ephemeral. In many cases, a practical consequence of gift-giving for the giver may simply be the reinforcement of their own sense of self (Simmel, 1971). Put differently, what we often receive from gifts that are apparently nonreciprocal is some of the "raw" cultural material of identity. Donileen Loseke and Kirsten Fawcett (1995) found that in order to be deemed "worthy" of charity, the potential recipient must demonstrate commitment to the ideological values of the giver. In this case the "return" on the gift appears to be a (more often than not) private affirmation of the giver's commitment to a political, economic, or cultural order. When we construct and deploy a moral hierarchy in the interests of determining another person's gift-worthiness—in any context—we reveal those ideals to which we aspire. The narrative of our gift-giving, even if never made public, is inherently social and thus has an impact on the self-concept of the giver.

Decisions about how to "treat" strangers or other individuals with whom we have only superficial interactions are fateful—whether in partial payment of services (like gratuities for wait staff), as gifts (a Christmas card and nip bottle for the local mail carrier), or in more ambiguously defined circumstances like offering money to buskers and street performers. As I began writing this essay, that moment in London kept returning to my mind. In line with Simmel's comments, my students expected that a gift be reciprocated in some way. Clearly, I perceived the presence of music in public space as worthy of "reward" in a way the students did not. There is a notable difference in the socio-economic backgrounds of the students and myself—I grew up working-class and briefly received government assistance, as opposed to most of my students, who come from reasonably secure middle-class families. Additionally, I was exposed to radical political, economic, and cultural critiques of poverty in grad school, and I tend to view the unemployed and un-homed as the logical consequence of an unjust social order. For aesthetic, biographical, and ideological reasons that are (in retrospect) obvious, I acted in a way that I experienced as mundane but to others was noteworthy.

Tricky Treating

In this sense, the trick-or-treating ritual of Halloween serves as a help-ful vignette that demonstrates how we evaluate the treat-worthiness of people in multiple circumstances. "Giving" and "treating" function as particular examples of what Goffman (1959) broadly called our "presentation of self" or what Cahill (1998) described as "technologies of person production." As both authors note, the performances we deliver may not necessarily even be directed at others. When I treat a masked stranger with miniature candy bars or drop a coin into a home-less woman's coffee cup in a foreign city, I cannot honestly expect any overt compensation from those individuals; the interaction is fleeting and not added to their store of biographical facts about me, so it may even appear to be of no consequence for the constitution of an identity. Yet, interactionists remind us that we are our own audiences. Even when alone and anonymous, activities like treating help us formulate our self-concepts. It is now somewhat commonplace to state that the "personal is political;" the sociology of everyday life takes this a step further and reminds us that even those activities that occur in seeming isolation from others remain social.

Halloween 2013 was the first time I distributed treats from my home in Springfield, Massachusetts. That year, despite being a Thursday evening we received over 100 visitors and found toward the end of the evening we had insufficient candy for our guests. As the night pro-gressed, my partner and I began explicitly discussing our decisions about how to allocate the dwindling supply. As we reviewed our ideal criteria for trick-or-treaters, it became clear that we were identifying similar and specific elements in making this decision: we both preferred to reserve candy for younger kids (under 14) and in the event older children or teens came by, we tried to avoid relinquishing candy to those who had not put forth the effort to wear a costume. We both agreed that the parents who wore no costumes yet were collecting treats for small children were basically scamming us—the children in question were often too young to eat candy at all, and the adults who participated in this way often failed to offer even the basic courtesy of a "thank you." These people, we agreed, should not receive anything. In the end, we caved and gave candy to everyone who came by.

In speaking with neighbors, friends, and family afterward it became clear that the expectations we voiced were widely shared. Some had tricks for managing a refusal—those who are apparently less susceptible to social awkwardness than myself simply said to older kids, "Sorry, we only bought enough for the little ones." One neighbor said she always kept the bowl only partially filled to help with the fib. Some had two stashes of candy (expensive stuff for the "good" candidates and cheap, off-brand candy for the "bad" kids). A few did not seem to moralize about who received treats and gave the candy to everyone, although it often evolved into an issue of the quantity or quality of treats they handed out. Those who were very liberal allowed children to grab from the bowl themselves. Although all agreed some individuals were ideal recipients, the criteria varied. Perhaps the most universally agreed-upon standard was that the later it got and the darker the streets became, the stingier people were. The perception in play was that the kids who "this was really about" should not be out past 8 p.m.

Treat Yo Self,[1] or the Micropolitics of Treating

Erving Goffman (1959) wrote that what we call "the self" is a product of social experience. Through the process of internalizing and using cultural resources we establish a relatively durable understanding about what sort of person we are. Goffman (1959: 253) likens the physical body to a "peg" upon which "something of a collaborative manufacture will be hung for a time." This includes even those behaviors we regard as private, idiosyncratic, or bereft of higher meaning. Even those activities that occur in seeming isolation from others remain social in the sense that they are added to our self-concept, informed by previous interactions, and inform subsequent ones. In our daily lives, we are subjected to the evaluation of other people in ways that hold us accountable to commonplace cultural assumptions from our gender (West and Fenstermaker 1987) and to the way we are expected to smell (Waskul and Vannini 2008).

Spencer Cahill (1998) explains that normative prescriptions for social behavior act as interactive "technologies" that construct and communicate a legible person to others. Thus the "normal" individual is one who reproduces the social world and its interaction order. This indicates that social interaction (and even the possession of an identity) is thus "political," if we can define politics simply as the use of power. More specifically, *micropolitics* may refer to the forms of social power seen in action "on the ground" via the shaping of our personal tastes and way of seeing the world (Bourdieu 1984; Goffman 1974; Zerubavel 1997). Fittingly, Cahill (1998) notes this was Goffman's own concern when he wrote that sociologists must attend to the "various ways in which the individual is treated and *treats others*, and deducing what is implied about him through this treatment" (Goffman 1971: 342, emphasis added). If we consider the ritual of "treating" masked candy enthusiasts on Halloween in this light, it ought to be obvious that the decisions we make—about whether to distribute treats, to whom, in what number, and under which conditions—reveal the social values held by the treater, acting as one of many incarnations of those ideas as the basis for social action.

In "Halloween and the Mass Child," Gregory Stone (1959) characterizes trick-or-treating as essentially consumerism with training wheels, normalizing the accumulation of useless commodities in order to recruit these children into a lifetime on the work-spend treadmill. Years later, Joel Best and Gerald Horiuchi (1985) addressed the contemporary folk devil of "Halloween sadism" in which children are injured or killed by treats that have been purposefully contaminated (with poison, sharp objects, etc.). Best and Horiuchi (1985) point out that empirical evidence to the contrary does not hold up against the *usefulness* of people's belief in this story. Together, Stone (1959) and Best and Horiuchi's (1985) arguments reveal that being "treated" in the manner of Halloween simultaneously underscores the allegedly egalitarian and civic dimensions of contemporary American culture while revealing the limitations of our belief in the altruistic aspects of that image.

Whereas Stone (1959) was concerned with the decline of productive activity (the move from "tricking" to treating"), Best and Horiuchi (1985) suggested that the fear of the sadist often culminates in our culture's suspicion of homemade (non-commercial) treats. In other words, strangers ought not be trusted unless those relations are managed under the auspices of capitalism. Since the nature of trick-or-treating requires interaction with strangers but threatens the capitalist basis of exchange, it therefore becomes the source of anxiety. One might argue that the homemade treat becomes the ultimate boogeyman in the story because it represents a form of creative, expressive labor (antithetical to late capitalism) and it is offered freely without an explicit demand for material reciprocity (which undermines capitalism more generally).

In 2014 I had committed to give candy to everyone (I am both a communist and a bit of a wimp when it comes to confrontation), but determined to be judicious in terms of who got what. My partner and I both value homemade or DIY costumes over the store-bought variety, for instance. Yet in 2014 this became complicated by what were clearly very poor children who could only afford a plastic mask worn with their everyday clothes. For instance, about a dozen children in my mixed-class neighborhood wore Batman t-shirts with makeshift capes as "Batman costumes." In these cases, especially if they were young, I found it difficult to enforce the "homemade" standard and often gave to these children the same amount I had to the children in "good" costumes. There was also a not-so-subtle preference for children we knew or recognized from our own block (whom we even encouraged to stop by again on their way home).

The following Halloween in 2014 I asked people again about their decision in treating the children and got a range of responses:

"I flat out refuse if they are taller than me."
"I can't help but give to everyone, it's sort of an egalitarian holiday that way."

"They have to say 'trick-or-treat,' that's my rule."
"The teenagers out at 9 [pm]? Come on, fuck that."

As Kawash (2011: 164) noted, Halloween is generally viewed as a holiday oriented around "charity, generosity, and neighborliness." Despite Stone's (1959) general animosity toward trick-or-treating, even he reveals degrees of disdain for the so-called "urchins." Stone, for instance, also seems to place some slight premium on the homemade costumes over the store-bought. Additionally, he illustrates using newspaper editorials that an age-specific character was enforced, including the temporary placement of an older youth in police custody for trick-or-treating at age 17.

The most fascinating anecdote was from an individual who decided to take a stand against treating people who were not in costume. After giving one kid a "hard time" about not being in costume, the teen boy responded that he could not afford one. The treater in question softened, but offered the young man a single piece of bubble gum. In our conversation, they expressed deep remorse about their decision: "I gave him crappy candy … and now I'm always going to be just another mean White person who made him feel bad about being poor." I argued that I always *liked* getting bubble gum as a kid, that "crappy" candy is subjective, and that by treating the kid at all they should be free of guilt.

In sum, "treating" others carries deep implications for the self. The act of giving is infused with moral, ideological, and cultural values that inform our decision-making practices. In this way we can understand treating or gifting as a micropolitical endeavor: one that affirms our identity and values and imposes that moral reality upon others. This is perhaps most obvious in the anxiety or regret we experience when we realize that we have unintentionally "shorted" or "stiffed" someone.

Conclusions

The ritual of trick-or-treating at Halloween serves as a useful illustration of how we evaluate the gift-worthiness of people in multiple circumstances—how we decide to "tip" wait staff at restaurants, whether we give money to homeless folks, and gift-giving during birthdays and special occasions to name a few. Arguably, even less overt forms of gifting are implicated: when to compliment a person, whether to let a distressed driver ahead of us during traffic, or (as a professor) when to give a merciful passing grade. In each case, this decision involves processing the raw materials of the situation—the potential recipient of generosity, the circumstances of the exchange, and (perhaps most importantly) the social values by which the treater operates. The act of "treating" is autobiographical and a micropolitical gesture that enforces a moral vision of the world.

When second-wave feminists asserted that the personal is indeed political, part of the goal was to reveal the structures of domination in which we unwittingly participate. Sociologists of everyday life help advance our understanding of the meaning-laden quality of even the most mundane activities by articulating their relationship to institutional and cultural stocks of knowledge. The decisions we make about whether and how to "treat" are among countless acts of self-construction in which we confer to others a value relative to our own. In determining an individual to be treat-worthy, we secure for them a legitimate place in our social universe.

William Ryan Force is Assistant Professor of Sociology at Western New England University (MA). He is a student of social life. His research and teaching explore the accomplishment of identity at the intersection of culture, power, and language. His work covers a variety of areas including punk/indie rock, transgressive TV, bar culture, and queer visibility.

Note

1. "Treat yo self" is a ritual of lavish consumption (including "massages, mimosas, [and] fine leather goods") practiced by the characters Tom and Donna in the TV series *Parks and Recreation*. Sociologically, it functions for Tom and Donna as a ritualized affirmation of their decadent, consumerist selves. Furthermore, when fiscally sensible Ben attempts to join in, it is incompatible with his self-concept.

References

Best, Joel and Gerald T. Horiuchi. 1985. "The Razor Blade in the Apple: The Social Construction of Urban Legends." *Social Problems* 32(5): 488–499.

Bourdieu, Pierre. 1984 (1979). *Distinction: A Social Critique of the Judgement of Taste* (trans. Richard Nice). London, UK: Routledge & Kegan Paul.

Cahill, Spencer. 1998. "Toward a Sociology of the Person." *Sociological Theory* 16(2): 131–148.

Foucault, Michel. 1975 (1977). *Discipline and Punish.* New York, NY: Vintage Books.

Goffman, Erving. 1959. *The Presentation of Self in Everyday Life.* New York, NY: Anchor Books.

Goffman, Erving. 1971. *Relations in Public: Microstudies of the Public Order.* New York, NY: Basic Books.

Goffman, Erving. 1974. *Frame Analysis.* Boston, MA: Northeastern University Press.

Kawash, Samira. 2011. "Gangsters, Pranksters, and the Invention of Trick-or-Treating, 1930–1960." *American Journal of Play* 4(2): 150–175.

Loseke, Donileen and Kirsten Fawcett. 1995. "Appealing Appeals: Constructing Moral Worthiness 1912–1917." *The Sociological Quarterly* 36(1): 61–78.

Simmel, Georg. 1971. *Georg Simmel on Individuality and Social Forms* (Donald Levine, Ed.). Chicago, IL: University of Chicago Press.

Stone, Gregory. 1959. "Halloween and the Mass Child." *American Quarterly* 11(3): 372–379.

Waskul, Dennis D. and Phillip Vannini. 2008. "Smell, Odor, and Somatic Work: Sense-Making and Sensory Management." *Social Psychology Quarterly* 71(1): 53–71.

West, Candace and Sarah Fenstermaker. 1987. "Doing Gender." *Gender & Society* 1(2): 125–151.

Zerubavel, Eviatar. 1997. *Social Mindscapes: An Invitation to Cognitive Sociology.* Cambridge, MA: Harvard University Press.

27

STAYING IN HOTELS

Orvar Löfgren

Travel and tourism are often pictured as an escape from the everyday, getting away from it all, becoming a different person, playing the role of "the holiday me." But vacationing too has its own routines, micro-rituals, and trivialities (often overlooked in studies of tourism). While searching for the great travel experience, tourists spend a lot of time exposed to delayed trains, bad weather, missing boarding passes, ill-fitting walking shoes, or the occasional dingy hotel room—so different from the slick digital image on the Web. I explore this mundane side of Paradise, focusing on one basic institution: the hotel, which also occupies a prominent space in popular culture.

To be a tourist hotel guest is to constantly move between mundane activities and mediated fantasy worlds, as well as negotiate the transits between everyday life and holiday adventure. My own interest in hotels comes from an ongoing project on the materialities and affects of travel and tourism—from baggage and train compartments to moods and modes of mobilities (Löfgren, 2015). In the following I will use the hotel as an arena to analyse a classic tension in everyday life, that between private and public spheres.

Home Away from Home?

We are in the car on our way to the airport, ready for a vacation in Barcelona. I had trouble sleeping last night, having a strong bout of travel fever—that special nervous and footloose state that blends antici-pation and euphoria with anxiety. It is still with me. Did we lock the front door? Have I got the passports? I have to stop the car and check the baggage to be sure.

The flight goes fine, but it is still a relief to get into the hotel room and close the door. Outside the traffic is intense, but in here we are safe—our own miniature world for a weekend.

"Esterilizado Sterilisé Sterilised Sterilisiert" reads the reassuring four-language message on the plastic ribbon stretched across the toilet seat. Similar promises of pristine order are found in room number 1003 at the hotel *Presidente*. But otherwise our room shows many traces of hard-drinking and hard-smoking generations of earlier visitors. The carpet is faded. The 1960s modernist interior has taken its knocks too. But, still, there is magic in opening the hotel door: a new place of temporary residence.

There is the weightlessness of a clean start, bolstered by all those small gifts waiting for us: from shampoo bottles to note pads. There is a childish pleasure in recording these details, going through the basket of toiletries and opening the tiny piece of chocolate resting on the pillow. Maybe we should treat ourselves to a drink from the mini-bar?

How is this hotel room euphoria created? As one of the characters in Douglas Coupland's novel *Shampoo Planet* defines it: "In a hotel room you have no history, you only have an essence. You feel like you're all potential, waiting to be rewritten" (1992: 32). This weightlessness also has to do with winding down from the stress of all the departure preparations and the actual travel, but it can be a fragile euphoria. As Daisann McLane points out in her book *Cheap Hotels*:

> Hotel rooms, even the most pleasant ones, contain within their walls a hint of melancholy. When you arrive in a place the room is your new friend, all important. You open all the drawers, turn all the lights on and off, play with the faucets, and begin a new relationship (2002: 159).

She continues to say that hotel rooms often lack staying power, every night the magic may fade, as people discover and explore the territories outside the room.

Tensions and transformations like this illustrate why hotel rooms can be such a rewarding arena for studying the paradoxes and contradictions of everyday life. The hotel balances so precariously between a number of polarities such as private and public, intimate and intimidating, adventure and routine.

"Private" is associated with a cluster of related words: secret, exclusive reclusive, isolated, but also intimate, informal, warm, and small-scale. As such, the home is often cited as the classic example. In a discussion of the home as a cultural project and moral arena, Mary Douglas (1991), simply categorized home as "everything a hotel is not."

The ways in which hotel and home are linked or contrasted tell us something about how cultural polarities may be organized in complex ways. The hotel is an institution that is twisting, mixing and reframing this tension between public and private. The ways in which this is done varies with what kind(s) of hotels we are talking about—from small pensions to gigantic establishments. My focus here will be on larger hotels, like resorts (Löfgren 2000) and four- to five-star hotels (Volland, Greenville, and Rebick 2013).

Welcome to the Hotel California

Moving into a hotel is also moving into a mediascape. Consider, for example, all the hotels one has visited in television, movies, novels, and other media. Daydreams and flashbacks to earlier memories or images are entangled in the actual hotel experience—such interweavings are a constant part of everyday life. People rather effortlessly manage to live simultaneously in the past, the present, and the future—in first-hand, mediated, and re-mediated realities.

Hotels are often used as a scene and storyboard in all kinds of popular culture. There are musical hotels like Eric Burdon's "Hotel Hell," The Doors' "Morrison Hotel," The Eagles' "Hotel California," and Elvis's "Heartbreak Hotel." There are hotel soap operas from all over the world and a genre of "hotel novels."

Hotels are also popular in Hollywood. There are hundreds of films using the hotel as their setting, from the Marx Brothers' first film from 1929 about the Hotel de Coconut in Florida, mismanaged by Groucho Marx with the assistance of Zeppo, to Wes Andersen's nostalgic *The Grand Budapest Hotel* from 2014. Hollywood hotels are used for all kinds of genres.

In thrillers and horror stories, what looks just like an ordinary hotel slowly takes on a more threatening presence. Deserted, endless hotel corridors, unfriendly staff, rattling windows and dripping faucets. Think of Hitchcock's *Psycho* from 1960, with Norman Bates (Anthony Perkins) as a crazy motel manager, or Stanley Kubrick's *The Shining* from 1980, where Jack Nicholson goes mad in the isolated Overlook Hotel, running along empty corridors, knife in hand. The hotel also becomes a strong emotional backdrop for romance and passion (*Maid in Manhattan*), drama and conflict (*Le Week-end*) melancholia or homesickness (*Lost in Translation*) slap-stick and farce (*Some Like it Hot*). For filmmakers it is often a starting point that people behave differently in a hotel. The setting does something to activities and affects. It is as if the minimalist blandness of the hotel room makes the drama of conflicts, feelings, or longings stand out more clearly. Movies thus tend to aggrandize, parody, transform life in hotels. They make certain themes very visible and this can be a real help when one is embarking on a study.

Secure or Hostile

I will start with one dimension of the polarity of public/private: the hotel as a safe and private haven, a miniature home-away-from-home and, on the other side, the fact that people are not at home at all but moving in alien territory. Indeed, in a hotel room the feelings of secure coziness can disappear all of a sudden.

In Roman Polanski's thriller *Frantic* (1988), an American surgeon and his wife arrive in Paris one rainy day and hurry to claim their hotel room. Their marriage is due for a boost. They inspect the clean and perfect room, full of happy anticipations. They order breakfast and put out the "do-not –disturb" sign. But first the husband (Harrison Ford) needs a shower. We watch him rinse off the travel fatigue, singing happily while shaving and wrapping a thick white towel around him. He walks out of the bathroom only to find out that his wife is gone. In this moment the hotel room is transformed from an intimate honeymoon cocoon into an inhospitable, hostile space. With mounting desperation he tries to orient himself in this alien Parisian world through the hotel phone and an unhelpful hotel staff.

Leaving home for the hotel can be a balancing act between the safe and predictable and the adventure of moving into a new setting. The hotel industry is constantly mediating this balance. On the one hand, there is the attempt to produce an architecture of reassurance, a "home-away-from-home" feeling of a space that is safe and predictable. On the other hand, a hotel should provide a holiday experience; something new and out of the ordinary.

"No surprise is the best surprise" was the motto behind the Holiday Inn, the motel chain that was developed to give American families on vacation a safe, predictable, and orderly alternative to earlier settings on the road—with greasy spoons, drab rooms and shady managers (Kirn 2003). Another American hotel empire, Hilton, aimed at creating "Little Americas" all over the world.

Hotels work hard to create a backdrop for carefree leisure and vacationing. Relax; you are on holiday, no mundane worries will bother you. Fresh towels will appear out of nowhere, your bed is made, and breakfast is waiting. In a sense what tourists pay for when staying at a more expensive hotel is the trappings of a Victorian upper-class home where servants take care of everything. This smoothness of the operation may also do something to the guests, as Walter Kirn suggests:

> Every corporation does one thing well, and in Marriott's case it's to help guests disappear. The indistinct architecture, the average service, the room temperature, everything. You're gone, blended away by the stain-disguising carpet patterns, the art that soothes you even when your back's turned. And you don't even miss yourself, that's Marriott's great discovery. Invisibility, the real vacation (2001: 215).

Already in 1906 a critic complained that the modern hotel had become like a fairy-tale land, where all wishes will be granted—as long as you pay—but your individuality is erased in this process. Wherever you go there is standardization and "an hour after you leave the hotel you are totally forgotten" (Harper 1906: 85). The feeling of "home-away-from-home" evaporates quickly; this is not a home but a machine for hospitality.

The Lobby

How does one start observing a hotel at work? Writing a dissertation on
hotel life Maria Strannegård (2002) started by spending time in hotel
lobbies. She writes about the strange in-between position of the lobby,
open and public, yet semi-private, a kind of liminal space between the
bustling city life outside and the quiet privacy of the bedrooms. Her
example is a Copenhagen tourist hotel, close to the city attractions. The
first thing she notes is the subdued atmosphere. The silently-revolving
doors and the red wall-to-wall carpet mark the entrance. The soft carpet
makes people slow down and lowers their voices. The high ceiling—
typical of many lobbies—and the soft upholstering of chairs and sofas
arranged as little islands also helps to set a mood: quiet and sophisticated. People are constantly taking in all the comings and goings. She
notes that the lobby is a perfect place for eavesdropping on other guests,
hiding behind a drink or a newspaper, and this mix of public and private
is why Hollywood loves lobbies. In 1932 the movie *Grand Hotel*, set in
Berlin, created a tradition, by using the lobby's potentials. In the movie
a guest sits in the lobby complaining, "People coming, going. Nothing
ever happens." On the contrary, the movie goers can follow a lot of
happenings: romantic meetings between strangers, secrets exposed, and
shady deals that are made. The camera juxtaposes the extremely public
and the intensely private.

This is also why cultural analysts are attracted to this space. In the 1920s
Siegfried Kracauer (1995) used Berlin hotel lobbies as a way of catching
what he saw as important social and cultural changes. He described the
lobby as a void. Here people are removed from the bustling urban life outside. They are distancing themselves from the everyday; they sit idly, doing
nothing, noting strangers. It is an extremely public space; every move, every
word is observed or heard, and at the same time people withdraw into their
private bubbles. There is no community here, Kracauer observed, and he
contrasted the lobby with a house of God. There is the same shared silence,
but it doesn't draw people together as in a church, but pulls them apart. It
is not a bad idea to combine a reading of Kracauer's essay with a viewing
of *Grand Hotel* in order to to catch the new social climate he described.

Sixty years later another influential cultural analyst sat in a hotel lobby
and used it as an entrance to capture the new mentality and politics

of postmodern life. Fredric Jameson (1991) wrote about the lobby of the Los Angeles Hotel Bonaventura as a postmodern icon (featured in many Hollywood movies). He described it as an awfully designed "miniature city," a kind of hyperspace of late capitalism, where the setting choreographs and disorients people's movements and interactions, creating a world set apart from the city outside it (he could have found similar qualities in casino settings).

For Kracauer, as for Jameson, the lobby is the place to go to capture what is happening in a turbulently changing social world—in the Berlin of the 1920s or the L.A. of the 1980s—and also to get analytical distance from everyday life. For both authors the lobby had an attraction as a special territory that illuminates patterns of social change, in this case becoming a kind of dystopic scene-setter. Indeed, sometimes hotel lobbies carry a heavy symbolic burden.

Although the cultural continuity of the layout and staging of life in hotel lobbies seems strikingly strong, changes also tell us about different views of public and private space in hotel life. The fear of hotels becoming too home-like or predictable has constantly fostered attempts of redesigning the hotel experience to achieve re-enchantment. Good examples are the boutique hotels or design hotels pioneered by people like Ian Schrager, who started to build new lifestyle hotels in the 1980s under the motto: "You are where you sleep!" Strikingly enough, this meant a focus on the public sphere of the hotel: the lobby. It became a new kind of theatre scene. The redesigned Great Eastern Hotel in London called for people "to feel at home in the lobby," but at the same time the lobby was decorated with domestic objects like telephones, pans, colanders, oversized versions in striking blue plush textile. It was like an artistic parody of the home. In these new lobbies guests were supposed to be self-conscious co-creators of atmosphere, hanging out with other cool people. The private hotel guest is turned into a public actor (Strannegård 2009).

Frontstage/Backstage

The lobby brings up another polarity, that of frontstage and backstage, an analytical approach to interaction developed by Erving Goffman during his fieldwork in a Shetland tourist hotel. The hotel organizes public/private in special ways. There are several private spheres in a hotel, not only the bedrooms but also the backstage regions. When Maria Strannegård (2002) was doing her ethnography, she struggled to get access to the backstage regions. The constant refusal of the management to let her in had not only to do with the grimness of that region—fluorescent lighting, plastic chairs, makeshift arrangements for the staff—but also that they did not want to expose this bleak underworld of hotel life, with bad working conditions and stressed staff. This is a territory best kept private.

A Hong Kong hotel manager I talked to remembered interviewing a job applicant—a girl who enthusiastically stated that she loved staying at hotels and had been looking forward to working in one. "She had no idea of what backstage work in a hotel looked like, and I told her to think of another career."

The bestseller *Hotel Babylon* (also a BBC soap opera), written by an anonymous hotel manager excels in such folklore (Edwards-Jones 2004), which often is about disclosing saucy details from the private life of celebrity guests. Rachel Sherman (2009) explored the Janus-faced world of luxury hotels, which mixes different forms of public and private spheres, especially the frontstage personnel of door men, receptionists, concierges, and managers, who learn much about the guests while, at the same time, showing a friendly façade. Unlike the guests, the hotel staff has access to all public and private territories, including the bedrooms (when guests are out) and thus create their own private sphere of knowledge about the guests, their secrets, and their habits. They love to comment on vulgar behaviour, bad dress, or tastelessness of guests, but they keep on smiling. The best companion film to Sherman's book is, however, the Hollywood romance *Maid in Manhattan* (2002), which depicts the tricky relations between staff and guests, if you can tolerate its extra dose of sentimentality.

Artist Sophie Calle became fascinated by these transgressions into private spheres and took a job as a maid for three weeks in a Venetian hotel. As a maid Calle explored and photographed the ways in which her guests transform hotel rooms into their private spaces and spheres of intimacy. She goes through their luggage, their drawers, checks the contents of the wastepaper basket. Everything is noted down, photographed, and then presented in images and catalogue text in an exhibition called

"Under the Skin" (Calle 2001). What kinds of taboos is Calle transgressing? Hotel visitors are suddenly exposed, their privacy invaded, habits, degrees of orderliness, and secrets are all out in the open: an empty whisky bottle, a porn magazine, a diary, a used condom, tattered underwear. Calle shows how productive the hotel room is for exploring boundaries between public and private and touches on the fragility of these boundaries. As Danish novelist Jens Christian Grøndahl noted: "the intimacy of an inhabited hotel room can seem more private than in a home, vulnerable as it is for curious looks. The provisional private life of a hotel can almost seem shady, because the surroundings are so anonymous" (2001: 158).

But as Sherman (2009) also points out, some guests find it difficult to live up to the public expectations and pretentions of hotel life. They may feel intimidated by the sophisticated settings. There are awkward moments when guests are standing by—in their "private" rooms—as cleaning is going on in the room, or when guests try to prevent the bell boy from taking their luggage ("Should we tip?"). Or situations when they feel belittled or scrutinized by the head waiter in the restaurant or the elegant front stage clerk ("Is this really a place for us?"). They feel that they cannot live up to the public behavior expected in the sophisticated frontstage of the hotel, and prefer to hurry to the privacy of their room.

Please Make Up My Room

Opening the door of a new hotel room can feel like both a routine and an adventure. People may know what to expect, but at this very moment all kinds of ideas and feelings may swish through their minds. There may be romance or homesickness in the air.

The hotel room and all mediated hotel impressions from popular culture help people to organize their new life. Even after an hour or a day some have created their own hotel routines, trying to personalize the anonymity of the setting or as one woman I interviewed put it: "We hurry to put out candles, flowers, and books in order to make the room more home-like—turning it into 'our room'" On the other hand, the fact that the hotel rooms do not segregate spaces like a home—all space (apart from the bathroom) is multipurpose—opens up for playful improvisation, breaking home routines.

I started out with the idea of the hotel as a very productive setting for studying a number of tensions or polarities. First of all, it is about the interweaving of mundane practices and images from popular culture—all the pre-understandings people bring as extra luggage into the place. Secondly, there is the tension between everyday predictability and drudgery and an opening up of a new, temporary world of carefree leisure. There are a number of paradoxes here. Many hotels aim to provide an out-of-the-ordinary experience with the help of an extremely routinized and hidden backstage activity. This is but one example of the ways in which the boundaries between public and private constantly are defined, twisted, or transgressed. In a hotel setting, the private may become public in certain situations, and the public scene becomes a territory for creating a very private space.

So next time you check in, put on the ethnographic glasses. Start scanning the terrain for everything hotel-like or home-like: objects, role-playing, moods, and rituals. How are situations and scenes defined (and experienced) as private and public? A hotel weekend may give a much more nuanced understanding of the workings and non-workings of everyday life than weeks at home.

Orvar Löfgren is Professor Emeritus of European Ethnology at Lund University, Sweden. The cultural analysis and ethnography of everyday life have been the focus of much of his research, with special attenton to themes like home and media, travel, and transnational flows. Currently he is directing an interdisciplinary project on managing overflow in affluent societies.

References

Calle, Sophie. 2008. "The Hotel." In: Stephen Johnstone (Ed.), *The Everyday*. Cambridge, MA: MIT Press, 190–192.

Christersdotter, Maria. 2002. "Hotell Öresund." In Dina Maria Arnesen and Line Hjorth (Eds.), *Come In, Go Out—10 billeder fra regionen*. Copenhagen, Denmark: Informationsforlag, 103–108.

Coupland, Douglas. 1992. Shampoo Planet. New York: Washington Square Press.

Douglas, Mary. 1991. "The Idea of a Home: A Kind of Space". Social Research, vol. 58, 1: 287–307.

Edwards-Jones, Imogen and Anonymous. 2004. *Hotel Babylon: Inside the Extravagence and Mayhem of a Luxury Five-Star Hotel*. New York, NY: Bluehen Press.

Grøndahl, Jens Christian. 2001. *Hjärtljud*. Stockholm, Sweden: Wahlström & Widstrand

Harper, Charles G. 1906. *The Old Inns of Old England*, vol. 1. London,UK: Chapman & Hall.

Jameson, Fredric. 1996. *Postmodernism, or The Cultural Logic of Late Capitalism*. London, UK: Verso Books.

Kirn, Walter. 2001. *Up in the Air*. New York, NY: Doubleday.

Kirn, Walter. 2003, December 28. "Birth of a Vacation. Holiday Inn Made It Safe for Americans to Go on the Road." *New York Times Magazine*, 12.

Kracauer, Siegfried. 1995. *The Mass Ornament: Weimar Essays*. Cambridge, MA: Harvard University Press.

Löfgren, Orvar. 2000. *On Holiday. A History of Vacationing*. Berkeley, CA: University of California Press.

Löfgren, Orvar. 2015. "Modes and Moods of Mobility: Tourists and Commuters." *Culture Unbound* 7(2015): 175–195.

McLane, Daisann. 2002. *Cheap Hotels*. Cologne, Germany, Taschen.

Sherman, Rachel. 2009. *Class Acts: Service and Inequality in Luxury Hotels*. Berkeley, CA: University of California Press.

Strannegård, Maria. 2009. *Hotell Speciell. Livsstilskonsumtion på känslornas marknad*. Malmö, Sweden: Liber.

Volland, Jennifer M., Bruce Greenville, and Stephanie Rebick (Eds.). (2013). *Grand Hotel. Redsigning Modern Life*. Ostfildern: Hatje Cantz Verlag.

28

(NOT) SMOKING

Justin A. Martin

The delicate forefinger of a Hollywood starlet curled around the sleek, slender cigarette holder from which a trace of smoke drifts up from a just-lit Chesterfield. The broad shoulders, rugged chin, and cowboy hat shading the eyes of the Marlboro Man. Idyllic visuals of smoking, imagined variously in black-and-white or lit only by campfire, permeate the collective consciousness. But so, too, contemporary understandings about the dangers of smoking and second-hand smoke inform our conception of the smoker. From the glory days of smoking, to public reaction, to the perils of smoke, to new forms of nicotine delivery: the transformations in the public's acceptance of smoking follow changes in advertising and legislation, bringing us to a new, liminal space for electronic cigarette users.

This essay examines the link between advertising and tobacco use. I outline the transition in the frame of tobacco use from one of glamor and normality to deviance and, eventually, the construction of the deviant, stigmatized identity of the smoker. Finally, I consider the effects of new forms of nicotine delivery, the use of nicotine vaporizers, and calls for the regulation of vaping and vapor advertisements.

Smoking: From Normative to Deviant

The normalization of tobacco use through advertising and television and sports sponsorship had a short life but a lasting effect. Faces from the field and the screen peppered cigarette advertising: Chesterfield had the lion's share of celebrities with the likes of Ronald Reagan, Willie Mays,

Frank Sinatra, Betty Grable, Bob Hope, and Jackie Robinson; Lucille Ball smoked Phillip Morris cigarettes; and John Wayne and Hank Aaron would walk a mile for their Camels. Who would George Burns or Groucho Marx have been without their trademark cigars? Iconic images of Santa Claus smoking his pipe were featured in Chesterfield and Lucky Strike print advertisements. Appeals to a hierarchy of credibility were made by Kent, Camel, and Lucky Strike: "More scientists and educators smoke Kent …;" "More doctors smoke Camels than any other brand;" and "20,679 physicians say Luckies are less irritating." The *Flintstones* prime-time cartoon was sponsored by Winston, which also sponsored NASCAR for 33 seasons. For seven years, from 1949 to 1956, presenter John Cameron Swayze smoked his way through the 15-minute *Camel News Caravan* on NBC (National Broadcasting Company).

There was as much smoking on the silver screen as there was in the studio theaters. There was Holly Golightly's elegantly slim, black cigarette holder. Would Mrs. Robinson have been so seductive without a little trail of smoke curling from her fingers, along her graceful neck, to her bouffant bonnet? Modern satirists have edited the smoking scenes from Bogart and Bergman's *Casablanca*; the new runtime is about 18 seconds (YouTube 2010).

If we are to believe contemporary depictions and modern interpretations of life a few decades ago, then we can only surmise that smoking was ubiquitous. Even Andy Griffith would take a few drags on the small screen, but that was nothing compared to the tobacco use in Don Draper's suite of offices. According to Centers for Disease Control and Prevention figures, approximately 42% of Americans over the age of eighteen were current smokers in 1965 (Rock et al. 2007). And yet by 2010, the CDC reported a decline in smoking to roughly 19% of the population (Syamlal and Mazurek 2011). What occurred to cut the rate of smoking by more than half? I would argue that there was a shift in the frames concerning smoking, a shift from a frame of glamour and seduction (see Vannini and McCright 2004) to a medical frame, which constructed smoking as dangerous, unhygienic, and deviant. Initially the glamour and medical frames were in competition with one another; however, the mounting medical evidence began to sway public opinion, and the medical frame came to be dominant.

On January 11, 1964, the United States Surgeon General issued a report entitled "Smoking and Health: Report of the Advisory Committee to the Surgeon General of the United States." Through their review of extant literature the committee definitively linked the use of cigarettes with an increase in lung cancer, heart disease, emphysema, and chronic bronchitis (U.S. Public Health Service 1964: 25). The report brought to the public's and policy makers' attention the health effects of smoking. The golden age of the cigarette was now officially in the decline. Stars of the large and small screen and playing field started to disappear from cigarette advertising. The report put tobacco manufacturers, particularly the cigarette makers, on the defensive about their claims that cigarettes were not addictive and that they were unaware of the deleterious health effects of tobacco use. It would not be until 2014, 50 years after the Surgeon General's original report, that tobacco manufacturers would agree to terms admitting their deception of the American public about the health effects of tobacco use (Zajac 2014).

Following the Surgeon General's report was a wave of changes and new advertising restrictions aimed at stemming the tide of smoking. Hollywood celebrities and sports stars who populated earlier advertising were replaced with caricatures and nameless faces. One of these nameless faces went on to embody an ultimate icon in masculinity: the Marlboro Man; a lone cowboy in a flannel shirt working the range. At the same time, Virginia Slims, a longer, slimmer cigarette, were marketed to women with the slogan, "You've come a long way, baby." Their advertisements attempted to link cigarette use among women with a wave of feminism that recalled earning the right to vote with the Nineteenth Amendment and women's increased participation in the workforce. The last such television advertisement, indeed the last cigarette advertisement to air on U.S. television, was billed as a "60-second review from flapper to Female Lib" advertising Virginia Slims on NBC's *Tonight Show* (Buck 1971). The reason for the cessation of cigarette advertising on television was a law passed in 1970, which made cigarette advertisements on television and radio illegal. Entitled the "Public Health Cigarette Smoking Act," the act also required labels on cigarette packs to inform users that "cigarette smoking *may* be hazardous to health" (15 United States Congress 1970, italics added). The transition from a frame regarding tobacco use as glamorous to a medical frame was well under way in the 1970s; however, the medical frame would not win out until new evidence began to suggest that not only was smoking a deviant act but alsp that the smoker was a deviant identity.

The Smoker as Deviant

From the glamorous days of Hollywood stars and sport legends appearing in tobacco advertising to the present campaigns of smoking prevention and cessation, the use of tobacco, particularly cigarettes, had gone through a process of deviantization. Backed by the medical establishment, the power of the U.S. Congress, and the rulings of the court, the American public became an audience not for the promotion of tobacco use but for a campaign highlighting its ill effects. While it had once been the norm to see tobacco users on screen, in restaurants, and in the office, tobacco use would be pushed outside of public buildings, off college campuses, and relegated, in some cities, to the private home. Tobacco use was beginning to be seen as deviant; it violated the norms of the health conscious; it was judged negatively and the noncompliant user suffered harsh penalties. However, the smoker was not a full-fledged deviant until the mid-1980s.

In 1986, the U.S. Surgeon General issued a report on the health effects of second-hand smoke. The report, entitled "The Health Consequences of Involuntary Smoking," had three major conclusions. The first of these was that second-hand smoke was a cause of disease, "including lung cancer in healthy nonsmokers." Second, children of smokers were at increased risk of "respiratory infections, increased respiratory symptoms," and decreased lung development. Third, simply separating smokers from nonsmokers in the same airspace did not "eliminate the exposure of nonsmokers to environmental tobacco smoke" (U.S. Public Health Service 1986: 7). Given that the risks of first-hand smoke were well-established in the medical literature and in the public consciousness, this new report singled out the ill effects that the smoker could have on the nonsmoker. This report marked the beginnings of the deviantization of the individual smoker. Smokers not only put their own lives at risk, they were now endangering the health of nonsmokers, their own children, and the general public.

The line drawn between the smoker and the nonsmoker was made clear: Nonsmokers do their best to stay healthy, and smokers put lives at risk. The smoker had become a species in the sense that the deviantization of the act of smoking became the deviantization of the individual. Foucault (1976) noted a similar transition from a person who engaged in homosexual acts to the speciation of the homosexual. In much the same way that the smoker prior to and just following the Surgeon General's 1964 report had been a normative "temporary aberration"—someone who smoked after a meal, at the office, or during the movies—the smoker had become a "species," one with an identity, one who could and did, seemingly willingly, inflict harm on the blameless nonsmoker, child or adult (see Foucault 1976: 43).

The 1986 report on second-hand smoke sparked debate while fueling smoking prevention and cessation advertising in the United States. Anti-smoking campaigns in the United States had medical credibility and Congressional approval to wage war against the tobacco manufacturers. The campaigns made significant progress in their efforts, such that in 1998 tobacco manufacturers entered into the "Tobacco Master Settlement Agreement" with 46 states, which funded anti-smoking agencies like the American Legacy Foundation, which runs advertisements though initiatives like truth.com about the ill effects of tobacco use and shames cigarette manufacturers and cigarette users (Legacy for Health 2014). The efforts of anti-smoking advocates throughout the 1980s through today have made certain that the American public knows the ill effects of first- and second-hand smoke. They have made smoking a deviant act and the smoker a deviant identity, someone who willingly puts at risk their own health and the health of others. This has given the smoker a discreditable identity, one which must be managed when dealing with the nonsmoking normal.

Erving Goffman (1963) differentiated between three types of stigma. The discredited identity consists of "abominations of the body." Tribal stigma is transmitted through the family and may include stigmas of race, place of origin, or religion. The discreditable identity, the one most applicable to the smoker, is the "blemishes of individual character, perceived as weak will ..." (Goffman 1963: 4). It is the weak will of the smoker, the lack of will to stop smoking, that is discreditable. The smoker may, to a certain extent, hide his weak will from public inspection: he may wear a nicotine patch when around others he does not wish to know that he smokes; remove traces of cigarette use from his personal front by meticulously washing the hands to hide nicotine stains, attend to oral hygiene to cover the smell of smoke, and apply deodorants to cover the smell on clothing; and generally "pass" (Goffman 1963: 73) as a nonsmoker. On the whole, however, the smoker will give himself away at some point in his association with nonsmokers. Today, this seems to take place largely outdoors. The United States has no national indoor smoking ban, although at least half of the States are smoke-free. Having no national ban is a marked difference from most other countries in Central and South America, Western and Eastern Europe, and parts of Africa. Where bans are in place, the smoker is obliged to engage in the deviant behavior in full public view of the nonsmoker and his fellow smokers. It is during these public displays of their deviance that one hears nonsmokers deride smokers for being too close to doors and windows and exclaiming to others that they have just had to walk through a cloud of smoke on their way indoors to class. These public humiliations harken to the spectacle of the punishment of criminals in which the "body of the condemned" (Foucault 1977) was the locus of scorn.

Having been singled out for their deviant behavior, smokers develop some sense of community. In between classes, on coffee breaks, and in between drinks at a bar, smokers congregate in their outdoor smoking areas, if they are available, and indulge in their discreditable activities. If this is done with enough frequency, patterns of deviancy develop: friendships are formed or reinforced, associations with those to whom one would normally show deference slacken in their formality, and sharing relationships are established when a smoker is caught short of cigarettes or a lighter. Because deviance is reflexive, a certain normalcy to the deviant act of smoking develops among smokers on their cigarette breaks that serves to neutralize the in-group stigma of using tobacco. However, individuals who will openly smoke in one circumstance will do their best to hide their smoking in other situations. My students frequently tell me that, while smoking is something that they do while on campus or at work, their parents have no idea that they smoke.

New Forms of Deviance and Acceptance

While popular images of smoking have shifted from glamorization to stigmatization, there is a group of nicotine users that the public, and even members of the medical profession, find ambiguous: people who are using nicotine vaporizers. Nicotine vaporizers, also known as electronic cigarettes or e-cigs, heat some combination of oils, the simplest recipe being propylene glycol and vegetable glycerin, flavorings, and various levels of nicotine into a vapor that is inhaled by the user. Among smokers of cigarettes, these "vapers" are seen as nonsmokers, or people who have quit smoking. They still, however, receive criticism from lifelong nonsmokers. A local vape shop, which sells the vaporizers and their liquid nicotine, has a "quitter's board" on which those who have switched from traditional cigarettes to nicotine vapers can sign their names.

Medical professionals remain vague in their opinions concerning vaping. The most recent Surgeon General's report on the health effects of smoking (U.S. Public Health Service 2014) devoted attention to vaping, but the conclusions it drew were mainly cautionary, stating that the use of, and advertisements for, nicotine vaporizers should be regulated and that the net effects of vaping versus smoking cigarettes are as yet unknown. The report did express concern about the use of nicotine vaporizers among the nation's youth, but offered little guidance as a means of smoking cessation. Medical practitioners seem to be at a loss as to how vapers should be categorized. One of my doctors said that she had no way to identify vapers in her medical records, and another told me that they would categorize vapers as former smokers.

Vapers appear to operate within a combination of the glamour and medical frames regarding smoking. On the one hand, they are complying with the recommendations of the medical frame by limiting their exposure to the harmful ingredients found in traditional cigarettes and operating on the assumption that they are not passing the harm of addiction to others through second-hand smoke. However, contemporary advertisements and other cultural displays of vaping appeal to the same tropes as earlier cigarette advertisements. Television star Katherine Heigl introduced *Late Show* host David Letterman to vaping in 2010 by using her electronic cigarette on air, proclaiming its benefits over traditional cigarettes, and sharing the experience with Letterman.

Former *Playboy* bunny Jenny McCarthy stars in advertisements for blu eCigs (electronic cigarettes) and stresses that users should enjoy the "freedom to have a cigarette without the guilt." She calls the electronic cigarettes "cool," "sexy," and "hot." Similarly, Aviator electronic cigarettes advertise that users have the "freedom to smoke anywhere." E-Lites, a UK-based electronic cigarette manufacturer, implies in its advertising that users will not miss their grandbaby's first steps (which will look like a Gangnam-style dance) by using their product.

Such appeal to freedom addresses the health and hygiene concerns raised in the medical frame, while a definite sexual undertone is used to promote individual products. These television advertisements harken to the glory days of cigarettes and entice users to enjoy the freedom that vaping offers them. They suggest that vaping will be welcomed indoors as a safer alternative to smoking traditional cigarettes. The appeal to the medical frame that electronic cigarette manufacturers make in their print, television, and online advertising places vapers in a liminal state of deviance. On the one hand, they are concerned about their health and the health of those around them, but they are still engaging in a deviant activity. In some ways their identity remains spoiled in that their use of electronic cigarettes associates them with current smokers and marks them out, at best, as former smokers, and, at worst, as current smokers.

This essay considers the construction of a glamour frame regarding tobacco use through cigarette advertising in print and on screen, which normalized smoking. Hollywood actors, singers, comedians, and sports stars all lent their names and faces to the glamorization of smoking prior the 1960s. The frame shifted to a medical frame when legislation regulating tobacco advertising followed in the wake of reports from the Surgeon General that linked tobacco use to increased mortality and created smoking as a deviant behavior. Reports linking second-hand smoke to the same effects as first-hand use marked the beginnings of the construction of the smoker as an individual with a stigmatized identity. New forms of nicotine delivery blur the lines between smoker and non-smoker and create an ambiguous space in which the nicotine-dependent former smoker exists. While smoking rates overall have decreased, the medical profession fears that increased advertising of new forms of nicotine delivery will entice nonsmokers to try electronic cigarettes and become addicted to nicotine. Through the shift from a frame of glamour to a medical frame, smoking moved from normal to deviance in the collective consciousness. The smoker, with the revelation of the harms of second-hand smoke, moved from a person who engaged in deviant acts to being a deviant identity. By appealing to the medical frame, electronic cigarette manufacturers are touting the health benefits of traditional cigarette cessation. With the uncertainty surrounding the health effects of new forms of nicotine delivery via electronic cigarettes, users are in a liminal state of deviance: not quite normal, but not wholly deviant.

Justin A. Martin teaches in the Department of Behavioral Sciences at the University of Tennessee at Martin. His published works have appeared in *Symbolic Interaction* and *Studies in Symbolic Interaction*. These works focus on new social media and its relation to the body. His most recent research efforts have been examinations of issues within the sociology of education, particularly on the application of social cognitive models of job satisfaction to teacher turnover. His current research extends expectation states theory to the classroom.

References

15 United States Congress. 1970. "Public Health Cigarette Smoking Act." Government Printing Office: Washington, D.C.

Buck, Jerry. 1971. "Friday Was the Final Day of Cigarette Commercials." New York, NY: Associated Press.

Foucault, Michel. 1978 [1976]. *The History of Sexuality, Vol. 1* (Robert Hurley, trans.). New York, NY: Knopf.

Foucault, Michel. 1977. *Discipline and Punish: The Birth of the Prison*. New York, NY: Vintage Books.

Goffman, Erving. 1963. *Stigma: Notes on the Management of Spoiled Identity*. New York, NY: Simon & Schuster.

Legacy for Health. 2014. "Truth: Youth and Young Adult Tobacco Prevention." Electronic document, available at: http://www.legacyforhealth.org/what-we-do/truth-r-youth-and-young-adult-tobacco-prevention, accessed 10/12/2014.

Rock, V.J., A. Malarcher, J.W. Kahende, K. Asman, C. Husten, and R. Caraballo. 2007. "Cigarette Smoking Among Adults—United States, 2006." *Mortality and Morbidity Weekly Report (MMWR)* 56(44): 1157–1161.

Syamlal, Girija and Jacek M. Mazurek. 2011. "Current Smoking Prevalence Among Working Adults: United States, 2004–2010." *MMWR* 60(38): 1305–1309.

U.S. Public Health Service. 1964. *Smoking and Health: Report of the Advisory Committee to the Surgeon General of the United States*. Washington DC: U.S. Department of Health, Education, and Welfare.

U.S. Public Health Service. 1986. *The Health Consequences of Involuntary Smoking: A Report of the Surgeon General*. Rockville, MD: U.S. Department of Health and Human Services.

U.S. Public Health Service. 2014. *The Health Consequences of Smoking—50 Years of Progress. A Report of the Surgeon General*: Rockville, MD: U.S. Department of Health and Human Services.

Vannini, Phillip and Aaron M. McCright. 2004. "To Die For: The Semiotic Seductive Power of the Tanned Body." *Symbolic Interaction* 27(3): 309–332.

YouTube. 2010. "Casablanca—Non-smoking Version." Retrieved from http://www.youtube.com/watch?v=boQBdgRYCqk, accessed 10/12/2014.

Zajac, Andrew. 2014, January 11. "Tobacco Companies Agree on Ads Admitting Smoking Lies." *Bloomberg News online*. Retrieved from: http://www.bloomberg.com/news/articles/2014-01-10/tobacco-companies-u-s-agree-on-ads-admitting-smoking-lies-1-.

29
CONSUMING CRAFT
Michael Ian Borer

The stare of a horned gargoyle, smiling mischievously at onlookers, is as haunting as his speech. "You're not worthy!" he declares. The unexpected pronouncement might shock the uninitiated onlooker as he or she peruses the continuously growing beer selection at liquor stores, bars, groceries, and gas station convenient marts across the United States. The gargoyle's taunt might appeal to some, while turning off others. That seems to be his point, which is made clear after picking up the 22 oz. "bomber" that houses his etched image, turning it to the opposite side, and reading the description of Stone Brewing's Arrogant Bastard Ale. "It is quite doubtful that you have the taste or sophistication to be able to appreciate an ale of this quality and depth," the label instigates. "We would suggest that you stick to safer and more familiar territory— maybe something with a multi-million dollar ad campaign aimed at convincing you it's made in a little brewery, or one that implies that their tasteless fizzy yellow beverage will give you more sex appeal. Perhaps you think multi-million dollar ad campaigns make things taste better."

Do we live in a culture where the simple and seemingly mundane act of buying beer can double as an anxiety-provoking assault on our identity by questioning our abilities to make "proper" aesthetic judgments while recognizing the dangerous social, political, and economic effects of corporate-controlled popular culture? Apparently yes. And, once we recognize the potential of craft production and consumption as acts of resistance, we gain a better grasp on what popular culture is, where it comes from, and what it can become.

As the mouthpiece of Stone Brewing—one of the most aesthetically and economically successful craft breweries—the gargoyle argues for, and even downright demands, a popular culture akin to folk culture. This type of popular culture stands in juxtaposition and opposition to the more common, yet often analytically incorrect, assumption that popular culture is mass-marketed, oppressive, mind-numbing and -dumbing mediated culture. But Stone's gargoyle clearly recognizes that popular culture works both ways, from "top-down" and from "bottom-up." From the top, Big Beer giants—namely Anheuser-Busch InBev and MillerCoors—dominate the market (about 90% of beer sales in the US) and, much to the chagrin of self-identified "beer geeks," inform the low status of beer. Counterintuitively, the growth in the number of craft brewers and brews has increased at the same time that the large commercial brewers have consolidated (see Carroll and Swaminathan 2000).

Beers from craft breweries like Stone and even smaller and more coveted ones like Russian River or Three Floyds purposefully stand in marked distinction to the brewing behemoths, yet their identities as craft beers—as not mass-produced beers—depends on them. Georg Simmel—writing in Germany at the beginning of the twentieth century, a time when practically all beer was local—noted an inherent tension in any culture between "elements which have a certain crushing quality of mass" and those "animated" and embodied by the creative acts of individuals (1997: 73). Any cultural object, mass-produced or craft-driven, relies on a symbiotic relationship between the objective and the subjective. This tension from the "tragedy of culture," as Simmel defined it, exists in the way symbolic boundaries are drawn within popular culture between products and those who both produce and consume them.

The social world of beer brewing and consumption embodies and signifies the tension between objective and subjective popular culture. Countering the ubiquity of Big Beer, craft brewers have challenged the traditional boundaries of styles and ingredients. All beers—from the lightest yellow fizz of a pilsner to the darkest black sludge of a stout—are brewed with some combination of water, fermentable sugars, hops, and yeast. The quality, variety, and amount of those ingredients lead to vast differences in taste and appeal. Add to that the variety of ingredients that today's brewers are putting into their fermenting and fermented concoctions, from all sorts of herbs, flowers, and fruits to bizarre additions like dust from lunar meteorites or oysters (Rocky Mountain and other varieties), and we might be witnessing a veritable revolution in taste—or tastelessness—depending upon, well, your taste.

Although revolution may be overstating what has happened and is happening in the world of beer, we are certainly in the midst of a craft beer coup of sorts.[1] The past decade has seen a meteoric rise in craft beer brewing as both a home-based hobby and a local business venture. Only 43 craft breweries were in operation in 1984. Thirty years later, there are about 3,000 craft breweries and an estimated 1.2 million home brewers in the United States. The market has changed dramatically since the ban against home brewing (an oddly resilient holdover from the days of Prohibition) was overturned and legalized nationally by President Jimmy Carter in 1976. Nearly all craft breweries trace their precursors to home brewing (Carroll and Swaminathan 2000), which has in turn created market demand and aesthetic desire for locally brewed elixirs. The "neolocalism" of brewing beer signals a fundamental shift in both beer production and beer consumption away from the corporate control of popular culture (Flack 1997). Yet, with their penchant for the new, the strange, and the authentic, craft beer brewers and consumers are part of a larger *translocal* "taste culture" (Gans 1999) that includes foodies interested in artisanal wares like cheese, sushi, or coffee and in "do-it-yourself" (or more appropriately, "do-it-with") (Vannini and Taggert 2014), initiatives that support collective creativity and an anti-mass production ethos (Campbell 1995).

Labels Matter

The visual imagery of labels either glued or etched on bottles and cans has become a popular technique employed by craft brewers to differentiate their goods from those brewed by the Big Beer giants. From Stone's intimidating gargoyle to the action-packed harlequin-themed cartoons of Clown Shoes to the various poker players garnishing the bottles of Las Vegas's Bad Beat beers, the artistry of craft beer labels serves two functions for the craft consumer. The physical labels serve as symbolic markers of craft (as opposed to mass-produced) and as engaging visual stimuli, intended to illicit an aesthetic or sensuous interpretation and response.

Craft beer labels help reinforce a symbolic boundary between craft-produced and mass-produced popular culture. Not only do they provide more information, from ingredients to quirky and comical narratives, the labels set these beers apart from Big Beer. They often scream "local!" with references to local places, landmarks, and folklore. They also scream "craft" which remains the most dominant label for artisanal brews.

Though the boundaries of art and craft are often ambiguous, spurious, and sometimes downright dubious, the practices that produce them are similar. In his seminal work on art and art worlds, Howard Becker (1982) noted that "art" is an honorific title intended to separate certain products and practices from mere craft. In a culture that has been littered with mass and machine produced "schlock," "craft" itself has come to signify something "authentic," handmade, and artisanal. As such, distinctions and symbolic boundaries between art and craft are less important today than those between craft-produced and mass-produced. Art and craft, then, serve similar purposes in a time and place where machine and machine-like production and labor are the overwhelming norm. In such times and places, "the artist craftman (or craftswoman)" (Campbell 2005: 25) stands out not only as a premodern Romantic, but as a late-(post-, hyper-) modern *bricoleur,* cobbling together old and new practices for the sake of creation and re-creation.

The artist, artisan, or craftsmaker engages in a type of creative and aesthetic entrepreneurship that forges the new and the novel out of already existing cultural objects and ideas. Such objects and ideas can pay homage to the past or seek to destroy it. Some even embrace the paradox of honoring the past while ushering in the new. New Belgium—a popular and successful craft brewery from Ft. Collins, Colorado—is best known for its mass-distributed amber ale called Fat Tire. But the name of the brewery is intentionally referential and reverential. New Belgium was the first American craft brewery to re-create and specialize in Belgian-style beers, mimicking seventeenth-century Trappist monks with their Abbey Ale. In the early 1990s, the American beer scene was unprepared for the arrival of this and other rich, malty ales, so much so that the Great American Beer Festival had to add another category—simply called "Mixed, Specialty"—to make room for them.

Novel beers are popping up in small, independent breweries and hobbyists' basements, elevating the complexity, diversity, and status of beer to levels that rival, and arguably surpass, the traditionally highbrow connotations of wine. Ratings and classifications provide order to complex social worlds and the products that emerge from within them. Such distinctions often appear as natural or inevitable, which tends to add to their power (Bourdieu 1984). Higher status products tend to generate fascination, awe, and a desire to consume them in those who accept the distinctions. The more complex and diverse a social world becomes, the more powerful the need for distinctions will be for individuals and groups, and the more consequential those distinctions will become for shaping that social world. As the popularity and ubiquity of "beer culture" rises, so does the need to makes sense of its contours and contradictions. Craft beer labels, in part, serve that need by functioning as boundary markers. Like Stone's gargoyle, they tempt and urge the potential craft consumer to move beyond the typical or mundane toward a presumably more authentic product and, in turn, a more authentic, sensuous engagement with popular culture.

Craft beer labels attempt to engage and elicit the interactional pleasures of frivolity, fantasy, and whimsy (Lofland 1998). Relief from the stresses of everyday life can begin even before the bottle is bought and opened and its sumptuous offerings are poured and glided along the tongue and down the gullet. India pale ales are known for their overabundance of hops, historically used to preserve them during long, water-bound trips from England to British-ruled India in the the mid– eighteenth century. Brewers today tend to adorn bottles of India pale ale with bundles of enticing, green hop flowers.

Oregon's Deschutes Fresh Squeezed IPA is brewed with Citra and Mosaic hops, both of which offer fruity overtones that temper the bitterness of traditional hop varieties. The label shows a vice pressing a bundle of hops, slowly unleashing milky citrus drops toward the beer holder.

The appearance of hops or the various incarnations of bourbon/ rum/wine barrel-aged this or that only resonates with those who can correctly read these signs as cues of craft. Craft beer aficionados have added to the power of these labels by photographing them and posting them on the Internet, Instagram, or beer-centric social media apps like Untappd where beer drinkers provide ratings, comments, and often pictures of the labeled-bottles or cans next to their current beer. These activities elevate the label as a means for differentiating craft beer from Big Beer. But the labels wouldn't matter, or wouldn't matter as much, if there wasn't a difference between Big Beer's products and those of the craft brewers and breweries. When it comes to the quality and variety of ingredients, recipes, and finished products, there is a difference, one that is exploited and accentuated by both craft brewers and craft consumers.

Tastes Matter

Though "common sense" tells us that an individual's taste is solely his or her own, individuals are socialized and re-socialized into particular contexts that both enable and constrain choices and aesthetic judgments. Invoked throughout our everyday lives, taste exists at the precipice of nature and nurture every time we claim to like or dislike something. Priscilla Parkhurst Ferguson (2011) points to the duality of taste as a sensuous property and a means for making choices. "Humans are omnivores; individuals and peoples are not. No society consumes more than a fraction of available edibles. Not simply a pleasure or even a possibility for the omnivore, choice is an obligation" (311–312).

Taste both unites and divides people into clusters around various consumable products. Judgments about taste emerge from within particular social contexts whereby all "sensory judgments are grounded in social relationships, face-to-face negotiations, social structures, and organizations" (Fine 1995: 246). The desire to produce or consume craft beer, then, is not merely a matter of subjectivity. Such feelings, ideas, and judgments are not random. Instead, they are part of a broader crafting ethos that, far from being totally consensual, may still vary in effect and consequence from one person to the next.

Taste judgments are not only made about popular culture but are a necessary part of it because of its ubiquity and the overwhelming choices individuals have to make about what they choose to consume day-to-day. In a pluralistic culture, taste is a form of social distinction that is often shaped by status competition. "Good taste" is a mark of distinction, in the double sense of setting apart from, and conferring honor to, those who claim to possess it. Pierre Bourdieu (1984: 6) claims that "Taste classifies, and it classifies the classifier." Along with attitudes, preferences, manners, know-how, and educational credentials, taste is a component of cultural capital that is transmitted by a complex process of socialization through the family and the education system. As part of class *habitus*, taste is one element of a set of preferences that are perceived as choices by social actors but, instead, are primarily cultivated rather than innately derived.

In the same way that "dining out" is "a perpetual experiment" (Warde and Martens 1998: 120), craft beer consumption requires intricate negotiations of personal taste and social status. Taste is turned inwards to define membership, even if that membership is not fully defined or articulated and may be more temporary than other attributes. Still, we recognize like-minded folk through the things we eat and drink, and where we eat and drink them. Both permanent brick-and-mortar brew pubs and tap rooms and temporary places-based events, like festivals, have emerged as sites for craft consumption; "these places are more than simply grist for the 'cultural' mill; they are, in actuality, where [popular] culture is empirically located" (Borer 2006: 181). Such places help define taste cultures and, in so doing, reinforce the distinctions of *crafted* taste. And they have become so popular and ubiquitous that, according to the Brewers Association, almost all Americans live within 10 miles of a brewery.

The proliferation of brew pubs, tap rooms, and craft beer festivals, as well as the growing availability of craft beers in grocery stores and at restaurants (some of which have beer lists that are as lengthy as their wine counterparts), implores consumers to engage in "somatic work" (Waskul and Vannini 2008) on a somewhat regular basis. Not only are their sense perceptions on call, but their consumer choices are then implicated in "aesthetic and moral dimensions of sense-making and impression management" (Waskul and Vannini 2008: 55). As such, craft beer consumption becomes a means to perpetually experiment with taste, identity, and popular culture as consumers confront feelings of alienation and anxiety through their choice of drink.

Brewing Popular Culture

Like the organic yeast cultures that are boiled with malts, barley, hops, and an increasing variety of ingredients (from ghost peppers to bull testicles), popular culture is a living thing. And it remains so, in part, through the processes of craft production and consumption. The variety of craft beers brewed today caters to contemporary individuals' cravings for novelty, local identity, and a buzzed escape from the often banal routines of everyday life. Recognizing their appeal and increasing share of the market, Big Beer offers "phantom craft beers" that look and sometimes even taste like artisanal wares (e.g., Blue Moon is a Coors product). This has simply pushed craft brewers and consumers to experiment further. The visual presence of quirky craft beer labels and the increasing variety of available tastes afford craft consumers opportunities to participate in the sensuous side of popular culture in ways that go well beyond the expected, contrived, or dictated. For example, some ingredients are culled from "ancient" recipes (like Dogfish Head's "Ancient Ale" series, which includes a beer made from a 2,800-year-old Italian recipe that includes heirloom Italian wheat, hazelnut flour, and pomegranates) or are part of nuanced concoctions like Evil Twin's Even More Jesus, which tastes like graham crackers dipped in coffee. Drinking such crafted beverages is an act of resistance and part of a "visceral politics" (Hayes-Conroy and Hayes-Conroy 2008) and of a struggle for aesthetic control of and over the practices, boundaries, and "tragedy" of popular culture.

Michael Ian Borer is Associate Professor of Sociology at the University of Nevada, Las Vegas. His specializations include urban sociology, culture, and the "sacred." He is the editor of *The Varieties of Urban Experience: The American City and the Practice of Culture* (UA Press, 2006), *Faithful to Fenway: Believing in Boston, Baseball, and America's Most Beloved Ballpark* (New York University Press, 2008), and co-author of *Urban People and Places: The Sociology of Cities, Suburbs, and Towns* (Sage Publications, 2014). His work has been published in *City & Community, The Journal of Popular Culture, Religion & American Culture, Social Psychology Quarterly*, and *Symbolic Interaction*, among other journals and edited books.

Dr. Borer was elected and served as the 2011–2012 Vice President of the Society for the Study of Symbolic Interaction. He is currently working on a book entitled *The Intoxication of Craft* (New York University Press) about the cultural contradictions of the Las Vegas craft beer scene.

Note

1. As of the time of this writing, there are at least three books published since 2013 that have used the phrase "Craft Beer Revolution" in their titles. Two are by journalists and one is by the co-founder of Brooklyn Brewery, one of the most successful craft breweries in the U.S.

References

Becker, Howard. 1982. *Art Worlds*. Berkeley, CA: University of California Press.

Borer, Michael Ian. 2006. "The Location of Culture: The Urban Culturalist Perspective." *City & Community 5*: 173–197.

Bourdieu, Pierre. 1984. *Distinction: A Social Critique of the Judgement of Taste* (trans. Richard Nice). London, UK: Routledge & Kegan Paul.

Campbell, Colin. 2005. "The Craft Consumer: Culture, Craft, and Consumption in a Postmodern Society." *Journal of Consumer Culture 5*: 23–44.

Carroll, Glenn R., and Anand Swaminathan. 2000. "Why the Microbrewery Movement? Organizational Dynamics of Resource Partitioning in the U.S. Brewing Industry." *American Journal of Sociology 106*: 715–762.

Ferguson, Priscilla Parkhurst. 2011. "The Senses of Taste." *The American Historical Review 116*: 371–384.

Fine, Gary Alan. 1995. "Wittgenstein's Kitchen: Sharing Meaning in Restaurant Work." *Theory & Society 24*: 245–269.

Flack, Wes. 1997. "American Microbreweries and Neolocalism: 'Ale-ing' for a Sense of Place." *Journal of Cultural Geography 16*(2): 37–53.

Hayes-Conroy, Allison, and Jessica Hayes-Conroy. 2008. "Taking Back Taste: Feminism, Food and Visceral Politics." *Gender, Place and Culture 15*: 461–473.

Lofland, Lyn H. 1998. *The Public Realm: Exploring the City's Quintessential Social Territory*. Hawthorne, NY: Aldine de Gruyter.

Simmel, Georg. 1907. *Simmel on Culture: Selected Writings* (David Frisby and Mike Featherstone, Eds.). London, UK and Thousand Oaks, CA: Sage Publications, 55–74.

Vannini, Phillip and Jonathan Taggart. 2014. "Do-It-Yourself or Do-It-With? The Regenerative Life Skills of Off-Grid Home Builders." *Cultural Geographies 21*: 26–85.

Warde, Alan and Lydia Martens. 1998. "The Prawn Cocktail Ritual." In Sian Griffiths and Jennifer Wallace (Eds.), *Consuming Passions: Food in the Age of Anxiety*. London, UK: Mandolin, 118–122.

Waskul, Dennis D. and Phillip Vannini. 2008. "Smell, Odor, and Somatic Work: Sense-Making and Sensory Management." *Social Psychology Quarterly 71*(1): 53–71.

INDEX